IN THE MOMENT

The Zen of the Wild

Francis Sanzaro

Saraband

Published by Saraband
3 Clairmont Gardens
Glasgow, G3 7LW
www.saraband.net

ISBN: 9781916812345

Printed and bound in Great Britain by Clays Ltd,
Elcograf S.p.A.

1 2 3 4 5 6 7 8 9 10

Praise for Francis Sanzaro's books:

"Outstandingly good … It may be the single most insightful book about climbing ever written." —**Paul Sagar,** *Climber, writer*

"Simply put, this is the best book on climbing I have ever read! In this innocuously sized, un-illustrated paperback lies an incredible density of profound, thought-provoking and deep knowledge on climbing … beautifully written by a master of the writing craft." —**John Kettle,** *climbing coach and writer*

"Finding a climber who perceives bouldering as a moving meditation, or one who values form and style far beyond difficulty, is a daunting task … in this book, Francis Sanzaro takes a significant step in that direction." —**John Gill**, *American bouldering pioneer*

"A brilliant book that everyone interested in moving over stone should read! … Sanzaro manages to describe complex ideas without ever losing touch with the challenge and joy of bouldering—highly recommended!" —**Udo Neumann**, filmmaker and author of *The Art and Science of Bouldering*

"Francis Sanzaro presents some of the most thoughtful and interesting writing I've ever read about this sport." —**Andrew Bisharat**

"Written by a climber, and for climbers, there is no better book to get you started climbing with the right mindset." —**Adam Ondra**, *Champion climber*

"Simple but elegant, vivid prose … An inspiring book aimed at rock climbers and other athletes that's ideal for both spirituality and sports psychology sections. Its emphasis on the virtues of cultivating mind-body awareness will also appeal to readers interested in New Age wisdom." —*Library Journal*

Contents

I dedicate this book to my mother and father, both of whom died while I was writing it. They are in these words more than I know.

It is a shame we never really "meet" our parents until we are older, which is to say, when we are young they are just building us, developing us. Knowledge of who they are comes later, and nature designed it to be so. Our relationship to the wild is like that—by the time we look to it for guidance, it has already built us, and thus the task isn't so much to look for guidance, but what it has built inside of us.

"Tao exists in the crickets . . . in the grasses . . .
in tiles and bricks . . . and in shit and piss."
—Chuang-tzu, fourth century BCE

"If there is any religion that would cope with
modern scientific needs, it would be Buddhism."
—Albert Einstein

"Three things cannot be long hidden:
the sun, the moon, and the truth."
—Gautama Buddha

"It is not true that you came into this world.
You came out of it."
—Alan Watts

"Experiencing the present purely is being empty
and hollow; you catch grace as a man fills
his cup under a waterfall."
—Annie Dillard

Preface: Swimming Naked Just Past Midnight on a Tuesday

If you are unmoored, again and again, you are awake.

"Nature loves to conceal herself," Heraclitus said over 2,500 years ago, a statement pretty much summing up nature philosophy since: nature is mystical, non-conceptual, mysterious, beyond reproach, inexhaustibly sublime—and so on down the rabbit hole of enigmatic descriptions, each one every bit as abstract as God or spirit or soul.

I've spent most of my life trying to plumb the inner depths of the wild and I think I can now, in good faith, respond to Heraclitus. And I think he's wrong.

Allow me to explain.

There I was, standing on the muddy embankment of the blue-green Loch Raven reservoir, deep in the bowels of a Tuesday, just after midnight. I was thirty-four. Christy and I had moved back to Baltimore, where I was born, to raise two children; we were happily married. At this point, I had lived in Colorado and upstate New York, the latter to get a PhD in the Philosophy of Religion. After graduating from Syracuse, we moved to Baltimore. I got a job in ed-tech, opting against a university teaching gig that would surely take me away from good climbing. There are no mountains in Baltimore, that's for sure, but it was a tradeoff: I had a good job, good pay, great climbing partners and incredible immediate and extended family.

Behind me, my clothes—all of them—were piled in a heap: black nylon running shorts, packed-out shoes, blue t-shirt, socks and headlamp. My skin was pasty from the run there, and when a slight breeze whooshed I felt the way I imagine a lollipop does after being licked. Acorns and twigs popped and cracked beneath my feet. Tall oaks and birch leaned over the water's edge, leaves rustling as they do. The darkness was one of the reasons I came, and, as I am every time I'm in the woods at night, I was reminded how quickly the dark art of the wild embraces you, how it reverts the world to its primordial energy, where dreams easily puncture the illusion of our control over life. I was also reminded how this feeling, with its opaque and lustrous mysticism, can be found not far beyond your back door. Thoreau's Walden Pond was a measly two miles from the town of Concord. He found the wild just fine, I'd say.

I tried to soak it all in. Breathe deep—you know, *be there.*

The water was warm, as when you fill the tub and let it cool for five minutes. Silky gray mud squeezed through my toes like sandy toothpaste from the tube. I took a step—ceremoniously, you could say—and gingerly lowered myself in. The faintest of breezes whiffed across the water, carrying the scent of duck shit and late autumn leaves. The nearest city, Towson, about five miles as the crow flies, lit up the sky to the south like a reticent halo. Everyone was there, under those lights, in their beds and resting for their workday tomorrow, which of course I should also have been doing. But I have always loved stolen time, as it is time you never have to fess up to. I smirked on the inside. Lucky me.

I had been anticipating this moment all day, all my life really, though I didn't know the latter. Finally, it had arrived. Breathe again. Don't waste it.

I was on the bank of an inlet-ridden reservoir tucked away in the suburbs of Baltimore, where I grew up: a gritty port city about halfway up the Atlantic seaboard, a landscape defined by the ocean, bays, estuaries, marshes, humidity and dankness; old wharfs, old ports, old world. I worried about stepping on fish hooks, a real possibility. I worried about swimming in a place I shouldn't be, it being illegal—not that this has ever stopped me before. I worried that I was desperate. The last one caught me by surprise.

Huh.

* * *

This book is about figuring out where exactly my desperation came from, and, as would follow, this book is deeply personal, the result of a life-long, personal and philosophical quest into the heart of nature. You should know, I am a lifelong nature devotee, a climber and skier and trail runner of thirty years, someone who is in wild places three to four times a week, living deep in the Rockies, but also someone who chased a PhD in the Philosophy of Religion. Zen grabbed me at a young age, and Zen's teachings, along with my mother, have been among the most influential things in my life.

While writing this book, my work in the philosophy of religion, my tenure as a mountain athlete and my love of the wild would come together at the same time as my physical bonds to my mother, and father, would come apart.

As you will see, this book is equal parts philosophical, existential and first-hand frustration. It is replete with theology, neuroscience, biology, evolutionary psychology, nature writing, and, of course, myself. I am a firm believer that the modern specialization of knowledge has made it that much harder to see and write about the big picture, which is unfortunate, as the bigger picture is absolutely essential. We are the bigger picture.

As fate would or wouldn't have it—likely, fate required it—this book was written during a time of grave upheaval in my personal life. My father died of cancer as I was starting it. While I was in early drafts, my mother experienced frightening changes in her mind, which, much lost sleep later, would settle into a diagnosis of Lewy Body Dementia; the nastiest kind. She would die just outside of a year after my father. My wife's step-father, a great mentor of mine in the mountains, died from Alzheimer's, and, quickly after that, my wife's mother moved from our small town. I lost a job and very nearly picked up the entire family to move across the country. I had to confront some individuals I never wanted to confront again in my life, and I experienced a betrayal that I never saw coming. In short, just about everything I took for granted seemed to wobble, and when things wobble we tend to hold on tighter.

But rather than grasp, I learned to let go instead. And in letting go, we receive tenfold.

* * *

Once, a young monk by the name of Kyosho approached Gensha, a Zen master. Kyosho wanted to study under him.

"I have come over here seeking the truth," Kyosho asked. "Where can I start to get into Zen?"

The Zen master responded, "Can you hear the murmuring of the mountain stream?"

"Yes, Master. I can hear it."

"That is the entrance."

With any luck, the mountain stream is running through these pages. The aim is for you to hear it and, with better luck, bend down and take a sip. It tastes pretty fucking good.

But it is also not just the entrance to Zen. It is the entrance to a more complete way of living. To life. To finding a sense of peace that no one can take away. I have learned these lessons the hard way, but, as the saying goes, you need a rough stone to sharpen the sword.

Our Good Friend Adam

Paradise, as it is so called, has nuances.

Whenever I swim naked, I'm reminded of our good friend Adam, the one who hung out with Eve in that delightful garden. Sans garments, I can feel his shame, his exposure. Except I hadn't been *placed*, or created, that night. Quite the opposite. I had come here, on the water's edge, seeking to be re-created.

Adam wasn't a person. That we think he's just a character is one of great scandals in the history of philosophy and religion. The name comes from the Hebrew *adamah*, which means "soil" or "earth" or "ground" or "land." What's the story about then: the earth being ashamed of itself? Our self-styled exile? A story we tell ourselves of our disenchantment? It is about all of them.

I didn't know what I was seeking exactly. But I knew the general thrust—to be *returned* to that blissful place, the Garden, the wild. Adam, aka the earth, didn't want to leave it either, but on account of his knowledge and discernment of good and evil, via munching from the tree (what we can call concept mind) him and Eve were booted. In short, the earth—expressed as humankind—had acquired intelligence, become self-aware, started to see with God's eyes, and thus didn't deserve to be in the cradle anymore. Divine jealousy, I suppose. For me, the story is simple—at the moment of judgment, of oneself or of the world writ large, you leave a special place, a fragile, if beautiful, landscape of convalescence, repose and balance. To return, which isn't really a "return," we should try to reverse this course of action.

Paradise, as it is so called, has nuances.

That night, at the most basic level, I wanted to go for a swim in a place I loved, a forest I grew up in, the site of so many mythical, boyhood adventures. At a more sophisticated level, I wanted to feel the sensation of water, to have it surround me, to shed what of the day, or my job, remained on my skin, nerves, and screen-weary eyes. Deeper still, I needed a way to manage the stresses of life. The incessant meetings and red-flag emails. The acute exhaustion of having young children. We all know these things, and we all need to find moments when we are washed of them. At the deepest level, I needed to patch up the hole in my soul with some nature, which I had done successfully to date, for decades, week in and week out, without fail.

And so I was there, on the reservoir embankment, human driftwood from a land I didn't know existed.

Desperation has a profound ability to hide from consciousness right up until it can't any longer; until it spills, or swims, out into a reservoir at midnight and you can't help but notice it.

Standing there, in the water, did give me a peace like no other, like turning a corner and seeing a childhood friend. You just look at their face, not needing to say anything, because just seeing them is the point.

The water at my ankles, I took a few deep breaths. I tried to relax. It was hard. The air was body-warm, the night not having cooled a degree. My eyes darted from the dark forest to the water, the latter illuminated like the veneer of an old porcelain jar. I scanned the forest and some suspect trees caught my attention—that ancient impulse of the trees watching you; of the forest having eyes.

A flash of my wife and kids in bed slid into my consciousness. When I told my wife I was going for a trail run at 11:30 at night, she didn't bat an eye. "What a moron," I imagine she said to herself. She gave me a big smile. "Have fun," she said, and turned around and padded up the stairs. I was jealous of her contentment and her ability to sleep. I'm a horrible sleeper.

I guess I was trustworthy. I guess she knew I needed it. I guess she was used to it. A few months prior, I had gone for a run in a hurricane, and it was great. Even then, as our metal trash cans were tossed down the block in the manner of a toddler throwing a Lego, she sent me off with the same, "Have fun."

I inched into the water, my footing unstable. Blocks of black, broken schist littered the shallow break, boulders whose sharp edges refused to be dulled. I knew these boulders well, having learned to climb on them, in places just like this—ragged Maryland shorelines—but now I was meeting the rock anew, touching it with bare feet, not my fingertips, as a climber would. The water sipped at my ankles, then my shins.

I felt embraced. The water didn't smell like roses. Ducky, I'd say, for obvious reasons, the reservoir a haven for Canadian geese and all manners of fowl. It was *their* reservoir, really. We are just visitors. In the daylight, the water had a bay-water vibe, green in the sun, gray in the shadows, not murky, not clear; almost emerald, just not translucent or regal in any way. Clogging the cornered inlets, of which this reservoir had hundreds, was driftwood big and small, branches broken in the wind, or simply aged out, whom had retired to a small watery grave to live out their days, together with kin. The open water was typically clean and sumptuous. At this time of night, however, the water was black, like motor oil. I'd have to shower when I got home. The sky was black-coffee dark, the stars struggling to shine under a thin veil of clouds. I relaxed my shoulders.

I took a few more steps, savoring the moment. The water lapped at my knees, that silky mud even more fibrous, the sensation of smooth, water-logged down feathers. Just a bit more and it was time to launch into liquid void.

I think death is like this: we near a threshold where it doesn't make sense to keep doing what we are doing, where we sense the transition to another manner of being, and so we leap. Before he died, one of the final coherent things my father said to me was: "I'm afraid to let go." His eyes were sunk into his face, shadows like mottled skin under his cheeks. "I know you are dad, but it's ok. It's ok to let go. We are going to be ok. I am going to be ok."

Holding on is what life does. But to be with the dying, we need to let go. Let go of more than just the other person.

* * *

In Tibetan Buddhism, death is a time fraught with danger. When our last breath has been exhaled, it's believed our minds are finally unmoored from our bodies. For the untrained mind, it's crippling vertigo, and dangerous, our minds spinning around in a space without an anchor. If your mind is attached, and was so in life, you will be reborn—and you might not have a good rebirth. You are reborn for another round of lessons; to be taught something about the nature of mind: namely, that it exists before and after you, and that thinking you are the light is like the candle thinking it is the only fire. But if you have lived in a state of relative alertness and attention and detachment, you will get a good birth, which will further help you become fully awake in your next life. And then, once the candle knows it is *part* of fire, it doesn't need to be reborn. Being here, in a body, is essential to becoming awake.

Tibetans call death's doorstep moments the *bardo*, but the bardo is, in essence, lodged in each moment, because we have the capacity to be unmoored in each second of our lives.[1] Sometimes we are unmoored without asking for it.

I lurched forward, into the water. A Venus in reverse. I see now I was offering myself to death, to the bardo.

A magical thing called buoyancy took over. I kicked my feet, pulled the water to my chest, and made my way to the center of the reservoir, to the center of the universe, "and that center is really everywhere," according to Black Elk.

I was waterborne now, and it felt lovely. The stars hid further, the ducks quietened. I did worry about snapping turtles having a midnight snack on you-know-what. Christy would never believe me.

As adults, we can forget about the delicious joy of swimming. And that's sad.

Liquid Trance

Being in water reminds us we are in a medium all the time; the wild, however, is our primal medium.

Swimming is a true wonder, a state in which we are weightless on account of being surrounded, on every millimeter of our bodies, by a medium with just enough give and pull to almost short circuit the constrictions of gravity; not so much we feel contained, or blocked, and not so little we are helpless, as "swimming" in deep space would render us. On earth, water is a sweet spot for being in a body while tasting the sensation of being without one; a place on neither end of the spectrum: the middle way, as Lao Tzu counsels. This is, at least, the only rationale I can find for the near-universal thrill of being in water. Religions across the world use water for rebirthing rituals, to wash before ceremony, and it's not just because it cleans us. Before water meant cleanliness, it meant freedom. Freedom is only defined in terms of what you are free of; in water, we are lightened, symbolically "free" of the weight of the world. It's a womb, a landscape of shifting gestation, a pre-symbolic gash resisting our concepts—freedom before *and* after our birth.

Art theory researchers have found that when we view art depicting bodies in pain—think of a medieval mural of writhing figures—our bodies undergo those very same feelings. To an extent, of course. Relatedly, actors, yoga devotees and anyone in the body arts know that in order to generate an emotion, say, of fear, you must close up your body, or cower, creating emotion through body position. Water, however, does not put us in a particular body position, and thus provides a sensation without specificity, which is part of its charm, and, given that all movement is sensation, water is a pedagogical *medium*. It can instruct us to feel the mediums we are in *all the time*—in cars, stores, houses, and so on—and these places, these mediums, are acting on us all the time. Water merely calls to attention our entry and exit into mediums with clarity. The wild is one such inescapable element, *our primal medium*, and it is all the harder to notice on account of being pervasive. For me, being in the mountains is like being in water.

The Chinese character for swimmer translates to "one who knows the nature of water." It's not "one who swims," as we'd define it, but one who navigates the medium of liquid with knowledge, who knows the *nature* of liquid. When I first came across this fact, I thought it a lovely description, textured with tonalities of patience, intimacy, feedback loops, discovery—all things required for true understanding. A swimmer shouldn't just be thought of as a person who performs the butterfly or backstroke. A swimmer is able to perform these strokes on account of their bodies *knowing this medium*, their minds feeling and reacting to the play of water the way we sense how our loved ones will react to something; we don't know the medium academically, or in thought. We know it viscerally, in our muscles, our memories.

To be human, for me, is to "know the nature of nature," a task sure to take us inside and outside ourselves, but in such a manner the two become indistinguishable. What lovely ambiguity. Was it not this indistinguishability—this merging of self with self, human nature with nature, self without knowledge of self—that defined our brief stint in the symbolic Garden … and, perhaps, in the annals of enlightenment?

It was. And I was there, that night, to get back in. Or to get out. I didn't know at the time.

I swam to the middle of the reservoir, about a hundred yards, and flipped up, belly aiming towards the heavens. Distant flickerings of faded starlight mocked my insignificance. Cosmic insignificance therapy. I felt as if in the middle of the ocean, floating to parts unknown. Geese yapped along the staccato shoreline. They knew I was there, as did every animal in a half-mile radius. I was in the bardo between my attempt to savor the moment and my awareness of not being able to. I wiggled my toes. A soft breeze said hello. My body softly exhaled the tension it had been carrying. I forgot it was midnight and I'd have to get up in five hours to get the kids ready for school. I forgot where I was. Where was I? I was in the water. I swished my arms in the liquid, unable to float. That annoyed me, my need to do something. I had needed, and wanted, to do nothing, but I sank in the water.

Distracted now, I lifted my head and looked at my running shoes and clothes on the shore, perhaps the way a snake looks back at its skin after shedding it, ambivalent about the rumpled pile of a former life. It was a pregnant moment, to say the least. Then, like the bardo always present, my consciousness rose up, unmooring itself thirty or forty yards above me and the water, and suddenly, in the person floating there, I saw my sixteen-year-old self, standing outside my sister's bedroom door in my childhood home. I'm picking the lock. Young Francis is picking the lock. I'm opening the door. In my sister's room was my best friend and my girlfriend, frantically pulling up their underwear.

Where the fuck did that come from? No idea.

Had I entered a liquid trance? Kinda.

Bad feelings arose. The stars are not my friends anymore. The water is no longer warm. I want to escape, but there's nowhere to go. I don't know my medium. I am no swimmer of life in the Chinese sense.

What I saw was my story, the life-medium I had been swimming in. A story in which I ran into the wild to run away from myself, from the betrayed person who lost not just their best friend, girlfriend and childhood friendship group, but their self-esteem, confidence and sense of place. A story in which I ran from Baltimore and toward the wild—because of that fateful evening and because, perhaps, the wild didn't know me, and didn't seem to care.

Floating, I didn't like what I saw.

When the Student is Ready, The Shit Plant Appears

Just as the center of the universe is everywhere, the shit plant is everywhere too.

An hour prior.

The run to the peninsula where I would cast off was not

trivial. To get there I drove ten minutes and parked in the corner of an empty church lot, then snuck across the busy four-lane road. I was trying not to be seen, as it was illegal to be in Loch Raven at night—and it would just be weird to be driving at midnight and see a shirtless guy in running shorts cross the road. I guess I didn't want that guy to be seen. Adam and his shame again.

Once I crossed the road my body relaxed. I was in the protection of the woods now. I felt the coolness and quiet of dampened senses—the sound of a scurrying fox or racoon, the moisture of soil—like rolling the windows down when you get near the beach, so you can smell the salt and get excited. This was a liminal space. A bardo. I could feel the wild coming, and yet, at the *exact same time* my feet touched the first bit of trail and I took a deep breath, into my lungs plunged the foul, wretched stench of a shit plant, though in reality it was a pump station. A pump station helps human waste, through a series of pumps, go from a low elevation to a higher elevation. As you can imagine, it smells like a shit plant. The small plant was a hundred yards left, tucked away off the side of the highway in a nondescript white building. I didn't remember the smell, or even that it was coming, and so I had what felt like a thousand shits piped directly up my nostrils in the exact breath I had expected to be my entrance point into a landscape of repose, childhood and homeostasis. I tripped over a root immediately and nearly smashed my head on a tree.

It was rather shocking, the juxtaposition of the two. However, it is good Buddhist practice: it keeps illusion at bay, blunts the sword of the Romantic impulse of expectation, which I am forever guilty of courting. "We suffer more in our imagination than in reality," said the first century Roman Stoic philosopher Seneca. Indeed old pal.

* * *

What I've come to learn is this: just as the center of the universe is everywhere, as Black Elk so eloquently reminded us, the shit plant is everywhere too, part and parcel of our psychological landscape. The shit plant is not just a physical reality, but a metaphysical one. The shit plant is the inhospitable truth lodged within each moment we breathe, place we visit, or person we know—it is what fends off perfection and thwarts prediction, two mistresses of the mind. But you have to look close. Imperfection is in the wild as much as it is in our hearts. There's no such thing as perfect love, they tell us, but we forget this when we fall in love. There's no such thing as a perfect place, we are reminded, but we forget this when we feverishly seek a new place. There's no such thing as the perfect job, but we chase it. Then, like celestial clockwork, we see the wrinkles on a lover's body and their perfection is blown away with the gentlest of breezes. Our new boss disappoints. The crowds at the Grand Canyon annoy us. The food we ordered not what we imagined. The shit plant is what disagrees with us, what calls us out from our ever-fragile fantasies, germinated in discontent. The shit plant needs to be acknowledged and accepted. We become much happier beings if we seek discomfort and hard truth rather than comfort and soft delusion. *Kintsugi*, the Japanese art of the broken, is instructive here.

Kintsugi is the practice of repairing pottery with a resin made from trees. Its ultimate origins are unknown, but rumor has it a fifteenth-century Japanese Shogun broke a pot and sent it to China for repair, but when it came back with staples, he didn't like it. The Shogun turned to a local Japanese craftsman who used lacquer and gold to stitch it back together, accentuating the breaks, rather than hiding them. A formerly shattered bowl was now stitched together with gold-sprinkled resin. It was a hit, and the aesthetic caught fire, dovetailing with the existing Zen aesthetic of seeing perfection in imperfection. And vice versa. Many started breaking bowls and repairing them in *kintsugi* style.

Kintsugi does not so much highlight the shit plant, but rather makes a whole of perfection and imperfection.

Perfection, symmetry, harmony and balance—these are the bulwarks of Western classical aesthetics, witnessed in Greek temples, Medieval cathedrals and modern skyscrapers. We are comfortable around these shapes and ratios, and our minds have been shaped by this aesthetic, causing us to have negative reactions when we see something antithetical to these principles. This even applies to what we eat: 33.3 percent of food produced for humans is wasted.[2] One reason for the waste, as uncovered by researchers, is that we think deformed fruit is "suboptimal." I.e., not perfect. Our evolution is to blame, as symmetry has been singled out, across cultures, as a top factor when determining attractiveness, and thus, mates.[3] Apparently, we apply the same attraction impulse to fruit. Consciously, we might reject the idea, but the preference, and judgment, happens on subconscious levels. This preference has led growers and food engineers to be constantly selecting for traits of symmetry.

We do to experience what we do to fruit. Can you imagine turning your nose up at 33.3 percent of human experience because you judged it unnecessarily, because you brought a needless and illusory concept of perfection to bear on it?

But that is exactly what we do. That's what I did. I was the broken vase in search of a gold lacquer. The wild had historically been my lacquer, but the problem was I couldn't see the vase.

Our brains are natural faultfinders. Most of our avoidance is born from the desire to get rid of imperfection, so as to "optimize" our experience. But optimization is fantasy. *Kintsugi* doesn't so much eschew these principles, but redefines them: *perfection as the blemished*, an acknowledgement of the impermanent; symmetry as a correspondence of broken and unbroken; harmony not as the absence of conflict, but the presence of history, and time, in the ahistorical;

balance as the manner in which life finds a way to challenge our expectations.

The art of *kintsugi* is more than an aesthetic of the broken, rustic, ragged line, and more than a mere physical manifestation of the Japanese, and Zen, love for the worn and impermanent; it is a philosophy of nature and an intentional sword to defend against faultfinding, one of the most basic reflexes of the human mind, one of the biggest causes of our discontent. *Kintsugi* is an expectation-management aesthetic, and a key to the nature of our nature. *Kintsugi* defends not by buttressing perfection-expectation, which is what we typically do, but crafting imperfect-expectation, a fundamental acknowledgement of the ever-abiding unpleasant abnormalities in life's things, loves, apples, people and experiences. It works. When you expect imperfection, and your mind releases the fantasy of its opposite, what you'll find is, ironically, a higher form of perfection. Perfection in *just as it is*, not as you want it.

And that's just how it is, isn't it? Imperfection, impermanence, all around, everywhere. *Kintsugi* isn't exotic, or foreign. To claim it is a philosophy of Japan is to miss the point entirely. The idea pops up in Islam, Christianity and Judaism's insistence of the perfect imperfection of humanity.

Kintsugi is right in front of you, in fact. The imperfections in this book. Your dinner tonight. Yesterday, now, tomorrow. The annoyance you feel from your husband or boss. It applies to our nitpicking of people and our intolerance of their misalignment with our expectations. A deep appreciation of *kintsugi* doesn't just allow you to appreciate the things you didn't before, it allows beauty to germinate in experiences and people (yourself included) you didn't know existed. This beauty is what is revealed when you remove the shadows of your thoughts blocking the real thing in front of you. Or inside you.

Some of this I knew then, that night at Loch Raven. I knew, intellectually at least, that you need to appreciate what is around you. You need to embrace the moment. You need to be present and if you are always expecting, you are not in the present. But there is nothing like a shit plant up your nostrils to bring you back to reality. When the student is ready, the shit plant appears. To know something in thought is to merely hold it; to know something in your body is to have eaten it. One can look at maps of a mountain range all day, but unless you've walked its hills and waded its rivers, you've never experienced it. My life had come to a head—out of the maps and into my mind.

* * *

I smelled the shit plant, and its golden, putrid, lacquer ribbons loosened me up. I had exited the car rather intently, full of dreams and fantasies of escape, but the horrid scent burst the ceramic bowl of my experience-expectation. Two types of nature had just been combined—the nature qua nature and nature qua humanity—that which we go to, the wild, and that which we hide, the stuff of our body. The bubble I had kept the wild in, the experience of myself in the wild, had burst. It was a lesson I'd have to learn again and again.

In the darkness, I gave my repulsion and annoyance some energy. A few cars went by, their headlights casting shadows of yellow light in the canopy, illuminating the still bodies of trees. My thoughts stopped me; I looked at them. I did some self-talk. *That's pretty shallow of you. What did you expect?*

I picked up the pace. In seconds, I got to a better place, which isn't to say the smell went away. Rather, I brought the smell into the fold of my experience. A minor victory. The disappointment faded with this new reality.

After a minute or two of running on a gravel trail littered with moonlit shards of broken green and clear glass, I brought my head up to look into the woods. A final few cars passed by. I stuck to the shadows. The proscenium of the forest. The shit plant, still with me, is two hundred yards behind.

Trail running here is a hopscotch of finding the dirt amongst the stones, crossing a few streams here and there, maybe some downed logs, but overall, an up-and-down gentle forest path, idyllic running. The streams are humble, small, and trickleish; they are easy to dam and fish around for crayfish in, a favorite hobby of mine as a kid. The rocks are schist, which means they are sharp and they sparkle. The trees are just magic—tall slender beech, maples, hemlocks and elms with a porous, high canopy, their trunks typically the diameter of a human waist. In the fall, when the leaves descend and pile onto the trail, and before the rain matts them to the forest floor, running is treacherous on account of the constant fear of spraining your ankle. It is not a dark forest, generally, nor an airy one as you'd find in the High Sierras. Enough clouds and rain keep the sky gray, which, presumably, allows the trees to give each other space, fifteen-to-twenty feet or so between trunks. These are the types of trees whose trunks branch only slightly, which leaves your line of vision in these forests almost unobstructed, except, of course, for other trees and rolling hills. Deer are the predominant wildlife in these forests, along with racoons and squirrels and ducks, and are tolerated, hunted and feared when driving in the dark on two lane roads; I've known many people who totaled their cars when hitting them, and even a few who died when swerving off the road to avoid them. The deer are not afraid of you, but not friendly either. They prefer their own acre. There is no thick brush carpeting the forest floor, as scrub oak tends to do in sub-alpine parts of Colorado, but impenetrable thickets appear now and then, where the soil is waterlogged and water runs in small natural ditches or channels.

I was in the full dark now, and out of the sight of others. I clicked my headlamp and a bright yellow-white beam exposed the path. I slowly found my pace, my feet tip-tapping on the trail's sandy, waterlogged leaves. I focused on my feet. The forest welcomed me. An old friend to be sure.

The magic was returning.

Intersecting in all directions and crossing the main trail were fisherman's trails, trails made by young kids that lead to forts, trails blazed by teenagers to do the things teenagers do; smoke weed, make out. But I knew every trail, every inch of this forest, which was why I was there; this place is special to me, as deep as I can go on my brain stem for rehabilitation. Getting lost, at least practically, wasn't a worry.

It took me a few minutes of running in the dark to be ok with it. It's not that I'm afraid of the dark, though I think everyone is a little, but rather something about being in the woods at night makes you feel vulnerable and stripped of just about everything—the ability to see in front of you, for instance. On par with the fear of falling, losing one's sight is a primal fear. Sight, I've come to learn, is an essential component of our brain. Rob it of sight, and you change the brain and its basic functions. From our eyes we discern security, calculate the future, calibrate for danger; sight grounds us practically and symbolically. Darkness isn't just the lack of light—for our purposes, it is the emotion we get when all the formers are robbed of their breath by a stripping of the senses. Fantasy abides in the absence of assurance, and that goes for good and bad flights of the imagination. Every rustle of the leaves provokes outsized attention, every snap of a twig rivets my consciousness with caution. I tell my brain not to react, but it doesn't listen. Our brains are hardwired to react; our quickness meant we'd have a greater chance of survival during a time when we were prey. We get a little irrational in the dark, without sight to ground us.

The only thing hunting us today is, of course, ourselves.

I settled into the strange beauty of night running in the forest, as I have to do time and time again. Slowly, the patter of my steps and I descended off the main trail, down, down, down through a two-hundred-foot section of single-track switchbacks, each turn with angled banks for mountain bikes.

These make the trail even better to run, allowing you to go fast and take the turns with an aggression not possible on the flat. After the switchbacks, fluorescent green ferns carpeted the forest floor, which is uncommon, but makes for a soothing few strides, as you can feel coziness of the ferns, much in the way you feel the hominess of a carpeted room. Remember: the medium. This little section, because of the knee-high ferns, retains water, and the moisture hovers over the area like a sticky yet invisible fog. After the ferns, you run down the throat of a wide peninsula; it is hardly deserving of the descriptor, I must admit, but it feels nonetheless apt once you arrive. A few hundred feet more, over exposed roots and tangled fishing line, and you hit the water's edge. When you do so, the forest curtseys and takes a step back as the water takes a step forward, to bow. As with any shoreline—the sheer absence of something is powerful. And in the dark, the absence is filled.

On the sloping embankment, leaves of maple, birch and elm were strewn about, leaves dry in the clearings and soggy and clumped in the shade. After the sun is gone, warmth remains in what it has touched during the day. Acorn shells loitered about, snapping when I stepped on them, like nature popping its knuckles.

I'd been coming to this point on the earth for thirty-plus years. The haze of familiarity overcame me. Nostalgia sinks us so deep into the cobwebs of memory we can no longer see what is in front of us. I was both there and not there.

I slipped off my running shorts and stepped into the water.

The Bigger the Beauty

The bigger the beauty the greater the experience, right? Wrong.

As a result of work, life, stress, and so on, I had built up this moment for days and developed it in my mind the way a dreamer fantasizes when they are stuck, when the dreams just come and come and come. I had "chosen" the setting, the time, the spot, and from that I had extrapolated the experience I wanted to have. I could feel the expected sensation in a forward-facing memory all days prior. Tonight was transactional. I needed something the wild had.

We all design our experiences. I had done what hundreds of thousands of us do on a daily basis—I turned to nature for some solace, to fresh air for some peace, to a familiar place to draw me back into myself.

In retrospect, I had hoped that, in doing all of this, the wild would speak to me with greater clarity. Why was that essential? Despite having a coveted position at work, where I managed a big team and even bigger budgets, and, in general, had a career with all the makings of success and comfort, I wasn't able to be myself, and this *not being able* haunted me. I can recall one conversation with some coworkers in which they were talking about running. There was a local race over the weekend, a 5k I think, and a few coworkers had run it. After they had exchanged stories about the run, someone turned to me and said something like, "Do you work out?" It was a question I'm normally fast at answering, but I oddly found myself paralyzed. My ego whispered, "Do I work out? Pssshhhh. I made the cover of climbing magazines. I've been a high-performing athlete most of my life." I really wanted to say that. Of course I didn't, but the power of the self-talk revealed to me one thing about myself—I had kept myself hidden, and, despite the power I had at work, something in me was powerless. These individuals, whom I had worked within ten feet of for a year, didn't know my life virtually revolved around sport. In hiding myself, I had tried to rewrite the person I thought I ought to be.

After what must have been an awkward couple of seconds, I answered, "Yeah, definitely." The conversation moved on, and I breathed a sigh of relief. What I saw in myself, however unclear and unwilling, was a disconnected person, a classic case of having it "all"—a good job, healthy kids, loving wife, family and friends—and yet suffering at the core. What else do you need!?

Turns out, whatever that *else* was, I didn't have it.

Not long after that conversation at work, I went for the midnight run, to get something back I had traded out, to prove something to myself, to reestablish a secret bond. Nature was always my go-to. I needed to find my place in this town again, on the earth again. I hadn't lived in my hometown since I was seventeen and left for college in Colorado with a lone backpack on my shoulders, and mentally I hadn't lived there since I opened that bedroom door and found my friend and girlfriend with their pants down.

My childhood was spent in the Maryland woods, climbing rocks, damming streams, romping here, galumphing there. I was in the woods a lot. Every child, in some way, has their imagination born from a landscape, and hence, their heart will always be fed by the hills on its back and the birds in its air. Children are extremely vulnerable to place because they play in it, get intimate with it, pick up its bugs, eat its mud and bark, and, in general, touch the body of the wild the way young lovers do. Delight under every rock, down each trail. That was me. We remember place as children to the extent it feels boundless, because when you are a child you run up against boundaries on a daily basis: what you can and can't do, how late you can stay out and what you can and can't eat. The life of children is one of supreme frustration. By necessity then, nature becomes seared in our imagination when it feels boundless and we are able to express, or cultivate, our deepest desires in said place.

When I was thirteen, my friend Pete invited me on a climbing adventure out in Colorado. It was an organized trip, the kind parents booked their disgruntled kids on all summer, lest they get into trouble hanging around, which he and I were sure to do. I think Pete's parents sent him off on back-to-back trips for two to three summers in a row, and it is Pete to whom I give the credit for opening me up to the West, to Abbey, to the smell of burnt sage. On that first trip, aged thirteen, the vast spaces of the Colorado Rockies blew me away—not just the mountain tops, but the broad valleys and clear rivers and brown-gray bluffs, sights that would have been pure marvel for me back home, but were here just another curious landmark on the endless mountain passes, roads which bowed to the curves of the landscape rather than willed themselves through it. It was love and shock and freedom rolled into one. A child of the East Coast, of concrete valleys and congestion, I didn't know places like this existed. The air. The vastness of a prairie going and going and going into a horizon, which, for itself, also went and went and went. Over each mountain pass was another valley wider and more verdant than the last, long fat fingers splayed into hidden other valleys. I remember staring out the window a lot. On long drives, packed like sardines in a long white van, listening to Neil Young for the first time, I sat with open eyes to make sure I saw the last of the deep valleys, sure we'd be dumped back into a greasy suburban sprawl around the next bend. But the moment never came.

Years later, I'd come across this feeling again in a story recounted in Antoine de Saint Exupéry's *Wind, Sand and Stars*. In the book, there is a story of a pilot taking a few men, born in the harsh and waterless deserts around Port Etienne in northwest Mauritania, to the French Alps for a visit. He takes the men on a hike to a waterfall. I imagine it was a typical mountain cascade, the water clear and cold and impatient, ragged at shoreline, cobbles polished, rushing down. Their heads wrapped in sand-crusted turbans, the men are transfixed and can't believe their eyes. They stare and stare. After a while, it's time to go. The guide lets them know as much. The men don't want to leave. Born in a land of sudden storms and flash floods, the men have never seen so much water. The guide presses them. "We must go." But the men's eyes and feet are planted.

They are waiting for the waterfall to stop.

The mountains affected me like the water these men. I was a different person thereafter.

With each passing day of that summer in the West, the world seemed to change up on me, reveal a second act. It is for all these reasons that I can say today I was conceived in Baltimore, but was born in the mountains. A gymnast at the time, I was introduced to climbing, and I took to it immediately and with deep familiarity. With trepidation and foreboding, my mother and father supported me along the way until, at last, I'd go there for college, fulfilling my childhood dream of being a climber.

* * *

From a childhood in the hills to an adulthood in the mountains—for the past thirty years, four to five times a week, every week of the year, my life has been one of feverish climbing on frozen waterfalls, spires of rock, alpine boulders and limestone cliffs ... or of running, or skiing, in the nearest mountainous terrain. My body craves mountain ledges, tabletop summits, exposure and cold winds like sugar. Over these decades, my body adapted to the rigors of these sports. When I look in the mirror, I see decades of moving in the hills—my arms are made to hang off edges for days. My legs ready to haul me up steep inclines. I take pride in this fact, of what my body allows me to do, and so, because of this body, I thought for years it was the best way to enjoy the wild, to keep doing what it was I knew how to do. What I knew how to do, of course, was be extreme in nature, alone, in a remote spot, pushed to my limits, sometimes with no recourse or rescue. And so, I had thought I was well suited to receive whatever it was that nature wanted to give on that Tuesday, midnight in the forgotten black of Loch Raven, outside Baltimore.

As I cast off in the liquid ether of memory, floating there under the stars, a set of basic questions arose from my floating body:

What is he looking for?
The question arose because the person wasn't finding it. I felt sad looking at that person down there.

Didn't they know they wouldn't find what they were looking for?
I was sixteen opening my sister's bedroom door again. That boy would lose trust in everyone. He'd feel ashamed, embarrassed in public, like a fool. He didn't want to go out in public for months. So he didn't. He didn't want to tell his parents. So he didn't. He didn't want to talk to anyone about it. So he didn't. He'd still feel the pain of those moments about thirty years later, now in fact, while writing this. It was easy to discount the damage done to my psyche then, to repress and walk away from it, but it is hard to sidestep now. At that moment, a plan was hatched in my teenage subconscious to leave Baltimore and never come back. And yet, here I was, in the city again, looking for the mountains, for the wild. I had returned.

What was this boy, betrayed, doing here, now? Why is this betrayed person betraying my experience tonight?
I needed the wild real bad, and he was blocking it, spoiling it.

Though running, I couldn't run away anymore. I was betrayed twice. Then, outside the bedroom door, and now, by my own psyche, on the water-door's edge, in the same town. Experiences in nature were what I could depend on. I was at home, felt alive there. I needed those feelings. How was it possible that I, with such a long and deep relationship with the wild, suddenly felt so rejected by it? There had, it seemed, been no warning signs. As with all existential diseases, you notice a symptom here, a dysfunction there, but it's all very fragmentary and disconnected until you get diagnosed in what oncology researchers term a symptom cluster.

The symptoms had just reared their heads. I felt like my soul had been put in a trash compactor.

* * *

Less than a year after my swim, the malaise lingering, we moved back to Colorado, and I took a job managing a few rock-climbing magazines, thinking I could outrun the disease. I spent as much time in the mountains as I could. I thought, like so many of us do, that just *being in* drop-dead, postcard landscapes would be my panacea. Like living near a guru, all you need to do is be there, soak it up, right? Finally, I could be in the heart of nature again and there was no excuse. Nature would have to arrive. And so, into the deep valleys of the Rocky Mountains I ran, light and fast, always alone. I drank direct from every stream I came across. Two to three times a week I entered mythical landscapes. Through and in the slick-rock canyons of Moab I climbed and explored, along with my family, swimming in the watering holes, crawling through the slots … and so on. The good stuff. Magazine cover landscapes. I was healthy, strong, with a good job and a good family.

I believed all this face time with nature would repair my relationship with the wild, because the bigger the beauty, the greater the experience, right?

Wrong. I was searching. I was desperate. The wild was there. I was there.

But where?

* * *

There had, literally, never been a time in my life when I had gone into the woods to run, climb or hike, and it hadn't given me what I had asked of it … and this was because what

I had asked of it had been rather shallow. I had, in essence, lacked imagination.

While I didn't even know the right questions to ask, of myself or of the wild, I did have inklings, from books. In high school, a Catholic boys' school—which I attended not on account of faith, but because I got into too much trouble in public school—I came across Ralph Waldo Emerson.

At the time, I was an insecure reader and a horrible student. I could barely understand anything I read and the reports coming home from my teachers confirmed as much. I remember telling this to my mom and she sat me down at the kitchen table for an experiment. I was fourteen or so. The kitchen was empty except for us, my dad at work and my sister self-quarantined in her room. I remember our red table mats, the polished wood table. The window over the sink. The room was quiet. My mom read a page from a history book, American history, and then she had me read it. After I was done, she asked: "Now, what do you remember?"

I remembered nothing.

"Nothing?" she asked. She couldn't believe it.

I could read the words just fine, but, as the saying goes, in one ear and out the other. Even more of a reason to pursue adventure sports. I read less as a result. But my reading challenges vanished—poof!—when I came across Emerson and the Zen poets. Because it was a college-prep high school, I had blocks of free time, which I increasingly spent in the library by the big windows overlooking a courtyard of maples and elms. Emerson was an American nature writer and philosopher, and he spoke about the wild in a way I had only felt inklings of, but, because I had inklings, it was as if he spoke to me directly. My soul thirsty, I read everything I could get my hands on by him. From Emerson I absorbed personal transcendence via a romantic and intimate embrace of decaying logs, green moss and New England leaves. Emerson spoke of a world I knew well, all so well; his and my landscapes were geographic cousins. In *The Poet*, he wrote: "For, as it is dislocation and detachment from the life of God, that makes things ugly, the poet, who re-attaches things to nature and the Whole, — re-attaching even artificial things, and violations of nature, to nature, by a deeper insight, — disposes very easily of the most disagreeable facts." The poet feels, sees, communicates, re-attaches the artificial and violations (*kintsugi*) and, thanks to the latter union, disposes of disagreement (discontent). Beauty is the poet's goal, the altar in which she worships. The altar is the wild. This would be the basis of how I'd identify myself for the next twenty years. I'd already been a poet when I discovered Emerson, but he taught me that to be a poet of nature you need to see with clarity, sobriety, honesty. You need to feel. You need insight. I'd nearly major in poetry in college until a late game switch to journalism. My father successfully convinced me a job in poetry wasn't waiting for me after graduation.

I was amazed Emerson could talk about the woods in the way he did, with such majesty for the details and unbridled curiosity and poise and astonishment. He pulled something from bark and bugs that I wanted. He elevated the wild and communicated to me, over so many hours and pages, that it was worth looking into. He took my childhood woods and turned them into an object of philosophical and spiritual reflection; the church at my school was replaced by the temple of the forest. For Emerson, the wild was personal and delicate and emotional, and because I was a climber, I was aware of a growing ability I had with the wild: my fingertips knew stone, my legs knew the hills, my eyes knew how to navigate terrain. I had an in.

Lines like this from the New England sage seared into my young mind and became permanent fixtures in my mental life: "Most persons do not see the sun … The lover of nature is he whose inward and outward senses are still truly adjusted to each other; who has retained the spirit of infancy even into the era of manhood. His intercourse with heaven and earth, becomes part of his daily food. In the presence of nature, a wild delight runs through the man, in spite of real sorrows." I felt that delight. I didn't need to try. In Emerson, there is a lot of "he," nature doing good work for *this* person. Emerson portrayed the wild as a romantic interlude; we touch, it touches back; our eyes reach out like tentacles; our bare feet become native. He writes, "In the woods, we return to reason and faith." In Zen, however, the "he" is absent. In Zen, nature is equally poignant, but impossibly understated, and you never found reason and faith in nature. Quite the opposite—nature pried you from a reliance on reason and self, and Zen has no tolerance for faith. Basho, a Zen poet, scribes: "The snow of yesterday / That fell like cherry blossoms / Is water once again." Simple, sober, immutable laws of the wild, unadorned with sentiment. There was, indeed, a formless obsession in Emerson at times—an obsession with the invisible, the beyond, the thing without form—but it was often balanced with a tangible sense that he just loved the woods. I related. In Zen, however, there was nothing to find, and the idea of a *person who finds* is a barrier to finding. In fact, the very act of *trying to find* is, more often than not, the thing keeping you from what you seek. The desire to find, you could also say, is a guaranteed way not to find anything. I related to that as well.

These two traditions loitered in my subconscious for decades.

* * *

I can see it now, but I was the dumb money at nature's table, caught in universal mythos and stories predating me, like a lot of us are. This was the essence of my state of mind at the time, but it is also the essence of how millions of us do, and don't, perceive and interact with the wild today. Our perception is broken. Our bodies are short-circuiting.

Let's run through how we think of her today—Nature is stressed, her animals lost, ecosystems in decline. It's not a coincidence that as she is broken, we can't see her. The wild is a place of singular beauty, but whose beauty we know not what it does nor what it is for. We mythologize her curves, her valleys and vistas. Studies tell us nature is good for our health;[4] the sound of rain relaxes us, gives our attention-deficit minds an eddy to wade in; spiritual without the spirit. Coke without the caffeine. Nature is the place of former magic, dark and light spirits alike, but today it is without the stories told by our ancestors of mountain gods, fish spirits, trees with eyes. We have in our unconscious the ghost of this nature mythos, a long-dormant expectation whispering to us today about the majesty in her hills. We idolize the wild in wilderness, but fail to see the wild all around. We are, as a people, unable to rewild ourselves.

We want from the wild badly, to cure so many ills, to remind ourselves of what we are not, to counter our toasted modernity with the syrup of the ancient. We valorize the Indigenous relationship to the land as a panacea for our alienation from it. But in these wants we are trying to leverage nature for a benefit. And whenever one thing is leveraged for another, you can't see the thing for itself. And so, the very same impulse driving record National Park visitations is the thing preventing us from establishing a lasting, intimate relationship with the wild. I speak from experience. And while those National Park visits are increasing, the data shows the duration of the visits is shrinking. We are, simultaneously, going to National Parks more but there for shorter periods of time. We are like kids forced to go to church by our unconscious. Glad to have gone, but not much to see.

In so many areas, we are trying to bring the wild to us. The wild has become medical prescription of sorts, a consumable for the disgruntled soul: green architecture, bigger parks, community gardens, more trails, reintroducing species, conservation. Real estate with a mountain view or access to nature is becoming even more of a premium. In my area, with Aspen not far away, people build 30-million-dollar mansions with panoramic views of snowcapped peaks and hillsides dotted with dark-green Douglas fir. But our experience of the wild, our connection with the real spirit of the mountains, is not enhanced by a wraparound porch and a hot tub.

Which brings me to Albert Sutton.

Microtopia

Nature often reserves great thoughts for no one.
Emphasis on no "one."

After laying eyes on Columbia Island for the first time, in 2007, the late multi-millionaire Albert Sutton was bewitched. About an acre in size, though it shrinks at high tide, Columbia Island was unkempt, raw and derelict, and just north-east of New York City. The island sat just off the coast of New Rochelle, New York, about a five-minute boat ride from shore, a thirty-minute drive north and east of Manhattan. Along with Rat Island, Pea Island (which Sutton also owned) and Huckleberry Island, it is part of a string of rocky islands in that part of Long Island Sound, a large estuary in the shape of a finger, which, as it happens, points at Manhattan. A few media conglomerates used it in the 1940s, and the ensuing two decades, to host radio transmission towers. There was nothing remarkable, at first glance, about the small island. More than anything, it was an eyesore for passing fishermen. Sutton, however, saw what could be, rather than what was, despite the rusting radio tower and ugly one-story administrative building calling the island home. Sutton saw the waters encircling the island. Smelled the salt-laden air. Admired the island for being in the middle of the tide. He got a good Emersonian feeling.

He promptly bought the island for $1 million.

A pathologist turned real-estate developer, Sutton had dark, inset features, a slightly offset neck that kicked his head to looker's right, and, from the few images I found of him online, a melancholy seriousness; he doesn't seem willing to smile, nor frown. For someone who would make another zag into acting and filmmaking—notably in films with a strong ethical bent—he does not have a robust online presence. Reflecting on when he saw the property for the first time, Sutton thought, "Wow, what a Zen experience this could be."

So, he went about designing a Zen experience.

After acquiring the island, Sutton proceeded to pour another $8 million into renovations over the course of a decade: pumps, solar panels, water desalination systems, hurricane-proof windows and walls, marble in the bathrooms, stainless steel fixtures in the kitchen, exposed brick, etc.

From the outside, you'd mistake the current 5,600 square-foot luxury mansion for a small administrative building, which, of course, it once was. With a dull brown exterior in the shape of a square, a luxury eco-paradise it does not look. The inside, however, is exceptional—Euro-modern minimalist with large swatches of white, exposed ceilings and clean, thoughtful lines throughout. It has a minimalist Zen vibe, and he designed it to be self-sufficient too, truly an island unto itself. Beyond its bulwarks, the North Atlantic nips and flows; unharried birds, fisherman and day yachters chug by; and tree-lined shores—not unlike the one I stood in that night when going for a midnight skinny-dip—stretch out across the vista. That landscape would have swooned me as well.

After ten years of renovation, flooring installed, landscape designed, Sutton didn't get the Zen experience he was looking for.

"I thought I would have great thoughts out here," he said.

He slept in the house one night, then put it up for sale. I could relate. I felt like I wanted to put my life up for sale.

Before he decided to sell, I imagine there was a moment when the home was finished—the last bit of trim nailed on, the paint barely dry and the reclining chairs on the patio unpackaged—and he anchored his boat to his private dock. He walks up to the deck, peers around like a new father, proud of his creation. He takes a few breaths. It is quiet but not silent. The water laps at the stone barriers. A few seagulls. He has waited for this moment to arrive.

He sits, perhaps a coffee in hand. He has sunk a decade, and $8 million, into the moment.

I stood there, outside Baltimore, about to cast off into the liquid ether.

His eyes scan the horizon.

It was after midnight, on a Tuesday.

Boats hum. A vague, if ill defined, sentiment of completion washes over him.

Us.

He slides his hands in his pockets.

I didn't have pants on. I slide into the water.

The sun's rays splintered on a few wakes from passing boats.

A midnight moon threw silver.

He waited, but nothing happened.

I waited, but got myself, defunct, in return.

Nature had, apparently, reserved great thoughts for someone else.

Night Run

You will find that when you imagine a future, or past, version of yourself, you are always in a place. Study that fantasy carefully.

To get to any *ground zero*, a place in which we hope to heal, have those great thoughts, and find the deepest layer of ourselves, we have to go on a *night run*. A ground zero is a place we imagine, along *with an idealized version of ourselves in that place*. The night run is what we do to get to our ground zero. Some night runs are fun and juvenile, others are illicit and the stakes are high. My night runs have always been somewhere in the middle.

Ground zeros are not good or bad, but a function of our brain, which, once formed, becomes a central actor in our minds. *Brain* I understand as the hard-wired biological organ within our skull; *mind* is closely related, on most fronts, with brain, expressing it in an odd ether we call consciousness. But mind and brain are not the same, a sentiment shared by a few top brain scientists.[5] "The mind is separate, yet inseparable from, the brain," writes neuroscientist Caroline Leaf.[6] It's a sentiment held by meditation masters for thousands of years as well: "Just as the physical organ of the eye is not site, and the physical organ of the ear is not hearing, the brain is not the mind," said Mingyur Rinpoche, echoing thousands of years of meditation-fueled introspection.

Mind is generally felt as aligned with our brains, the latter engineered by evolutionary biology and cultural input, but it can inhabit a place and power outside our skulls where it is privy to sentiments, vagueness or even "experiences" of places and times beyond our brain's purview—it's not mystical, just misunderstood. That it can do so is unmistakable for those who have experienced it.

A ground zero is a desired identity in a place, aka in a landscape. This notion is critical because we forget that our future and past visions of ourselves are always in a place, fully situated and embodied, in relation to surrounding things. A ground zero, and my naming as such, is an attempt to bring place into conversations about identity. Who are you? What kind of person do you want to be? What is the best future version of yourself? Most of us work toward cultivating this person, with varying degrees of awareness and intentionality. In fact, feverish self-cultivation is one of the most common tropes in the contemporary obsession with self-mastery and self-optimization. You will find that when you imagine this future person, such as who you want to be, you are always *in a place*. You look a certain way, feel a certain way, have certain things around you; you are in a scene, as if a set stage. Place-based selfhood is what defines a ground zero, over and against the empty concept of identity. When we think of what our identity is, we don't try to imagine a landscape; rather, our mind does it automatically. Mind, being born and cultivated in a body *in a place*, needs place to think, to solve problems, and since *we* are a problem to ourselves, we imagine ourselves in a place. A ground zero is a solution we present to ourselves. As for your future self, perhaps you imagine yourself sitting in a spacious room with a desk, overlooking a leafy park. You are unharried, financially secure, in control; or you are painting in a studio, the sun filtering through broad windows, finally having the time to scratch that creative itch; or, you have lost fifty pounds and you're running through the tape at your first marathon. The crowd cheers. The sun is shining. These ground zeros give us good feelings because they solve the bad ones in the present. Ground zeros can take shape very early, as mine did, such as the wish to be a good son, a climber, a nature-whisperer. Or, the type of person who owns and relishes their private island, like Sutton.

Ground zeros are cinematic, scripted by our imagination, cued from the world we know, constructed using the social and cultural tools at our disposal and populated by the narrow range of objects, values and spaces dear to us. The night run is merely how we get to a ground zero; *night* because it's a game of being in the shadows and of chasing phantoms. How else, other than in darkness, can we chase ghosts? *Run* because of the often-mad pitch to arrive. Think of ground zeros like existential psychodramatic landscapes we expect or desire to inhabit, except we are not them, can never be them and can never arrive on account of the fact that, once we inhabit our zero, should we be lucky enough, we automatically imagine another ground zero; expectation and prediction are the fuel, but they are also magicians. The magician reveals it was all just expectation, all mind, from inception to completion. Nonetheless, we chase them. We might have been in them in the past, when we were happier, or more successful, and so we might look back to them as an idealized model for going forward, as I did with the wild. As such, they can be nostalgic or aggressive, but never conservative. They indicate a change we desire, like an "index" in the language of investing—they track a change in performance.

Many of us are motivated, inspired and driven to align our current selves with these future selves, and some of us appear to get "there." We run that marathon, we lose the weight, we get the nice job or the fancy house, but whatever state of being we get from arriving is as fleeting as morning frost in the sun and it never, *ever*, aligns with the person we thought we'd become. A new zero, or a modified, more optimized one always awaits. It's just a trick our minds play on ourselves.

Alex Honnold, the first person to climb El Capitan without a rope, a high achievement if there ever was one, recently remarked that after achieving his once-in-a-lifetime goal, he thought he'd be different. A different person with different feelings. Perhaps a different outlook. But, as he said, he was still the same person the next morning. Michael Phelps, one of the most decorated Olympians of all time, with twenty-three gold medals to his name, struggled with severe depression, wondering "Who was I, outside the swimming pool?" In the back of his mind, he felt more gold medals would smooth over life's jagged shorelines. He thought he'd be somebody with the most gold medals in the world, but, as it turns out, once he got those medals, that person never appeared along with them. Selfhood is always empty, which is why we can change our versions of it so much.

It's like this for all of us. Dissatisfaction with the "here" is what causes us to chase the next "there." Most of the time, the dissatisfaction begins in the now but becomes more pronounced the closer you get to the zero, as with Phelps, which is ironic, because you'd think the opposite would be the case. But it isn't so, because he got closer to the truth instead. Not everyone is lucky enough to see through the cycle. One of the most talented, respected and successful musicians in our lifetime, Avicii, said before his death: "I was running after some idea of happiness that wasn't my own. I didn't like being a persona, I didn't like having a persona. I didn't like having to be Avicii and then having to be Tim. I wanted to be the person who was up on that stage liking it." Avicii seemingly found his zero, got so close to it that he almost was it, but then, like Sutton, like Phelps, when the music stopped, the person you wanted to be doesn't arrive. Avicii would end up taking his own life. Sometimes, we chase our zeros so far it is hard to turn around.

Because a ground zero resides in a place, we mistakenly chase the place and the accoutrements in this psychodramatic fantasy, which means we are leveraging today for tomorrow. When you leverage, you lose.

In military terms, a ground zero is the spot where an explosion occurs, sometimes the exact point where a bomb strikes the earth. Hiroshima was the ground zero of a US-dropped nuclear weapon. In seismology and disaster protocols, a ground zero is where the epicenter of disaster occurs, say, the place where an earthquake inflicts the most damage. More generally, it can mean a starting point, and more recently, it has become synonymous with the former site of the Twin Towers, lost in 9/11—Ground Zero. A ground zero isn't necessarily a pleasant place upon arrival.

I've borrowed the phrase because all the nuances of the term—starting point, epicenter, trauma, past/present, memorial—are captured. We typically establish a ground zero as a result of suffering: a lost loved one, a lost piece of ourselves, an event rendering us unfulfilled, exiting the womb. I chased the wild because I felt I had lost everything else—my girlfriend, my friends, my place of home—and I left for the mountains. I figured I'd be safe there, find the peace and wisdom I was looking for, where Emerson and the Zen poets said it was.

The idea of a ground zero first came to me after my failed run and swim in Loch Raven, as it was that moment—lying there face up in the water, the stars above, a vision of myself floating below—along with the ensuing confusion that caused me to look deeper into what I had created in my mind, why I had created it, and what the contents of the psychodrama I was working out that night were. Or, more precisely, what this psychodrama was forcing me to perform. I hadn't, I realized, been in control of my mind. I was at its whim. I also realized my experience crystalized the desires of generations of romantic nature warriors, wild lovers, nature devotees, and those striving day in and day out to crack the shell enclosing nature's Heraclitean veil and great wisdom—a wisdom I hoped to apply to myself. When I began looking at my failure carefully, I realized I wasn't alone in this imaginative enterprise, and yes, I was swooned by the nature bards, but as I dug into the neuroscience research I realized it was also a function of how our minds work. Not only that, the way our minds use place in the imagination doesn't just illustrate a mechanism by which we think, but an essential truth about how our brain has evolved in concert with landscape, eventually leading to our minds today. In short, we can have no thought *without that thought being in a landscape*.

That's interesting. And it has, in so many ways, led us to the mistaken belief that nature hides, that it is always, somehow, one step away. How could anything be closer? But to see it, of course, we need to see clearly.

The idea of the ground zero is born from the fact that nature writing and all its adjacent mystical romanticism needs more neuroscience, more evolution, more science to balance it out. Neither shall rule. With the two, we not only learn more about the wild, but about our minds in the process, and there is no nature experience without mind. Every experience of the wild occurs in the mind, first and foremost.

The ground zero uses landscape for a curious reason—the mind was born in and of landscape, literally, from tens of thousands of years in the wild. "Even planning mechanisms (such as "consciousness"), which supposedly deal with novel situations, depend on ancestrally shaped categorization processes and are therefore not free of the past."[7] Our minds have a specific shape and talent like all parts of our bodies, like the thickness of our bones or the color of our blood; the latter has a purpose and is just so for a very good reason. It could have been otherwise, but it wasn't. As it was born in the wild, in land, the mind has no choice but to imagine itself in place. In color. In scene. Place is the medium of self-centered mind, or "small mind"—to be distinguished from "big mind," which is the awareness level we tap into when our small minds, our minds of self, come into view.[8] When I am talking of mind in this book, it will typically be of small mind. That mind is forced to imagine place, out of biological necessity, and thus reveals a trace of the wild in us, a trace so faint and thus so easily taken for granted it might go forever unexamined, like dark matter, which is all pervasive and yet, to date, undetectable. It is my assumption too that examining the fundamental ways the wild engineered our brains and minds and ground zeros helps pry loose assumptions we have of our distance from the wild.

We needn't shy away from the violence of a ground zero. The destruction. The loss of life. That too is essential here, since it is the ground zero to which we are running on our quest to chase a phantom. And chasing phantoms, a human trait if there ever was one, is always destructive: to ourselves, others, the time we've been gifted. Truth has no better hiding place than in the folds of self-deception.

Though it's a terminus, we think life begins in our ground zeros. We memorialize ourselves, draping self-statues in gold lacquer. *Kintsugi.* And yet, in the quest to find it, the journey degrades, the shit plant arrives, and the destination too. A vacuous crater.

In a ground zero, we are not really dreaming of *a being*, though that is indeed the form it takes, but of a being *in being*, the verb, a gesture of what it means to live. Life presents no other journey, no other ask of us. To live. To live well. Place. Story. Discovery. Place is the foundation of story, and, as Yuval Harari reminds us, we think in stories. We act toward our zeros, tell ourselves narratives of where we've been and where we're going. These stories are existentially satisfying, adding structure and the promise of resolution to issues that are, in essence, chaotic and not resolvable. As for my own story, and so many others, this is precisely where the desire for the wild, or to get on the inside of nature, springs from, since we believe we can *be* more freely in the wild, as it is *there,* in untrammeled terrain and vast solitude, where humanity is *not*, thus we can escape ourselves with greater facility. It's a very old story. You see this impulse in the very origins of nature writing, mountaineering writing, one of stepping *outside* ourselves—intellectually, spiritually, culturally—when we step *into* the wild; it is the foil of civilized societies. The technical definition of wilderness involves a place where humans don't reside, and yet, we pass through hoping to find something which can't be taken from us. This is echoed today in various studies and research about the nature cure, nature deficit disorder, and the varieties thereof.[9] We become enriched, we become engaged when in nature. Nature is good for us. Nature is curative, therapeutic. We want to improve our attention. Our lifespan. We want to relax. We want to brag that we've been some place. Increasingly, the natural world is being positioned as the curative for the increasing unnaturalness of our lives: our processed food, our decreasing vitality as a people. Where do we look to escape? There's only one place, we think, that is *not us.* It's part of the truth. But we still have an extraction mentality, not much different than strip mining, and we are still leveraging nature for *our* benefit, which means we are only seeing the wants of small mind. As the saying goes, if a thief met Mother Teresa, he'd wonder what was in her pockets. We are psychologically mining nature's perceived riches to possess them for ourselves, put it in our wellness back pocket, as it were. Experience is a resource like any other; except it isn't.

The wild is not us, right? It's complicated. Can the wild deliver? Also complicated.

The wild is not just in us as if *we* are here, and *it* is outside our window, but it's in us in the way you can see in a newborn the eyes of the mother, the eyebrows of the father. You can separate a child at birth, but you can't erase its provenance. Discovering this wild provenance is crucial to understanding our brains and minds, who we are and what, ultimately, we can expect from the wild.

What I needed to do, in the wake of my failed encounter with the wild, is figure out *why* I thought it would deliver the wisdom I needed. To do that, I needed to go back.

* * *

Building off my high-school LSD and magic mushroom-induced journeys with Emerson and Zen and Muir (books before drugs, for what it's worth), I always nurtured an image of myself as a writer and a climber, and, as such, I had to manage dueling versions of myself, which I would indulge in to varying degrees, on different days of the week. Both sought intimacy with the wild, but via different methods. Sometimes the two ground zeros interlocked, such as in my first climbing philosophy book, but, in general, they squatted in my psyche like guests in a small house with an even smaller hallway, such that each time the writer was called into the kitchen (the world) from its bedroom (my unconscious) it would have to awkwardly scoot and shuffle past my climber zero. Their uncomfortable interaction calls to mind Marina Abramović and Ulay's 1977 *Imponderabilia*, a simple piece of performance art where the two artists, one a woman and one a man, stood naked facing each other at the entrance to an art exhibit. In order to enter, visitors had to squeeze in between their naked bodies, through a space big enough for a person to walk, but small enough so that you'd be brushing up against both of them.[10] Abramović called the piece "living doors." Some visitors just couldn't deal, and either turned around or found a side door. Police were called. The exhibition shut down. There's a lot more to say about the piece of art, of course, but I can't help feel it is the most accurate representation I have of the zeros that lived inside me, and I think it's interesting, and better, than the old "two selves" or "two versions of subjectivity" inside the human mind, because these selves have bodies, personalities, desires, wants, and they squat in landscapes and have to look at each other. I'd shuffle down the hallway of my life and squeeze through nakedness, the climber and the writer, each aiming for the same wild, laughing, crying, trying so hard, giving up.

Rinse and repeat. Samsara. The cycle.

My climber zero sought remoteness, adventure, difficulty, hardship, learning. He was good. He had goals. He achieved a lot of goals. He was driven. Success was pitched as achieving those goals. He was told he could become a pro. He enjoyed listening to the stone and became adept in the art of movement. He wrote a book about it. He thought his ability to move on rock and stone brought with it a wisdom of the wild, which it did, in a way; he did get to know, with great intimacy, a slice of nature, but whatever wisdom there was did not compensate for the feeling, or search, for an ultimate truth of the wild. This climber was propelled to repeat the climbing experience time and time again. The late Ueli Steck said it right when he stated, "Mountaineering is a transient experience. I need to continuously repeat it to live it." I was like a donkey with a carrot dangling in front of its nose and walking into the desert to my death just to get a bite of the carrot.

For my writer zero, I imagined traveling the world like a National Geographic photojournalist, flung to far-off places, visiting a remote tribe here, a secret community there. This person was not riveted to rock, but free. This person was learning from the wild, plucking wisdom from the earth like wild raspberries on a summer hillside. When I reexamine my perceptions of this self, this ground zero, I was always in places, and stunning places at that—big nature, big rivers, sprawling deserts, deep canyons. Nature on steroids. Luckily, my climber zero brought me to these places; not just to them, but in them, on them, as if one zero was delivering a package to another zero. Very convenient.

I imagined my writer zero standing or sitting, and taking notes, a romantic scribbler on the edges of civilization, like Wilfred Thesiger trekking through the empty quarter in Arabia, or Percy Fawcett hacking at the dense undergrowth in the Amazon in search of El Dorado. The feelings this person would have would be tremendous, catastrophically beautiful, crippling in their awe. He was more native than adventurer. The notes of this writer were little, hard-won truths pulled from the thickets of exotic adventure, and, even at this time, an image of nature as the skilled surgeon of my soul took root in my mind, as it does for so many of us. One of the more complicated influences for this zero, an endless task to entangle, would be the Native American. Like a lot of young boys, I was fascinated, enamored, curious and reverent towards this figure, and it *was* a figure, a product of my imagination, as I hadn't had contact with a single Indigenous person growing up. And yet, in college, I took courses in Native American literature and ritual, and the dots connected: one reason I was so drawn to this person was that here, in the Navajo on his horse on the dry bluff of the red rock, was the listener, the real steward of the land, who could read its signs, who knew landscape was life, and life was land. I projected in him, and her, or in the shaman, a depth of feeling and reverence I so badly wanted. Was this an "othering," a juvenile misunderstanding, a romantic fantasy? Of course. But it propelled me into the wild like nothing else. It was my karma working itself out, for better or worse.

My fantasies were cliches, archetypes, and the best models I had at my disposal to get to know the wild, to be an Emersonian poet in its court, in its grand medium.

It was for these reasons that, immediately after college, I got a shit job cleaning up flood and fire damage in houses, remodeling bathrooms and installing carpet, and occasionally cleaning up the bloody aftermath of violent death. I was saving as much as I could, ready to set off to southern Africa, Europe and South-east Asia with a lovely girl I now call my lovely wife. The climbing accomplishments somewhat achieved, with little net gain to the self I thought I'd be (a meta shit plant), it was time to hand over the torch. The writer zero could finally have his shot at delivering the panacea.

Big Nature

To be a climber, a mountain runner, a surfer,
to do anything in a natural medium—your skills develop only
in relation to your ability to read and react to a landscape.

To the Jordanian deserts we trekked, in the footsteps of Wilfred Thesiger, to drink from the same spring as Lawrence of Arabia. In Petra and Wadi Rum we rode camels, slept in the sherbert-colored hills of the Arabian outback. We climbed Mount Sinai in 100-degree temperatures, slept in the open air at the summit, and were treated to the most gorgeous sunrise I've ever seen. We went to the Kalahari; the jungles of Cambodia and Angkor Wat; to the Okavango Delta in Botswana, to Victoria Falls in Zimbabwe. We hitchhiked in northern Burma, in Syria, through the West Bank. And so on.

I was acting out my writer zero, because this zero was a nature-whisperer. And this zero liked big nature.

In the sprawling red sands of the Namibian desert, I remember seeing oryx for the first time, far off in the distance, below a snaking crest of sand. This was a creature I had seen countless times in nature shows as a child with my mother, and on the glossy print of *National Geographic.* But now, I was here. It was here. I could see it with my own eyes. I had arrived.

The oryx is an extravagant animal, with long, spear-pointed horns, a horse-like tail, and the face of a Georgia O'Keeffe painting; on its face there is a fur pattern that can only be described as skull-flower, a white patch painted dramatically down its face and coming to a point midway between its eyes and nose. The rest of its face is black, except the area of its mouth, which turns stark white again. It wears an organic mask. The main body of the animal is brown but under its belly is a thick black stripe extending down its legs, and then white socks.

When I first caught a glimpse of this beautiful creature, I was standing barefoot in a patch of shade in a gravel parking lot. The second I walked out of the shade, it felt like I was walking on hot coals. From walking about thirty feet on the pavement, I got blisters on the bottoms of my feet that would take a month to go away. In contrast, the oryx could walk carefree in the scorching sands, picking up its feet *just enough* to walk, but no more, a stride depositing a set of snake-like tracks where its hoofs would drag on the surface of the sand, leaving a distinctive V-shape. The animal did this because in such a harsh climate, where water and food were scarce, it couldn't afford to waste its energy. Anything more than dragging its feet wasn't needed, and, as such, this stride, though seeming inefficient and lazy, was the most efficient. That made an impression on me. I sat with that observation for a while, the slow cadence of the animal trudging along the sands of my mind, finding shade, so close to death. It was fully in tune with its environment. I was impressed anything could survive in that landscape, so inhospitable it was, as if nature was trying to kill you—which it was. In the lack of green or water or anything that felt verdant and luscious, this landscape was as extreme as the Arctic. I wondered what the oryx would be like in an area full of shade and rain, where it could run with no fear of wasted energy? What traits would come out? Did the oryx regret its decision to set up camp in the Namib desert? At the time, I felt the animal was in a jail of sorts, confined to a harsh and joyless life of survival, of eking out, and yet, it had thrived just fine.

As an athlete, I understood the oryx. We had a connection. On long days in the mountains, when your energy reserves are depleted, when your muscles are in full revolt, your attention dull and ethereal, your stomach empty and lips cracked, your body becomes extremely efficient, much more so than when it is full of strength. At first this seems counterintuitive, since it should be the case you can perform the most efficient movements when you are at full strength. But that's not true when it comes to endurance. When you are in lows, when the *S* word—survival—rears its head, the body takes over with an intelligence impossible to fully decipher and inhabit otherwise, with movement-conclusions, such as a running or hiking gait using the bare minimum. You become like the oryx, unthinkingly dragging its hoofs. The landscape, ever wise, wraps itself around your experience. It is not that your body is listening, it is that you have allowed your body to be played, in the manner of an instrument, by the wild.

This very phenomenon is a hidden gem about animal and human life. I'd got this body wisdom idea from Zen, through years of absorption, and I'd crafted it as an athlete, unknowingly in large part. For Zen, the body is the prime medium, as close to the mind as anything else, as Thich Nhat Hanh said. Nature, I'd soon learn, allows the body to experience itself fully and directly, without remainder. That's a leg up when you are trying to understand your mind.

I was jealous of the oryx, and since I had inside me a zero that sought to soak nectar from the land, to pull a philosophy from it, a new way of life, I was beholden to the wisdom of animal life, and full of admiration for how well the oryx's body was in sync with the landscape. This was something I clearly felt I lacked, but wanted, and did have in small portions.

Why is this important? Remember the Chinese character for swimmer: "one who knows the nature of water." To do that, as Gilles Deleuze would say, you have to become animal. My tactic was to go deep into the areas I knew well, to see if the part could become the whole. I'd try to leverage this *knowing* to enter the wild. What I didn't know at the time was that I was developing a skill I did want and need—listening to landscape—while at the same time constructing the walls of my separation from the wild.

As a climber, a mountain runner, any kind of athlete within a natural medium—your skills develop only in relation to your ability to read and react to a landscape. A climber needs to touch and see rock with the same amount of intelligence an astronaut needs to navigate space. To climb ice, you really need to understand the medium of frozen water at a very deep level—how it sounds when you swing your tools into it, how it vibrates, and doesn't, how it drips, its color—otherwise you are not going to survive long. To excel as a mountain athlete, I had to let the landscape in. I had to develop muscle that would allow me to go deeper, tendons and sinews that wouldn't leave me stranded in the mountains. I had to empty my mind so that rock and ice could enter, so I could listen to its language. I thought I was building a listening-machine, and I did for a bit—or so I thought—but years later, while standing naked on the shores of that reservoir at midnight, I'd learn a tough lesson: the things you own eventually own you.

Sometimes you invest in the wrong things. Investors bias is quite a thing, after all. You get too attached to your talents. You leverage the love of your life to benefit you.

I saw that the oryx was living in communion with its environment; it had an intuition inaccessible to any technology, GPS tracking device, or AI brain-mining software we could subject it to. Its inner life is, of course, a mystery. The oryx doesn't worry about getting a job, paying bills. It doesn't suffer from the constraints we put on ourselves. The oryx finds a nice spot to sleep at night, perhaps with a few others, and gets up in the morning, going on about its business for the twenty-or-so years it lives, finding a mate, swishing its tail (which it does constantly), avoiding hunters, licking dewy rocks for water, digging holes for shade, eating shrubs and grasses, particularly in the morning or evening. Who has it better—us or the oryx? Beauty in simplicity is a flow of life revered in Taoist philosophy. In one accounting, the oryx wins, lacking all the ups and downs, the simplicity; its evenness is meta-biology at work. On the other hand—and I'm speculating—the oryx does not have ecstatic joy when it births a child, nor, when it gets a tasty bite of food, does it do the happy dance.

Like the wild, the animals in it have forever been a sounding board for how we talk about ourselves. It was precisely observations like mine above—animals being driven by biology, automated and machinic—that led René Descartes in the sixteenth century to conclude that animals didn't have a soul. Since intelligence was the product of a soul—which we had—the lack thereof laid the groundwork for an inhumane stance towards animal life, *inhumane* in the strict sense of the world: lacking humanity. Today, we have a much more generous definition of intelligence, but remain largely indifferent to the plight of our non-human friends.

Nicolas Malebranche, a Frenchman living and writing in the seventeenth century, wrote of animals, "They eat without pleasure, cry without pain, grow without knowing it; they desire nothing, fear nothing, know nothing."[11] Malebranche's attitude sums up a lot of what we can call the genre of *thinking about animals* up until that point, including that of Descartes, but also a stance toward the wild that holds for a lot of people today, despite the vast research on animal emotions, the complexities of their intelligence, and so on.[12] In the twentieth century, Jesuit Priest and philosopher Teilhard de Chardin concluded, "The animal knows, of course. But certainly it does not know that it knows." The animal lacks awareness of itself, so the story goes. Human observation of animal intelligence leads us to supposedly obvious conclusions: animals are not paralyzed by self-reflection, and, as they bed down at night in a hidden patch of the forest, they don't think, "Man, those humans have it pretty good." Animals are just in their environments, of their environments. Our awareness of this difference is analogous to the awareness of our own exile, an exile from our basic nature.

For the majority of us, animals are loving pets, food, curiosities at the park or zoo, lovely things to ponder when we hike, or signs of an epoch slipping like sand through our fingers, and thus are magnificent on account of living on the edge of extinction. Our stance towards them reveals more about *our* animal life—how we think we are different, the limits of our minds in encompassing them—than it does them. With few exceptions, our denigration of *their* wisdom, *their* genre of embodiment, which they have by the truckload, is just not wisdom we have been able to recognize or respect. Though we marvel at them, animal life seems closer on the scale to self-moving dirt than divinely enfleshed human. But there is in all religious traditions a subtle nod to the brilliance of animal mind, whether this is a valorization of enchainment to presence, of deep sensation reception, embeddedness in the elements, the lack of a fear of death, or the inability to overthink a situation. Each one of these, however covert, carries profound weight in religious systems.

And yet, we don't want to acknowledge animal mind because we feel, as a species, we have overcome it, graduated, as it were, from the forest to the city, the latter a metanarrative of civilization if there ever was one. Animal embodiment is often cast as a biological yoke, a burden, *their curse*. From the city to the stars we are pointed, as if destiny. This is our story, right? As Gene Cernan, American astronaut and eleventh person to take a stride on moon, wrote, "It's our destiny to explore. It's our destiny to be a space-faring nation." Space is code for transcendence of the human, the latter *already* transcending the animal. Space is undiscovered, and, so the thoughts go, we will discover undiscovered parts of ourselves when we venture, which is ironic, since we would be skipping the party for the after party, and yet, when we show up at the latter, *no one* is there; no one as *no self.* We need to go down, not up, if we are ever, in fact, to go up.

I'm with Shakespeare and Siddhartha. The former: "It is not in the stars to hold our destiny but in ourselves." And the latter: "With our thoughts we make the world." The wild of the late eighteenth- and nineteenth-century explorers is now the space of twenty-first-century techno-cosmonauts, and the same mistake continues. Not long ago, I sat in my shed to do some breathing. The house was noisy and I needed some quiet. It was winter and very cold. I put on a hat and a big down jacket. Icicles hung from the shingles. A light snow fell. I closed my eyes. I imagined being in a Tibetan cave, or somewhere exotic. After a few minutes of indulging these fantasies, a fact became crystal clear: if you close your eyes, it doesn't matter if you are in Tibet, on the surface of Mars, or in your shed—you always bring you, and this 'you' often obscures everything else you try to put on top of it.

A curious fact of our biological existence is the unfortunate inconvenience of having to live in our heads and minds first, and planets and million-dollar island homes second. We might be a fundamentally exploratory animal (this seems like a reasonable statement), and Mars might be a good place to explore (also reasonable), and there's a thread in our evolutionary history of achieving greater and greater things by inventing and extending our reach (definitely), but we will have learned nothing if we migrate to the stars out of planetary exhaustion and the related inability to cope with our misdirected fantasies, only to discover we are the same person in Colorado or on Mars. Life will not get better for the living, and if our exploits can't pass that litmus test, we should stop until they do. It is also wildly paradoxical that another argument for leaving earth is because of its current state of disrepair, a paradox underscoring not just an ignorance and disrespect towards the earth, but of how we got ourselves into the situation in the first place. In other words, if we exit out of fear we will carry the habits that created the disrepair and fear. And then, we'd only be better off for a bit. Then the cycle continues.

The inherent worth of advancement is just a story we tell ourselves, a story born, no doubt, from the prediction-machine that is the brain, hardwired to always calculate the future, always think that around the corner is what we lack. Keep moving. Moving from the earth, from our animal life, from our bodies. To the stars! To digital downloads! Make better things to do better things and be a better thing. The traits of valuing migration and movement are baked into our DNA from our ancestor's interaction with the wild, but they are maladaptive today, once-valuable traits exercised now with deleterious consequences. A gun pointed at ourselves.

Foraging, plant identification and primitive hunting are things of the past in developed societies, albeit popular in some modern circles. And yet, perhaps we are mistaking one wisdom for another. Survival requires knowledge to thrive and this knowledge requires a wisdom of the body. This is the wisdom we are lacking. We can bracket as *not essential*, as most of us would, the knowledge of plants, a detailed understanding of the seasons, how to build shelters from scratch, how to herd or farm. But we are increasingly finding it difficult to bracket the wisdom of the body, to which all of these things relied on: touch, feel, interaction, the stuff of the body needed for understanding. We know more about the body now than we ever have in history, more graphs and data are born from its flesh than we know what to do with, and yet, the wisdom of the body concerns not its neuro-chemical composition, the mapping of its bones, all the various data points we can extract from watches, straps and such, but how to be with it, how to honor it and how to develop its ability to feel deeper, sense more, attune to its surroundings, find peace.

What is a body?

Just asking the question feels odd, doesn't it?

The answer feels painfully obvious. *Here it is,* we exclaim, holding up our hands. It's a machine for passing on genes. It's the product of evolution. It has an outer and inner skin, and some organs. It does stuff, like regulate our blood pressure, without conscious oversight. It waters from its eyes and produces emotions. It dances and feels fear and gets stiff after sitting for long periods. And yet it's one of the least understood entities we know of, witnessed in a simple fact: our vast and increasing knowledge of it has yet to produce better experience, yet to democratize happiness, greater contentment or anything resembling a heightened human sensation. No bliss, no mystical encounter, no top-tier human experience occurs outside the body. A body is a solution to a problem, however imperfect. It is the solution to the problem of survival. Survival, for our long history, occurred in the wild. The body is a medium in the middle of a medium—the medium of the wild. Mediums are not things; mediums are fields for interaction and potentiality. The point isn't to know this and nod your head. The point is to feel it.

The Stuff of Nature

Unless the wild becomes part of our nervous system, the way a parent feels the pain of a child, we won't succeed.

We couldn't have had nature writing, in its modern, literary form, without first a shift in perspective about the *stuff* in nature. An interest in the stuff of nature first expressed itself in the so-called natural philosophies of the sixteenth century: in the post-Renaissance interest in cataloging species—butterflies, elephants, maple trees—all hand drawn or physically pinned behind glass. This stuff of the wild laid the groundwork for later literary prose of said life in its environment, or nature writing.[13] Nature is interesting and worthy of study, reflection and appreciation: such is the base assumption of nature writing. Ancient philosophers did speak of nature, just not in the strict material form we do today, and the Middle Ages investigated the "book of nature" for signs of God, but such investigations were symbolic; the majesty of a plant, for instance, was only so in light of its creator. Any tracing of the deep origins of nature writing will depend on how we are defining nature, just as anyone who wants to trace the origins of monotheism could theoretically place the origins at the point when one of our primitive ancestors painted a human figure with wings or wondered where a relative went after they stopped breathing. Though a tantalizing rabbit hole to go down, the history of nature, or the concept thereof, should not concern us here.[14] More important is what we believe today, and whether our beliefs help in our quest to understand what we want of it, what it wants of us, how we can coexist with it … or whether the wild hides (Heraclitus) due to something we have done on our end.

History is alive inside us: its wars, loves, fears, and concepts. The good, the bad and the ugly. The contradictions. This goes for ideas of nature as well. We only need to look at our daily reactions, emotions or judgments to see this. We sign a petition to save the polar bears, but kill a housefly. We fertilize our grass with grossly manufactured petrochemicals, harmful for birds and nearby creeks, yet would never throw a candy wrapper on the ground. We support a new development of condos and concrete, yet we never miss recycling day. We put relaxation in the cart at the trailhead. We click on our headlamps and check out. We return a few days later. But we never really see what it is we are entering, and we are never told we should see differently. That's where we fail. It's not that we're wrong. Rather, we need to think about the reasons we've failed to address the health of the wild, because every day, we are making decisions through our bodies. We can teach people to make better ecological decisions, either through regulation or under the threat of penalty, and we can educate them with our top-line environmental messages—climate change is bad, mass extinction is bad, the Anthropocene is bad—but unless there is a connection in and through the body, unless the wild becomes part of our nervous system and we can feel its pain the way a parent feels the pain of a child, we won't succeed. This is because the wild, a body itself, speaks to our *body* the loudest. A parent watching their kid play at the park is not going to let their child go down a slide with nails sticking out of it. Should the child start down the slide, we jump and race to save our kid. We need that kind of reaction to the pain of the wild. But, as of yet, as a people, we don't have that reaction; our bodies don't feel it, having been told lies by our small minds. The motivation of the parent involves a life form they are invested in; mutual bodies. It isn't complicated, nor academic. Take the child away, and it doesn't matter. Replace the child with a rock and our emotions don't get triggered.

What is it about *the life*, the breathing body down the slide, we are reacting to? And what is it about the non-ensouled life of nature we are not reacting to?

* * *

We can try to answer the question with biology or anthropology, social norms or psychology, but each discipline offers only a sliver of insight. The only thing we know is that in our modern lives, nature has been sent down the slide. Unless we acknowledge the *life* it has, and develop our senses to feel it, we will not be motivated to protect it.

Perhaps we have it backwards. It might be wise to imagine how the wild is viewing us.

But nature has no eyes, no life, and so thus, how can it view us?

A living thing looks back at you. If it is alive, by our definition, it re-*presents* the world, and if it re-*presents* the world, it is "looking" at us. Today, everything is looking at us and judging—cameras record, keystrokes are logged, online friends gawk, clicks are measured—except for one. Only one thing, we think, is not looking: the wild. That you feel more watched by TikTok or your iPhone than the forest should strike you as incredibly odd, if not pathological. Most people are distraught when they get one negative comment online about a post. We ruminate. We feel shame, embarrassment. We calculate our response. We devote a considerable amount of emotional energy to managing this other wildness, the so-called internet of things (IOT), looking at us from all directions.

It would certainly strike the vast majority of our ancestors as a preposterous manifestation of indulgent self-awareness to worry more about a stranger's online comment than the ground on which we draw our water and grow our food. Before religious rituals took the form of pomp and circumstance, lavished with gold and silver, they were nature-based and aimed at preserving the harmony of the wild, a task that fell to human hands. There was a pattern: our ancestors sacrificed so the world could continue. They danced for the rain. They offered incense for meat. Our ancestors knew what it took to live and repaid that debt with their time, blood, and lightest touch. We knew the behavior of animals, and they knew us, sacrificing their life for ours. One never took too much, since the effects were immediate and unfortunate. The wild was a medium *in* which we lived, in which we were born, not a medium *on* which we live. As Alan Watts has said, "It is not true that you came into this world. You came out of it."

This leads me to a curious juxtaposition—just as nature's vitality is draining, we are increasingly dressing our world with technological life, or, at least, technology resembling life and lifelike processes. It's not a coincidence, and it resembles a giant cosplay convention. We have devices with language and understanding, which can write back to us, talk to us, empathize, inspire—and thus we engage with them as if they were alive. It's called technobiophilia.[15] It's as if we are replacing one intelligence with another, as if we are hardwired to thrive in intelligence-suffused environments (nature being the first one), except our brains are intent on replicating its own version of intelligence and refusing to acknowledge the intelligence that engineered us. Technobiophilia is a second nature; the great narcissism of civilization.

Attacking Planes with Arrows

The wild is the shadow of civilization. It is a habit we haven't been able to kick until, at least, we know who we are.

In 2008, I stumbled upon an article about uncontacted peoples in the Envira region of Brazil.[16] Carlos dos Reis Meirelles Junior, a Brazilian who works to protect the rights of Indigenous peoples in the Amazon, had a plane fly overhead to take pictures of the tribes, which he intended to leverage to decrease logging in the area. In the pictures, two men painted in red pull back long bows, their arms full of tension; worried others stand nearby. The men are leaning back, weighted on their back foot, indicative of the posture you'd be in to launch an arrow into the heavens. A dark figure stands behind them. Left of the warriors is their hut, a simple grass leaf A-frame, door and wall-less.

Certain political groups in the Brazilian government don't see the value in these ancient peoples living in their forests. They believe the country needs to support its growing population with agriculture and timber, and small groups of pre-civilized peoples are preventing crucial resources from being extracted. The health of many is being sacrificed for the lifestyle of a few, so the argument goes. As for those in favor of protection, what are they protecting? Indigenous peoples' right to life? Or are we protecting something we have imagined, a living relic, no different from the million-dollar security systems surrounding the Mona Lisa? And, if we are protecting a relic, isn't it odd we can't see it, experience it?

The premise of preserving something is, in many ways, to preserve an experience of it, even if that experience is absence. Think of that nice bottle of wine you have stashed away for future enjoyment and consider how much pleasure it has already brought you from not drinking it. But yet here we are protecting something whose status diminishes every time we get close to it. Do we see Indigenous people as mirrors of a "wild humanity" in us? Are our efforts philanthropic, or more narcissistic?

* * *

In the sixteenth century, Michele De Montaigne penned an essay, titled "Of Cannibals," and in it the archetype of the *noble savage* emerged. Appearing in a time of exploration and colonization, and thus exposure to radically different ways of being, the notion was a catch-all phrase for the fascination and repulsion Western culture at large felt towards Indigenous peoples. The idea persisted. In 1904, in a World Fair hosted by St Louis, more than a thousand Filipinos were brought Stateside to live on 47 acres for over half a year, on display as a "living exhibit." Their "wildness" and "animality" fascinated.

The noble savage was *noble* on account of living in tune with nature, not wanting more than they had, a sense of balance with the Earth, a vitality in their bodies and ritual and art. Much was made of the "specimens" of their bodies; strong, virile, etc. On the other hand, they were *savage* on account of their "primitive" nature, living from kill to kill, feast to famine, with no sense of history (at least our idea of it); no understanding of *our* rules, which were "obviously" superior; and without books, arithmetic or Mozart. The noble savage was a marker, of what the Old World had lost *and* what it had gained. It had lost its history, hundreds of thousands of years of intimate communion with the natural world, but it had gained refinement in society, the arts, science. We had progressed. The noble savage was an expression of a deep ambivalence towards ourselves, a product of our self-styled, and hyper aware, exile from a type of consciousness (or intelligence) we knew was valuable but didn't know how to retrieve.

I question my own fascination with Indigenous peoples and how I have romanticized them, like so many others throughout history, as living in a pseudo-Garden of Eden, in simplicity, without our modern ills of greed, the nation state, exploitation, and so on, their senses honed from living in the landscape, eyes able to see what I never could, able to feel what I couldn't, either medicine or toxin; no sense of private property, which, as Rousseau noted, remains a deep source of the "many horrors and misfortunes" afflicting us. I ascribed to them an "innocence," instinctual kindness and lack of cynicism. I wanted in! I was jealous when I read of their ability to track animals, identify medicinal plants, find food in the harshest environments. They were content to be who they were. I was jealous because they had what I wanted, what my listener and climber zero wanted. *What do I have?* I asked my college self. I had the mountains, the ability to go deep and fast into the mountains. I had read things. I had inklings. I had philosophy. I had a body fully equipped to go places in the hills that others couldn't. As I matured, I had, in so many ways, expanded the theater of my adventures: from my childhood forests of Loch Raven to the Arabian desert and elsewhere, I was stepping up my game in anticipation of *what was around the corner*, an explorer's disease if there ever was one.

And yet, just as I was reaching the point of taking my adventures to the next level—crossing the Sahara, for instance, a dream of mine; or rowing across the ocean, another fantasy—I stepped off the gas. It wasn't the first time I took stock and slowed down. I was in my early twenties at the time. I stopped because I felt I knew where the path ended, and, more importantly I guess, where it didn't end. Great adventures in remote places, and great climbing abilities, in no way were going to get me to where I wanted to be: only small mind can travel. I wanted to be awake, and big mind doesn't need to travel. I wanted to be free. Not just untethered physically or economically, the easy versions, but free in mind, beyond suffering, beyond desire. Was it possible? I didn't know, but Zen had me good alright. Even though I stopped, I still chased and puttered and wondered what my life would have been like if I did become a professional athlete or a full-time adventurer. I second-guessed myself for decades.

I know now that this wasn't giving up. It was simply putting energy into different places. Prioritizing. Content that I had sought a better path than slogging in Antarctica for months for a goal I thought would make me a better person, I sought the path of the mind. Still climbing, I nonetheless put my own mind front and center of the journey. I put everything into a PhD in the Philosophy of Religion, and for a decade I read the wisest books ever written. It was a sure bet, I told myself. And thus, content with my decision to pursue realization, when the wild retreated from me that fateful Tuesday night, I was crushed, as if I had made the wrong decision all along. As if I needed to start over.

How did I get it so wrong?

* * *

If "man is born free but is everywhere in chains," as Rousseau asserted in the 1700s, I, for one, wanted to be unshackled, to climb back into the cocoon of nature. My desire was more than just being in the wild. I wanted to be on the inside. The wild had spoken to me deeply and early. I was just trying to catch up.

Part and parcel of the Romantic imagination was not just the wild, but the people in the wild. It took me a while, however, to realize a simple fact—I knew nothing about these peoples other than my own fantasies of what I wanted to be. My ground zeros were the pair of glasses through which I saw, and attempted to leverage, the wild and so-called wild people.

The history of one people encountering another can go a lot of ways, but for European history, it resulted in war and murder, notably of Indigenous peoples, but also, in the same turn, fascination (the "noble savage"). In fact, *othering* their experience created the concept of religion as we know it, a phenomenon placing nature, and people in nature, front and center in how we think about *the religious.* As ritualistic practices were first being documented and studied, first by missionaries and colonists, then by Christian academics, it was thought Indigenous Peoples didn't have religion. They had spirits and deities with names, loosely organized belief systems and idols they worshiped; rituals aplenty; they had creator gods, and lesser gods. But while they had all the makings of religion, they didn't really have it—or so the story goes. Most importantly, and never glossed over by their Western observers, Indigenous practices were grounded in the wild: in using fire ceremony, feathers for adornment, claws for necklaces, ways and manners of being based in the gritty stuff of the wild. Through the eyes of anthropologists, Indigenous spirituality was all very generalized, superstitious and unscientific. In contrast, Europeans, according to Europeans, had religion, as theirs was organized, with books, universal morality, a written code of conduct, and they didn't run around naked, because that's shameful. Of great importance, Euros had a monotheistic god which, while awkwardly participating in the world through a shake of trinitarian chicanery or another variation of abstruse theological speculation, was wholly divorced from the trees and sky while also fully implicated in it (the incarnation), at least in some theological varieties.

The who has religion and who doesn't distinction was, in addition to follower count, largely premised on the proximity to nature; close for Indigenous peoples, and distant for intellectualized monotheisms. Religion also helped the "sophisticated" European define himself against the "tribe," and thus fed into a self-serving story of the civilizational triumph of, as Nietzsche would say, overcoming our baser selves, our innate and wild nature. Few read the tea leaves and called bullshit. Writing in the 1800s, Nietzsche, however, was one of them. Long before the second great war, he wrote, "I call an animal, a species, an individual corrupt, when it loses its instincts, when it chooses, when it prefers, what is harmful to it." For the German, we are the animal whose instincts were neutered, who chose to divorce itself from the *plein air* of the forest and, instead, surround ourselves by smog and traffic. For Nietzsche, nature was the cultivator of instinct; body was how it deployed. The great religions of the West were not achievements for Nietzsche, but liabilities. The equivalence of the wild with a lesser form of spirit continues to this day.

What, then, do monotheisms say about the wild? Christianity, Islam and Judaism—our big three—are surprisingly mute on the topic.[17] With very few exceptions, in all my religious schooling, including three masters degrees and one PhD, on top of obsessive learning before and after graduate school, I can't remember a single exhortation to go outside, walk in the forest or have a swim in the river, other than in general platitudes and insinuations to seek solitude, which might or might not imply being on a mountaintop;

or that, in *Genesis*, God took a break and said his creation was good, as if God's curt observation to his vast handiwork was enough—good. Just "good"? It would have been better to stop there, but, alas, God couldn't help it; quickly after, he gave us dominion over nature, turned it into our property. And if there's one thing to sour a relationship, it's the dynamic of power, which property inculcates.

The idea of owning land was a true toxic chemical leached into the spiritual waters of the West, one that would culminate, at least for me, in the eloquent words of Chief Seattle, who was puzzled at the very idea. He was transcribed as saying, "The President in Washington sends word that he wishes to buy our land. But how can you buy or sell the sky? The land? The idea is strange to us. If we do not own the freshness of the air and the sparkle of the water, how can you buy them? When you are born out of the land, and of the land, selling the land is selling yourself. The earth does not belong to man; man belongs to the earth." How, indeed, can you sell something to which you belong without, in the process, selling yourself? You can't, but that's exactly what we've done. What have we sold ourselves to? A bad idea.

Earlier, I said that Christianity had no response to the wild, with few exceptions. My namesake, St. Francis, was one of those exceptions. He influenced me in profound ways.

The 1181 Saint

Truth is not a proposition you remember—
it is what you find when you take away.

Francis was, and is, the loudest voice in Christendom regarding the beauty and bounty of the wild, the majesty of animal and plant life. He smuggled into the catechism a mysticism of nature misunderstood, if not outright repressed, until this very day. Francis was Shinto, a Jain, a Navajo, a thief of the desert. He tapped into it. He saw it. I grew up with small figurines of St. Francis in my bedroom as a child, him feeding a deer, watching a bird, and I think it sank in.

Giovanni di Pietro di Bernardone, also known as St. Francis of Assisi, was born in 1181 in Assisi, Italy, a small hillside village north of Rome. Born into wealth, he quickly saw through the trappings, and thus he would devote himself to teaching, service and the spiritual life. In what must have been a cinematic masterpiece, young Francis, distraught but full of confidence, stripped down naked and strutted about the main piazza. He needed nothing, he concluded, no money, no clothes, no books. The birds would do just fine. Perfection needn't be sought as much as recovered, taken back. Recovering and rewilding overlap in lovely and mysterious ways. He went primitive, you could say. The Buddha did the same thing.

Francis put birds, animals, and earthly vitality at the center of ... what? His practice? His philosophy? It was both, and the fact that we can't determine which was which *is the point.* His spirituality was act and action, unspoiled Zen, an emphasis not on memorizing scripture nor navigating the labyrinthine minefields of theological doctrine, as Thomas Aquinas did, effectively suffocating what was young and true about the Nazarene's discovery. Francis revived an ancient idea—philosophy as a way of life.[18] Philosophy was not about argumentation and logic, not about carving the world into concepts, not about just doing what you've been told. It was how you lived. How deeply you felt. Religion is to be lived, not studied, not just for Sunday morning. Trees are to be read, not books. The body is your compass, not the man on the altar. There was one true Christian, Nietzsche said, and he died on the cross. The rest of us are worshiping the man, rather than the message. Amen to that. Francis knew as much.

Francis paid attention. He spoke to animals, and they spoke back. He acknowledged them. He honored their intelligence and biological kinship centuries before science would admit as much. "The perfumed flowers are our sisters," Francis observed, "the deer, the horse, the great eagle, these are our brothers." Francis looked at the ears of a deer the way Zen masters look at the stream trickling below their hut; or the way a Taoist might gaze at a bamboo shoot growing in a shadow. In the same century, Francis in Italy preached to birds and deer, just as Dogen, in Japan, the founder of the Soto school of Zen, would write, "You should entreat trees and rocks to preach the dharma, and you should ask rice fields and gardens for the truth." A good preacher is always preached to. The earth saw them. The earth preached to Dogen and Francis. They were accountable to it. We need to reinstitute that same sense of accountability; in it is wisdom.

No one sees the same thing, or the same way, but these individuals turned toward *a* truth, just not *the* truth. The Greek word for truth, *aletheia*, literally means "unforgetting."[19] In Francis' case, undressing. That nudity is often linked to truth, with its own starkness, bravery and lack of adornment, is not a coincidence. Truth is not a proposition you remember, not an abstract concept; it is what you find when you take away *while living*. When you bracket small mind. It always manifests in the body; if it doesn't, it is not truth, it is righteousness. The litmus test for truth is how it moves you, and move you it will if a secret is laid at your feet. Truth is a historical, personal and cosmic remembrance. We remember in a body, hold our memories in place, and create new memories in one way and one way only—by living. And, as it turns out, we can only live by being alive, and we can only be alive by being in a body. The quality of a truth is only as good as to how it increases the quality of your life; living is accumulative, truth is subtractive.

Richard Rohr, a modern Franciscan, aptly observed: *"What you see is what you are."* This sentence is harder to wrap your head, and body, around than you think. What he alludes to is *capacity*, what *isn't* as opposed to what *is*. You *are* to the extent of what you can see; your being is defined by your capacity to see wider, deeper, which is, ironically, not a theory of personhood, but a theory of being in its classical sense, *a state of being*. The verb. Rohr means seeing with the entirety of your being (big mind and open senses), not just a part of your being (small mind and myopic senses). Small mind is limited in receptivity, whereas big mind is unlimited in capacity. When you define yourself by capacity, you are not defining yourself, it turns out, but making an equivalence between depth of experience and quality of existence; by your ability to thrive in the inescapable medium we are all in, together. Truth magnifies both. Truth is acting with vitality, and or swimming, in the medium of life.

For many of us, depth and or quality of experience is a difficult idea to swallow when paired up with the body. In other words, what is depth of experience in terms of bodily experience? Does this mean mind doesn't play a part in experience?

Soul Doctors

We are obsessed with our exit from the wild,
with conceiving it as a success, but we are equally
obsessed with our re-entry.

The phantom limb phenomenon occurs when a sensation exists in a limb which either does not exist or has been removed from the body. About 90 percent of amputees experience a phantom limb, often accompanied by pain. Civilization, in its march from the woods, suffers from a phantom limb. We have amputated ourselves from the wild. Edward Abbey observes: "A civilization which destroys what little remains of the wild, the spare, the original, is cutting itself off from its origins and betraying the principle of civilization itself." Notice how Abbey inverts the narrative of civilization, the one we are accustomed to: in trying to escape from the wild, we violate a principle of civilization. What is that principle? The principle of paying homage. Giving thanks.

The first cities, either Çatalhöyük or Uruk or Eridu, blossomed around 7000 BC. This means we have been urbanizing for the past 9,000 years, in fits and lulls, and with quite a bit of progress in the past 200 years, but that's a very small period of time, considering that it was roughly 300,000 years ago when homo sapiens first began their journey. For the vast majority of our brain's development, about 99.7 percent of the time, the wild was the theatre of our vision, the scent up our nose, the medium we swam in every night and day; our circadian rhythms, which are our body's 24-hour internal clock, and which control our sleep-awake cycles, digestion, temperature regulation and release of hormones, follow the movement of the sun. In short, light and dark, properties of the natural world, are the main influences for the main processes occurring in our bodies each and every day.[20]

Evolutionarily speaking, it was during this 99.7 percent of time when our minds and bodies were constructed, leading to our somatic emphasis on vision over smell; the ability to hear only a select range of sound vibrations; our upright posture; the thickness of our skulls, to protect our brains; our molars for an omnivorous diet; fine motor skills and gray matter in our brains; our fight-or-flight response; our predictive capabilities; our talent for cooperation and empathy, aiding in scarce times.

In the twenty-first century, with 83 percent of Americans and 75 percent of Europeans living in urban areas—numbers expected to grow—our senses have new objects: landscapes of concrete, corner stores, dimly lit restaurants, traffic, small city parks, trees in square holes on sidewalks, the insides of our homes. More and more people are spending more and more time indoors, in their homes. Our bodies are lost as a result, though our faculties are exercised nonetheless. As a result, there exists in us—in our organism—a sensation of pain, of loss, of subsequent memorial, a phantom limb of lost and wild life. We feel it. It is psychological because it is anthro-historical, the mechanism as varied and complex as anything studied in the mind and body sciences. We feel it in the joy and rejuvenation when we go outside, and or the horror of confinement. The phantom limb expresses itself in film, in research into the "nature cure," in our personal lives, our public policies, in the push to build more trails, in biophilic or green architecture, in forest schools, in common sense. Despite a few outspoken techno-optimist "oracles," the lot of us just can't shake the unnerving, and unconscious, feeling that we are inching closer toward disaster the more we edge toward the inorganic. But this doesn't mean we understand where, exactly, the wild is in us, nor, once we find it, what to do about it. We don't.

The right question is not, "How can we have this feeling after millennia of not living in closer proximity to the wild?", but rather, "How could it not be the case?"

We are obsessed with our exit from the wild, with conceiving it as a success, but we are equally obsessed with our re-entry. These two complexes haunt the global mind. A large swath of our post-apocalyptic storytelling is framed by the collapse of civilization, the degradation of norms, dystopic cities, and a return to a state of nature, or at least how we imagine a state of nature to be: tribalism, hoarding of resources, militias gone rogue. We become beholden to the biological, witnessed in the genre of infection, zombie or otherwise. *World War Z*, with Brad Pitt at the helm, paints a classic picture of biological imperative running roughshod over the bulwarks of civilization. Few scenes show zombies *in nature*, as they are the Janus face of nature, albeit in cosplay for didactic effect. The majority of scenes are urban, depicting the infection of people-to-people like a wave, growing, flowing and bulging, a tsunami over the people and, uncoincidentally, the urban environment. We, the urban, flee this genre of defunct nature by, as is so often the case, returning to nature, to the small village enclave, the necessary utopia; back into biological history, as it were. In a scene set in Jerusalem, the symbolic center of civilization, the zombies flow over god's ancient walls; the dam has been breached. A becoming of disease. An acknowledgment of our straying too far from the source—a source that now, unthinking, returns back unto itself for its own consumption.

The cairns of our mass exodus from nature-based living can be selectively summarized as follows. About 800,000 years ago fire was tamed, and as one paper observed on the origins and culture of fire, "Accordingly the wholesale anthropogenic modification of the biosphere did not begin with the industrial revolution or with the Neolithic revolution but with the hominid revolution announced with Promethean splendor by the capture of fire."[21] Promethean splendor indeed. Fire allowed us to migrate to different (and colder) climates, ward off predators, come down from the trees. Cooked food allowed for brain development. In fact, anthropologists are unable to find a tribe, past or present, that didn't use fire.

The victory over fire was practical and unceremonious at first, but was expressed in later cultures as a symbolic victory of our exit from the beasts, hence the Promethean reference.[22] Prometheus was a god in the Greek pantheon, known for bequeathing to humankind fire and metallurgy. There's also Maui and the keeper of fire; Ra, the Egyptian god of fire and sun; and Christ, a reinvention of the sun god Apollo, hence why early depictions have his face against a glowing halo background. These myths tell us stories about how we understand ourselves vis a vis the wild, courtesy of mastering one of nature's perennial marvels—the orange and blue flame.

Roughly 500,000 years after taming fire, modern humans emerged in the *homo sapiens* variety around 300,000 BC. The domestication of animals, a nature hack if there ever was one, would begin with the dog, circa 17,000 BC.[23] Agriculture started to surface around 12,000 BC, and allowed for permanent settlements and a steady supply of calories. This pulled us out of the rhythms of nature just a little, and caused the skills of food production, which require an intimate knowledge of land-based practices, weather and soil, to languish, to be outsourced, much as it is today, to food specialists—farmers, herders. Then came industrial agriculture, ever advancing, and ever reducing our need to work with nature in order to survive. It's no wonder contemporary return-to-farm movements, or even the idea of the organic writ large, are unconscious acknowledgements that we as a population are too divorced from the rhythms of nature and rely too heavily on others to meet our basic needs (needs which require a knowledge of the wild). The feeling of absolute dependence is unsettling. Modern-day American militias and organic farming co-ops agree on two things: self-reliance and nature as the place to find it.

Just as we didn't go from beating animals with a club to harvesting alfalfa in a day, we didn't go from the wild to the city in one swoop. The transition happened slowly, in fits and starts, courtesy of invention and ingenuity. It also never occurred the same way in the same place. Cities, as we know them in their modern industrialized version, didn't take their shape until the eighteenth century, but they had been a long time coming. Still, the broader sketch is of us knowing the wild for over 290,000 years—our minds directly shaping and being shaped by its landscapes—and then, in a rapid succession of events, walking into grocery stores.

This is the deep root of our phantom limb. Now, courtesy of the past 9,000 years or so, we are an organic fruit trying to pawn ourselves off as an iPhone, that is, *pawning ourselves off to ourselves*, in an odd self-convincing story that we've transcended nature; we've entered the post human age; we're rational, modern creatures; we're destined for the stars.

Ray Kurzweil, Director of Engineering at Google, has long been prophesying the moment—coming soon!—when we download our brains onto the cloud and either live there in digital wilderness or wait to respawn into new bodies. It is our destiny, he says.

I couldn't disagree more; we are destined for the earth. If we ever transcend anything, it won't be of the physical variety. In actuality, we remain wholly archaic, primitive in mind and flesh, of the wild and from it. We get angry when provoked, and our flesh fills with adrenaline, the cocktail prepping us to fight, a very handy evolutionary advantage. We shrivel without water, the very thing we are searching other planets for, as a sign they could support life. Small bacterial infections kill us. We need to be raised with love to develop a healthy brain.[24] We are willing to throw away security for small thrills, for a woman or a man. We are as impulsive as we have ever been, driven by the vicissitudes of instinct, craving, hormones, the desire to be held, the thrill to destroy. We are greedy and kind. Our achievements—all of them—are as fragile as a glass vase on a windy day, rocking to and fro in the annals of time. As evolutionary anthropologists Michael Tomasello and Hannes Rakoczy observe, "If we imagine a human child born onto a desert island, somehow magically kept alive by itself until adulthood, it is possible that this adult's cognitive skills would not differ very much—perhaps a little, but not very much—from those of other great apes."[25] Beneath our self-styled veneer of psychological and cultural complexity, our ancestors are present in us, unmistakable—born not into the wild, but out of it.

We are not heavenly creatures with human-body afterthoughts, we are earthly bodies who fantasize of being heavenly creatures. To be sure, we will place a person on Mars, on a rocket made of material yet to be invented, before we understand the true nature of sadness. Already, we can code AI to run incredibly complex calculations, maybe even manage civilization itself in the near future, and yet, we suffer astoundingly basic afflictions: depression, boredom, pity, jealousy, meaninglessness. According to health experts, these afflictions are growing at a rapid clip just as they are increasingly normalized. Our humanity is the complexity we want to understand, what we want to master. This isn't to say things won't change some day, in some twist of fate when we are actually able to download our consciousness onto cloud computers and send our digital avatars to space to travel for millennia. In that case, we shall bring our discontent wherever we go. If we are the same there as we are here, then, really, what's the point? But that's not even the good question. What is more important is why we want, or need, to believe we have transcended the wild. The need for a new place. The need to escape. What are we running from?

Nature is inescapable. Any notion of an escape from nature either has a myopic conception of nature, as some pristine patch of forest in Siberia to which we have "transcended" on account of being urbanized, or is delusional, since *our* nature (the construct of our minds, the composition of our loves), is but an expression of that Siberian forest. We are intertwined mediums, stitched together by a mad scientist with a loose agenda, good sense of humor and ample amounts of time.

One good question could be the reverse—why must we insist we *are* of the wild? Isn't that an analogous obsession, indicative of an inability to let go and move on? Denial exists, is a real thing, and not part of a homeostatic existence. When a partner or friend is in denial, say about death, or the fact that their boyfriend is cheating on them, you feel the urge to correct them. You want to correct them because they are not living with a truth; truth is a subtraction—you must remove, in life and in mind, to arrive there. Truth is not adding. Every good insight you will have is the removal of ignorance. A healthy mind confronts truth, bravely, turns toward it like a sapling toward the sun.

Cooking with Pathology

Into every future creation you bake
the pathology of the past.

When my father was in his final months I visited him a lot, as much as I possibly could, though flying to Baltimore from the middle of the Colorado Rockies wasn't always easy with two young kids, a full-time job and a wife also working full-time.

At this point, walking is hard for my father, so he basecamps out of his bedroom. It's a fine room, with tall ceilings, burgundy paint on the walls, ample room to make circles with his walker, and a nearby bathroom. The carpet is thick and plush. He has a tall chair he uses on occasion and devices of all sorts; an oxygen machine and other plug-ins I can't recognize are starting to collect mysteriously in each corner. They are the accouterments of modern death, techno-saintly figurines of civilization. He has some magazines on his nightstand, which he doesn't read, and a growing collection of junk: papers of this and that, old keys, his driver's license and a few credit cards rubber banded together, and so on. The neighbors are quiet. Two lovely windows offer a view straight through the dense-green canopy of healthy maple trees. The afternoon light is sea-foam phosphorescent. We watch the news together, eat steak and ribs and lick our fingers. We talk about baseball, the weather, and once in a while he will say something, piercing what has become a comfortable and familiar game of silence, and I'm struck by the oddity of it: "I'm just looking forward to being able to go golfing again." I don't respond at first. For the most part, he is grounded in reality. As a doctor, and a skilled geriatric doctor at that, he managed the end-lives of people just like him for decades; if anyone knows what the tea leaves are saying, he does. And the tea leaves are saying he will not golf again. He will not walk down the sidewalk again. He will not leave the house again.

My father has a crushing, terminal prostate cancer. It is in his bones now, never a good sign. Getting down four stairs is epic. I have to take half his weight. His legs shake when he stands, if you can call it standing. When he mentions golfing, I find myself in a predicament. I feel correcting him might be rude. Giving a dying man his fantasies, right? Let him have his dreams. I'll grant him that, because to correct him might take some precious joy—the mere thought of golfing—from his moment to moment. On the other hand, not correcting him could be irresponsible, because there is a truth out there and he needs to see it, and he has the capacity to see it. It is important to have a good death, to die in truth, to see it clearly, right? Yes, I think so. That's a legacy we have lost—giving our children a good parental death.

What do I say?

I say, "Dad, you are not getting back to the golf course."

I say it with compassion and kindness. I look him right in the eyes, with a resigned smile.

His head drops and shakes in acknowledgement.

"I know."

He knows.

"It's heaven when you are around," he says. "I've always been proud of you."

He appreciates, thankfully, my no bullshit approach. My seeing it allows him to see it and it brings him back. It's a hard truth, but truth always is. After I say it, we have cleansed the air. Moments like this, truth moments, allow him to confront his death and will, in the end, provide much more peace than the illicit fantasy of swinging a golf club again. Plus, a clear death, if reincarnation is a thing, sets him up a little better for his next go around. Truth-moments clean the lens of distortion. As we receive visitors in the end weeks, a lot of bullshit swirls about. Most people don't see my father, but rather what they are going to lose. It's understandable, but I can tell it's awkward, and exhausting, for him. He is trying to say goodbye, to me, to his wife and himself, and I see the tiredness in his eyes when he has to manage other people's fear, people who are there, but not really there, with him. It took years of build up, and work on myself, but I see him and I see his cancer and I see his imminent death. I feel it fully. I'm done hiding. I can't, and won't, be an emotional burden for him. I owe him that. He needs to focus on dying. I am not holding on anymore, and this not holding is exactly what allows me to square up with it all, to find such beauty in his final days. The more I let go, the more the colors out his window get brighter. Not metaphorically brighter, but actually brighter. On our last few meals together, I have never tasted food in the same manner. I hold his hands—and I had never held another's hand like that. On my walks around his house I start to see his energy everywhere. He is fading into the world. I'd take this same lesson into my mother's death a year later and it would save me.

Correcting denial is just as important on a societal scale, and it is, in many ways, the only real and true *raison d'être* for philosophy. As Martha Nussbaum, a contemporary philosopher, quotes Epicurious, of ancient Greece: "Empty is that philosopher's argument by which no human suffering is therapeutically treated. For just as there is no use in a medical art that does not cast out the sicknesses of bodies, so too there is no use in philosophy, unless it casts out the suffering of the soul."[26] Philosophers are soul doctors. Religious leaders once used to be soul doctors. Even science liberated us, for a bit.

But we are in denial. It is easy to be in denial about death because in death the mind finds its limit. We can't, of course, blame our minds for this, but we can learn from it. This is why death is fundamental to every religious or spiritual tradition on the planet.

Our Biophilic Phantom Limb

There is nothing in nature that isn't a verb.

Before written language, before agriculture, before cities, our distant ancestors saw the light go out in another's eyes after death and, as far as our current findings reveal, did something about it, perhaps as long as 500,000 years ago.[27] Nearly half a million years later, we know more about what makes something alive, but after the point when the lights go out, we are in the dark as much as the breathless person we are looking at. When someone passes, we are still performing the same basic rites as our ancestors, but we use shinier things. In these early impulses to acknowledge a life, or the life we have, we can see the inklings of reflection and prediction, two hallmarks of mind.

Prediction: where is that person and where are they going?

Reflection: who was that person and how to summarize the life they lived?

It's fickle, this life we live, and we go about under the delusion of permanence, living our lives as such. There are a lot of theories as to why the phenomenon of religion is globally pervasive and seemingly essential to our animal psychology, as if the mind has a thirst that religion quenches. Mathematics, democracy, written language—none of these can be found the world around. But religion, generally understood, can. This is not to say the basic purpose of religion is to make sense of death, since it equally attempts to make sense of life. Rather, "here one minute, gone the next" remains an inescapable mystery of conscious life, a mystery we are still talking about today, myself included.

When people disappear, we are forced to make sense of the struggle and suffering they underwent. The things defining them for us, their laughter, smiles, ways of being, have evaporated. We try to preserve, in video, images and reflection, the trace of a once-living being, but they're gone. Yet, in the things they built, and in our memories, vestiges of them live on. And so, as it happens, if someone searches religion or philosophy for strategies, or answers, to the problem of death, they may be pleasantly surprised. Thai Buddhists carry around death cards to remind them of what is coming, and Christians place as their centerpiece a dying, tortured man in a loincloth. Agrarian rites around the world mark the end of fall as a death, thanking the sun for its summer work. On the desks of corporate offices around the world, and on the home-screens of millions of people, are those who are no longer. On the screen saver on my phone, as it turns out, is a picture of my mother; on my father's desk, before he died, there was a picture of me. Every time I open my phone, dozens of times per day, I see a woman who is no longer with us, and I am reminded that my daughter will sit next to his own dying father someday.

Around the void *to where someone goes*, and to which *we will soon go*, we cloak rituals, philosophies, and concepts, in an attempt to make permanent the impermanent, to stave off the loss. We invest in the lives of others. Culturally and personally, we have a perennial, near-constant unease with impending unknowing, a panic in the genre of *not knowing* of any sort, and yet, we should cut ourselves some slack. Our existential anxiety arises on account of our brains being *hardwired to know* in combination with death being where "to know" finds its upper limit. The mind wants to know because it is designed to keep the organism alive; and calculating the future has proven useful, hence why the traits of calculation and prediction remain.[28] Calculation moves our bodies toward greater chances of survival. This is also why truth, of a subtractive and Zenlike movement, is so appealing, because it guides us toward the experience of not knowing, and, in many ways, allows us a sober glimpse at our mind at work; if we can't see our mind at work, it is working us. In fact, Zen puts a premium on not knowing to such an extent that some masters, such as Korea's Seung Sahn, consider the "don't know" mind an essential trait of the enlightened mind, "Don't hold anything, don't attaché to anything. Only go straight — don't know. This don't know mind will fix any sickness you have."[29] It might sound easy, but it can take decades to develop this mind.

When the mind can't predict, it feels it is doing the organism a disservice, and disharmony arises: stress, panic and anxiety. And yet, for our modern minds, what is one thing which has escaped the throes of death? What is this thing we acknowledge contains the coming and going of life; where beginnings and endings fade into the ether of becoming; where, for our minds, we acknowledge the abstract dance of life, knowing we shouldn't get too attached to the bloom, nor dismayed by the fungi?

Nature is that thing, at least the concept of nature. The very thing we'd like to believe we are not a part of. Truth and then delusion, in that order.

The vast majority of us learn about death from the wild, whether we are aware of it or not. Our ancestors sure did. Before we see our parents die, the lesson of death is pervasive in our houseplants and backyards. In all life too, but in the wild decomposition and rebirth are underscored. Everything is turning into everything else. Rotting, flowering, flowing, flooding: there is nothing in nature that isn't a verb. Whether it is on the nature shows we watch or the maple tree losing its leaves outside our window, nature is straightforward and generous in the changing of tides. It's the yin to our yang. To see deeply into the wild is to see deeply into death. Into impermanence. It is coming for your mind, and it will win.

Fuzzy Metrics

Because we are attracted to life, we are instinctively repulsed, or psychologically injured, when life is constricted.

Earlier, I asked an odd question—*what is a body?*

The body is a survival machine. The body knows how to live. As William Sumner aptly states, "If we put together all that we have learned from anthropology and ethnography about primitive men and primitive society, we perceive that the first task of life is to live."[30] The body was designed, in and through the wild, to live … and live well, because wellness helps us live. Animal life does not seek suffering; suffering and hardship and cruelty arise, but the nose follows the scent of tasty food and the eyes seek the horizon for greener pastures.

This is not to say cultural inventions, such as going to a museum to see a sculpture, aren't aimed at knowing how to live and don't give us a biological or socio-economic advantage. They do. But another aspect of "to live" has been added to the task of consuming enough calories for the winter and passing on our DNA. To live, or "live well," now means to *thrive with meaning*. This is modern survival. An ant can thrive with food and sunshine and collaboration; she does not have to know she is an ant. To live well, for us, we need to know who we are. It is a trait of our minds to know, and that trait is now exercised by turning inward.

To survive with meaning is also to allow meaning to survive. Which is to say, we need to understand why it is some things have meaning, and others don't, because it is in things we give meaning, but don't understand why the meaning is there, that we can find our shadow, our darkness. Until we put light onto the latter two—on the shadow and the darkness—we will be prey and hunter, as terrified as the horse running from a dead mountain lion that just happens to be tied to its tail. The horse runs and runs, to the point of exhaustion, but every time the horse stops to catch its breath, the lion is there. The horse dies, never having escaped. If only it knew what it was running from, it could relax and live its life.

One of those things we grant meaning without knowing why, is nature.

In 1984, EO Wilson, a biologist and naturalist, articulated the *biophilia hypothesis*. The thesis is simple: as a species, we are attracted to life and lifelike processes. A leafy view outside the window is preferred to the neighbor's driveway. A street with nice trees is preferred to a sun scorched sidewalk. We make art of mountainscapes, not landfills. We pay to visit luscious gardens on a sunny Saturday afternoon, not parking lots.

Biophilia makes sense. But it's also incomplete.

Let's extrapolate from the hypothesis—because we are attracted to life, we are instinctively repulsed, or psychologically injured, when life is constricted or injured. The purpose of life is to live freely, and life requires a broad sphere of potentiality to thrive, receive stimuli, adapt, and so on; life is a medium with the widest sphere of action we can imagine (it is the deep source of the idea of interdependence). When that sphere of action is limited, life suffers; when a bear's habitat is shrunken, the species suffers, for instance. This is not to say we always act on our better impulses, since we don't, but our repulsion to life's constriction could be a biological ideology, or part of our environmental psychology, an area of research attempting to wrangle how we respond to our world. Or, perhaps, our revulsion is a felt effect of "deep ecology", which involves crossing a threshold of self-importance and granting nature a "self," for lack of a better word. Then, we feel the suffering of the wild as we would a suffering child. The phantom limb returns.

In one of the founding documents of deep ecology, predating the biophilia hypothesis by over a decade, in 1973 Arne Naess makes a few curt observations on organisms, including us: "Organisms as knots in the biospherical net or field of intrinsic relations. An intrinsic relation between two things A and B is such that the relation belongs to the definitions or basic constitutions of A and B, so that without the relation, A and B are no longer the same things."[31] The relation Arne is referencing is not abstract: it is a description of nature as we understand it today—discrete "knots" of energy connected by an intimate relationship, biological in nature. The medium. Our relations with the wild are expressed in the anger we feel when our view of the park is suddenly blocked by a new development, and so, the place of our morning coffee, once having a view of maples, oaks and bird chatter, is now off-gray concrete and windows. A relation was changed. Because it is no longer there, and because of this set of "intrinsic relations," a part of us is no longer.

What is that part?

The part is qualitative, related to the depth of experience and quality of existence, but grounded in evolutionary biology. As to the former example, how we spend our time changes; maybe the trees were relaxing, and now we are short on relaxation, and so we develop a less effective habit that contributes less over a year to our mental health, which means, at year's end, the quality of our life is degraded. In our daily diet, it's the same thing; small decisions, such as no fries rather than fries, or baked chicken rather than fried chicken, add up over time to something meaningful. The effects might be seen in blood pressure and our weight. But when it comes to fuzzy metrics, the stuff of feeling and emotion, qualitative stuff, it's hard to say, right? But just because it's hard to say doesn't mean it's hard to understand. I'm always fascinated when I go to a restaurant with someone and the first thing they do when they request a table is scan the room. I can see their gears turning. They don't want the place near the bathroom, nor too close to the front door, where it's drafty and there's no privacy. God forbid they are near the table with two screaming kids, or are sat at the table that wobbles. They are experiencing shopping, weighing this and that factor, knowing full well the situation with the least amount of uncomfortable elements will produce the more memorable experience. This decision making, which we do all the time, isn't hard science, it's more important than that: it's soft qualitative calculation, and we do it much more frequently than any other cognitive act in life. We are basing our decision on fuzzy metrics.

Nature, and the loss thereof, is part of the fuzzy metrics

club affecting our daily lives. But because nature's field of action is so wide and pervasive, it's hard to see if you are in small mind. If you expand your awareness, however, you can feel it with greater acuity.

In New York City, parks are important, and it's important for those parks to receive sun for the sake of children. Isn't the right to play in the sun a basic right as a child? Of course it is, but it turns out, no one had thought about it. But they do now.[32] Tracking shadows is a thing. Lawsuits are popping up in big cities as a result of skyscrapers syphoning even more sunlight away from city parks. At the root of this is the assumption that parents and children need sun. Well, yes. As organisms, we are knots whose quality of existence lies not on our side, given the health of an other, nor on the other, given our health. True relationality, and wellness of mind, lives in the free, elasticity of the medium.

What we forget is negative compounding, or exponential loss. Any economist knows that small variations, over time, produce big results. Most of us know of the power of positive compounding when it comes to a retirement plan, but negative compounding refers not just to the loss of compounding's benefits, but negative trajectories. Adverse effects are multiplied. As for ecosystems, all you have to do is imagine a truck full of gasoline spilling into your local reservoir to understand negative compounding. Water needs to be brought in. Trees die. Fish die. Plants die. The ecosystem will struggle for generations. It is a biological fact we need biodiversity to survive, which means we need our animals and ecosystems to thrive.

We are attracted to other forms of life. This is the basis of story; we are hardwired to care about characters and what happens to them. Story is nothing without life forms struggling and overcoming, whether ourselves (our zeros) or others, in and out of constriction and freedom. This deep, archaic empathy, is the wild expressed in us. We thrive together, with and among other forms of life. We have an instinctual desire to know how other knots rise and fall, or suffer and don't, on account of it having been painfully obvious in our past. In our present, it's just not obvious enough. When natural forms, or systems of life suffer, a biophilic phantom limb becomes lodged in our mind the way a missing limb is still felt by an amputee. As for their absence, we can reasonably conclude we are removing opportunities for deep sensation, depriving our bodies of important input, likely increasing feelings of isolation and degrading the system in which we ultimately source our vitality. Contrary to common sense, we are sensorily deprived in our society of spectacle, not over stimulated. It may just be the biggest effect the loss of contact with the wild is having on our minds.

Starved Out of Plenty

We are a response to the earth, and intimacy misplaced is often camouflaged in anger.

A biophilic phantom limb is equal parts biological and psycho-philosophical, and a deeply misunderstood area in the mind, premised by the existence of a deep symbiotic embeddedness with medium-expressions (flowers; the savanna; the vista), which starts to die, germinating feelings of loss and guilt, but also a psychological frustration, since we can no longer express ourselves, and be expressed, in the mutually expressed medium.

Practically, there is a starvation of previous and bountiful sensations, a limb that felt the world now cut off. It's not abstract. We are talking about our eyes, ears, skin and minds unable to exercise themselves, to find the object which fits them like a puzzle piece. Sensation deprived is experience degraded. Pain originates at the source of the incision.

This *is* also to say, our mind is an inherent environmentalist. This is *not* to say we are practicing environmentalists.

We can see this lost limb, per the dynamics of guilt, projection and reaction, in staunch rejections of the wild, in unnatural aggression towards it or its people, or a public and adamant anti-protectionist stance, fueled by the power of our unconscious voice telling us otherwise. It is said the human mind is tribal, that we can't think many generations ahead, but this inability is very much the shadow of anti-wild civilization lurking in our minds; it's hard to think ahead on account of it being hard to think back. We can't think ahead because we haven't gotten here, as self-appointed industrial beings, without siphoning vitality from the natural world; from its subjugation we get our superiority; from its timber our homes; from its body our lime for concrete; from its oceans the fish on our dinner table; from the sky the air we breathe. To live requires this give and take, and our denial of it, expressed in ingratitude, is the greatest story never told.

We no longer have a visible relation with the wild. This blocks us from seeing the essential relation, which results in a psychological resistance to thinking about the dead, and a sense of guilt (often expressed as its opposite—pride) for the imbalance. Mind wants to move (sphere of action), and when mind cannot move, its essential nature is threatened. Mind is free, first, and only second becomes ensnared in our lives in the form of small mind. Our love and conception from the wild has no other outlet than for us to feel sadness about its systemic dismantling. Yet sadness manifests in no one way. We become frustrated, in the Freudian sense of the word, biologically, like racehorses stuck in the pen, or birds whose wings have been snipped. This generates anger, and thus distraction, and so many political or ideological attacks aimed at the wild could, in fact, be a product of repressed feelings of mourning, turned to anger, turned to aggression, over its loss and our accompanying guilt. It is not uncommon, to say the least, to take out your anger on the thing you love.

Intimacy unfulfilled is often camouflaged in anger.

It was an evolutionary yesterday that created not only the pathways for stimulation,[33] but also the necessity thereof and the pleasure we derive in situ of the wild. Our nervous system only *works* properly, and feels fulfilled, when it is *used* properly, which means we are optimized to receive certain types of natural stimuli. As a result, we desire these stimuli.[34] In arguably hyperbolic fashion, but no less correct, Thoreau observed, "The ears were made, not for such trivial uses as men are wont to suppose, but to hear celestial sounds. The eyes were not made for such groveling uses as they are now put to and worn out by, but to behold beauty now invisible." The pathways of sensation are our potential to be affected (capacity). This is the deep source of the biophilia hypothesis. Studies show we prefer blues and greens over urban grays.[35] We get great pleasure from the chirp of birds, brushing wind and gurgling water. Our eyes relax in parks (involuntary attention), like ginger between sushi rolls, cleansing our minds. We move toward the wild, but not all of it—fear, danger and insecurity are also felt in the wild, proof as well of our instinctual knowledge of it. Around the globe, the traces of the wild are burning out, and yet, you'd think we could recoup the sensations elsewhere, such as in our cities, which are sensation factories: signs, colors, billboards, skyscrapers, the beautiful and the ugly everywhere. Cities are beautiful. Yet we are increasingly turning to the wild for the sensations only it provides, like a penguin swimming 1000 miles in the Antarctic Sea to return home once a year, to pay homage. Habitat matters, literally and symbolically.

One of the great assumptions of our time is that we are overstimulated. I feel it, you feel it. You know the argument: screens everywhere, incessant emails and pings and buzzes and notifications like mad, multitasking to our deaths, shrinking attention spans and desperate attempts to save what mindfulness we do have. We are exposed to between 4,000 and 10,000 ads every day. No, that's not a typo.[36]

But this overstimulation hypothesis is wrong, and we have demonized sensation as a result, to the perils of the organism requiring it.

* * *

Despite feeling we are overstimulated,
the opposite is the case.

By 2030, roughly 70 percent of the world will live in urban environments; in 1800 the number was about 3 percent; in 2008 it was just 50 percent.[37] This is troubling given our brains are running on nature 1.0 software, whereas urban environments require city mind 4.0 software. A relatively new area of research attempting to understand how it is our bodies are ill-equipped to handle mega cities and ceaseless noise is called evolutionary mismatch.[38] Deirdre Barrett writes: "Our instincts—for food, sex, or territorial protection—evolved for life on the savannahs 10,000 years ago, not in today's world of densely populated cities, technological innovations, and pollution."[39] Just imagine putting a hippo in Alaska and you get the point. Where's the warm water? Where's the lush leaves? The animal has no applicable instincts, no sense organs adapted to the cold to keep it thriving.

Evolutionary mismatch needn't be theoretical. We feel it all the time. It is here, immediate. It is not affecting someone else. Sometimes we notice it, sometimes we don't. Sedentary screen-based life is a good example—our bodies were not made to sit and stare at a lightbox 1.5 feet from our faces for eight hours a day. As a result, our vision goes bad, our backs go out, our health and cardiovascular health suffers, and we die early. From an article in Yale medicine: "research has linked prolonged sitting or other sedentary behavior to diabetes, poor heart health, weight gain, depression, dementia, and multiple cancers."[40] Sitting is violent, but the point is that it's only violent to an animal who is made to walk. That's us.

We are hippos in Alaska. We need mind software in which our bodies don't generate stress from urban stimuli and noise; where we enjoy bland colors and the lack of green, or any green at all; where we are adapted to constant signals. Where concrete and muted grays are pleasing. Our small minds are confident we are already adapted, but our bodies, of course, tell a different story. We are adapting, it's just that our bodies will take a long time to catch up—as in tens of thousands of years, the same amount of time it took to adapt to previous environments. Our en-masse stress and anxiety are not a secret. City-park officials, urban designers, and focus groups the world over are working at a feverish pace to make cities "livable." When you see soft-edged architecture with plants growing from the outer walls, or organic shapes, or spirals trying to seduce us with the Fibonacci sequence (a pattern found in shells, trees, and flowers) you should stop in your tracks and try to soak them in visually, the way you'd suck fresh air from a paper bag in a room full of smoke. They are designed for your mind's health. When I walk and come across a building, or park, I do. I stop. I gaze. A nano-peace grows inside of me. Good examples of nature-based urban interventions are The California Academy of Sciences, Singapore's Nanyang Technological University (NTU), and the Lotus Temple in New Delhi. In these buildings are soft shapes and biological life growing on the building. In these structures, elements of nature are being borrowed and adapted to suit the animal that once lived outside.

We are trying to fix the evolutionary mismatch problem. Names abound for the valiant effort to greenify or bring nature, or nature-inspired structures, into our urban landscapes—green architecture, biomimicry architecture, etc. The effort is not just aesthetic, but related to large scale mental health projects, which is, from one side of the desk, a "cost of living" that governments are incentivized to solve because it is an externalization of centralized living, just as the public medical costs of cancer were an externalization of the private tobacco industry. City life comes at a medical cost to modern governments, and, as such, they are trying to pacify the effects. A study conducted in London discovered that residents who lived in neighborhoods with greater tree density had, on average, a lower rate of antidepressant prescriptions.[41] And then there's that famous 1984 Pennsylvania hospital where "twenty-three surgical patients assigned to rooms with windows looking out on a natural scene had shorter postoperative hospital stays, received fewer negative evaluative comments in nurses' notes, and took fewer potent analgesics than twenty-three matched patients in similar rooms with windows facing a brick building wall."[42] That study alone led to a change in postoperative building design. It makes sense, doesn't it. Who wants to stare at a brick wall? Not I. A view of a forest adds a small, but not insignificant, amount of healthy mind each day. But it has taken centuries, millennia even, for us to realize the negative effects go beyond mere fleeting discontent. We are literally becoming sicker as a result.

Research is coming out, and correlations confirmed, that city life has big health risks. A study from 2010, which brought together various substudies, found that people who lived in urban areas had a 39 percent increased risk of mood disorders; the same population has a 21 percent increased risk of anxiety.[43] The "city never sleeps" adage apparently also applies to us, except it is our nervous systems which can never quite shut down. The noise, the never-ending lights and traffic, and the lack of visual cues to trigger relaxation in the brain make us prone to stress. And, given the space constraints, "social contagion" of said stress passes from one mind to the next, like a yawn or a virus.

Boredom is a crisis in many parts of the world, tied as it always is to a loss of meaning, a sense of uselessness and, as one might expect, a dearth of stimulation.[44] We are not overstimulated. We are understimulated. It's not a new feeling,

I imagine, but exacerbated by evolutionary-based sensation mismatch.

The paradox, which isn't really one, stems from a poor understanding of what it means to be stimulated.

On the one hand, *we are stimulated* by being in a boardwalk arcade or in Times Square or downtown Tokyo—the lights, signs, traffic, people and noises enthrall. *We are stimulated*, in the sense of the body being in a heightened reactive state, pulled here and there. Stimuli are everywhere, especially visual stimuli. We are piqued by the spectacle, often delightfully distracted, carried as if on a river, from one street corner to the next, one ping, one image, life as a ceaseless scroll. The mind turns to sensation because it expects it to be meaningful. In reality, our attention is pulled, curtailed and fragmented to the point where stimulation has no psychological or biological or meaningful return and thus we are, in fact, understimulated. The noise of traffic triggers a reaction but not a response, and thus we become increasingly riveted to a reactive state, a quality which has been predominantly associated with pain, anxiety and adaptation to stress, all of which have negative health consequences.[45] Unconsciously cognizant of the lack, the modern world attempts to get our attention via ceaseless stimuli—to keep us "vital"—and it is cleverly, and always unintentionally, seducing our minds via very old pathways designed first by the wild; we think non-natural environments are those of plenty, but, in reality, for our bodies and minds, they are landscapes of scarcity. It is not a coincidence that there is a growing cottage industry of touch therapy and or tips and tricks of how to re-enter your body, which, on the surface, should strike one as odd. Don't modern environments cater to the body if nothing else? No, they don't. They cater to a mis-understanding of the body.

The leveraging of our need for sensate novelty is no secret and not a conspiracy. In fact, it's good business.[46] Social media was born hundreds of thousands of years ago when our brains became hardwired to seek our fellow tribal members' approval, to avoid shame, to wonder and chase the novel thing, to know the movements and feelings of the tribe. Contemporary forms of attention consumption, of which social media is just the flavor of the day, are not creating new desires but rather repackaging old ones and leveraging the pathways first trod by the river, the tribe and prey.

We need better stimuli. When I walk in the woods, I often close my eyes and rely on sound. Or, I will spend ten minutes just trying to smell. Slowly, this sense-practice has rewired my brain to draw in different information, which focuses and calms my mind. The environment is alive in new ways. Now, I smell things I wouldn't have ten years ago, and I hear with more intelligence. If you practice like this long enough, you start to differentiate the lengths and intensity of sounds which a minute ago flew in and out of your mind like swallows under a bridge. My mind is reactive, but what I'm reacting to is worthy. While it might seem reductive to base this reactionary impulse on hundreds of thousands of years of living in nature, it is a conclusion hard to avoid. The other night I was sitting with my children, watching a movie, and my phone pinged. I tried to ignore it, but I immediately felt the impulse to get up and check it out. I waited. I watched more of the movie.

"But what if it's important," my brain told me.

"It's not important."

But it might be.

I watched five more minutes, then, unable to let it go, I got up and checked my phone. The fact that it *could* be important was distracting me. The simple fact that it was there, that something had arrived for me, was enough to draw me towards it, in curiosity and in flesh. Millions upon millions of us are doing this every day. The inborn pathway is the only reason the technology is seductive.

Moving toward or away—what biologists call approach and avoid—is the most basic of animal responses.

If, in the middle of night, a picture frame falls over, and a thud echoes through the house, my body is jolted into a state of alertness. I didn't direct this alertness. It's not good for my sleep. But in the very distant past the trait of becoming alert, at night, as a result of a loud noise, proved useful. I don't wake up with a smile and think, "Ah, nice, there's a strange noise or perhaps a stranger in my house. Isn't that great!" My attention is riveted, immediately fearing danger. My heart races. I clench my fists. We take this so for granted it's hard to realize it could be otherwise. Researchers have found that our minds are hardwired to respond to animals.[47] When we run or hike or sleep in a tent at night, we react to the sudden sound of a bird rummaging in dry leaves as if it were a bear, even though we might be in Central Park. Our minds know better, but our nervous system doesn't, and the latter is in charge.

It is the same in social interactions. We are hardwired with the desire to get along, to work in groups. "We've evolved over millions of years to want to connect with people because it helps us protect ourselves from predators, use scarce resources, find a mate. One of the ways our brain gets us to make those connections is [to] release dopamine," says Anna Lembke, of Stanford University.[48] But social platforms, while trying to replicate ancient environments and leverage instincts low on the brain stem, are really maladaptive ones.

Our brains turn toward noise, not away from it; they crave social approval, novelty, posturing, jockeying for social status. We desire to know what is behind a signal—the ping of a text—just as we did the crack of a twig in the forest. We become alert instinctually. The world is, in a sense, becoming more *animistic*, a word, ironically, used in religious studies to define pre-modern worldviews in which the world was alive, full of alive things, rocks with spirits, trees with ancestor souls, places guarded by good, or bad, entities.

We've come full circle. Almost.

Things are "alive", but their aliveness means nothing if the sensations they produce in us are empty. Technology is packaged as sensation, but it is dead sensation, rotting on the floor of our minds.

Just as the worm reacts immediately to direct sun on hot pavement, sensing the danger, wiggling and writhing, a fundamental *property of the body is reaction* to stimuli. Not only is the shape and function of our body born in and from the reaction to stimuli, but reacting just might be the most primal thing an organism does. Toward and away. Toward our zeros, away from the shit plant. We will always need to move, but in order to be free, we have to see this clearly. Movement is part of our nature, but while it is in the nature of the worm to move automatically, we have the option. That we have an option is a fundamental property of complex consciousness.

All stimuli, however, is not created equal.

A potent alchemy happens when stimuli cross a threshold and become something else, when grass beneath your feet turns into *more than just grass under your feet.* This physical energy undergoes a transduction, becoming, down the line, a component of consciousness. What, exactly, is this transduction?

Stimuli vs Sensatio

The wild makes our bodies whistle.

Akin to high-quality and low-quality food, distinctions grounded in biology, there is high-quality stimuli and low-quality stimuli, also grounded in biology. We all know this and feel this in our lives, and, moreover, research has proven it. The sound of a stream releases stress and anxiety, whereas the honk of a horn outside our window annoys us, activating our amygdala, producing low-level stress.

We flock to the Grand Canyon for a view, but it would be preposterous to queue in line for a panoramic of a Walmart. We plant beautiful flowers, but scoff at heaps of metal and trash in our neighborhood parks. There's noise and there's music, rubbing a cat with the fur and against the fur, and while the precise boundaries shift across cultures and time, the phenomenon of judgment doesn't. Just as it has been shown that humans across all cultures have certain preferences for mate selection (men select for beauty, for instance, women for the ability to procure resources), we have preferences for place.[49]

Being drawn to stimuli is an outgrowth of biophilia. High-quality stimuli, as regards the effluence of nature, have a greater ability to give *affect*—a term defined as a power to give meaning, produce feeling—and so an ability to morph into *sensatio*, more than mere sensation. Like an empty bottle held into the wind: if you find the right angle, it will whistle.[50] We are the bottle, the wind is sensatio. A good litmus test for sensatio is if it creates a memory and you re*member* it, that is, re-*member*, put it back together in your mind after the experience has occurred; or if it produces the feeling of nostalgia when you encounter it, or something like it, in the future: a texture of skin, the smell of a room, a melody. The idea of sensuous things going deeper than the norm is, in fact, the basis of tantra (which uses sex in some manifestations) and it was a fundamental feature of Plato over two thousand years ago; beautiful things, for instance, can lead us to the Idea of the beautiful.

The wild makes us whistle. But the whistle is a between.

As for the biological need to be stimulated by natural stimuli, which is what the body is designed for, we are creating strange compensatory (and contemporary) mechanisms to remedy the evolutionary mismatch—the landscapes in which our brains were formed are nothing like they are today, and the brain doesn't evolve at the same pace—and it is almost as if, in an era of destimulation, we have created ways, such as those mentioned above, to make up for the lack of quality stimulation. In a strange twist of human psychology, our attraction to life and lifelike processes (biophilia) might just be fueling the technologies causing us harm, such as techno-biophilia or techno-animism. Because the body desires stimuli in one way or another, we create pseudo-stimuli in landscapes where natural stimuli are degraded, where sensatio is in short supply, and so, because attention *needs to be exercised*, we created television, advertising, green architecture and porn. We go about our lives from one stimulus to the next.

As they say, the road to hell is paved with good intentions. Attention is the new coal—it's the resource the most successful companies on earth are trying to extract from our lives. It's not even the new coal, it is old coal, but we need to *be stimulated*, not just put in front of things that stimulate us.

A body is nothing if not an organism designed to receive sensation, and frustration born of cheap sensation thrusts us forward into the future in strange manners. If you trim the avenues and methods of receiving sensation, which many of us are undoubtedly doing with increasingly sedentary, screen-based administrative lives, but attempt to remedy the lesser reception with substitutiary stimuli, you get the telltale signs of understimulation: frustration, lack of motivation, boredom, irritability, anxiety, distraction, depression, phobias, panic attacks, substance abuse.

Sound familiar? They are the most common afflictions of our time.

Wisdom of the Body

Every space is wild, absolutely wild. If you don't think it is wild, you are not seeing correctly.

The first step out of the morass of pseudo-stimuli, and into sensatio, into the wild, is to let your body guide you.

The wisdom of the body does not utter sentences, or use punctuation. Movement is the language of the body and the earth, and we are all in, whether we know it or not, a constant dance of repulsion, attraction, survival … often simultaneously. “The language of movement cannot be translated into words,” writes the dancer Barbara Mettler. “It must be sensed in the muscles.”[51] The senses are an easy path out of distraction; aka the monkey mind, aka a small mind without discipline.

All the language we have of seduction is based on this primitive to-and-fro, of any organism, of any mind. Toward and away. What would life be, or look and feel like, without this movement?

Inching. Pushing. Drawing. Toward. Out of the light. Into the darkness.

Seduction and attraction. Attraction and survival—ancient pairs for any organism at the cellular level and at our highest levels of complexity. Space is not abstract or preexisting. It is created when we move. In that movement, we also mark time—human time, to be precise. Time isn’t there prior. From it, memory and calculation are born, and from these, selves. In the mind awoken a world is painted, texture and scent assumed, and then, we are painted as well.

What then about the wisdom of the body? What does it move toward? It moves toward…

Loving; dreaming and waking with purpose. When our children wrap their hands around our waist and squeeze, when we are in our bodies fully, with intention. When creativity plunges us into its chaos and we ride, like Nietzsche, the shooting star. When delight knocks on our minds and we let it in, a cloudless day, a cool breeze on a late summer afternoon. When we are proud to be. When we catch a glimpse of our small mind, see it in action, and pull a truth from ourselves. When the grass is smooth underneath our feet. When the red rock canyon walls are tall. When we discover we have been lying to ourselves.

We know why we move toward children and pleasure and sensate delight, but why do we move towards nature? If you were natural selection, designing an organism needing to live in the world, an organism which needs to embody its immediate surroundings and embrace the world (attraction) with no reservations and yet with all the reservations (repulsion), then, over time, you would pass on the genes of the individuals who could do all this and more, because they have survived in greater proportion. The result of this is a selection for the trait of finding pleasure in the wild, because, deep down, those that first put their deft ear to the earth, did so because an intelligence of and in the wild helped them survive.

It is for the same reason that eating gives us joy. Natural selection favored the genes that found eating to be pleasurable, since animals who enjoyed eating ate more, and were more likely to survive and pass on their genes. I'm simplifying, of course, but the same goes for sex; we like it because the trait of finding sex pleasurable meant passing along genes with greater frequency. Social life is analogous; it was an essential tool in our past, linked to food sharing and survival, which explains why even today the vast majority of us find great meaning in social relationships and study after study has shown that doing things for others makes us happy, perhaps the happiest.[52] "For it is in giving that we receive," said Saint Francis. Likewise, natural selection favored traits of being outwardly attuned, with our minds engaged, fully embedded in our environments.

* * *

A body never stops moving. It can't. A fox toward the back of a den; a mother toward her children; us toward the fridge, toward sex, toward our fear. Away from a storm. Into shelter. Fresh water toward the ocean. Salt water to the sky; a bee to a flower. My father toward the earth. My mother toward the earth.

On one of my many visits to my dying father, my flight had me going from Aspen to Austin to Baltimore. I made it to Austin, but my flight kept getting delayed, and each potential delay in my flight brought its own frustration. I was moving toward something, after all. When I arrived, I moved toward my father, who was in the hospital bed. I could feel his skeleton—his muscle was gone. His body was leaving him. He was immobile, and shrinking in all ways, but the cancer was thriving, moving toward its goal. His wife Josephine moved out of the room, to give us a few seconds. Being with him, I was infused with sensatio. Sensatio because I was there, in the room, nowhere else, squared up. The air smelled of death. The dim light of sickness. The sound in his voice of failing lungs. The sight of tubes and monitors of end days. Sensatio because it was teaching me something, an opportunity to arrive. Many visitors to my father didn't want to have these sensations, to really look. Sensatio can be painful, and so visitors avoided looking, or filled the space with small talk. A few minutes later, nurses and doctors moved in to check vitals, and, while they drew close to him, I drew away, to give them space.

These sensations guided me, offered a guidepost to his exit, allowing me to say goodbye—goodbye to the father I could go out and eat ribs with. Goodbye to the father I could walk around the block with. Goodbye to the father I could text back and forth with. Each of his presences were no longer, and those presences were immediately felt. Rather than hold onto the being I was losing, I opted to move along with the impermanent being in front of me. From one emptiness to the next. "He who binds to himself a joy / Does the winged life destroy / He who kisses the joy as it flies / Lives in eternity's sunrise," as Blake wisely put it.[53] I unbound myself to the sadness. The days and nights imbibing these transitionary moments, not bound to the joy of my father as he was before, were joyful as a result. In the emotional thickness of a room with an individual on their last days, chaos and sadness want to take over. But I didn't let them. I calmed my mind instead. From this calm, a unitary power of experience, involving me and my father, each in a death of sorts: "When the mind is disturbed, the multiplicity of things is produced, but when the mind is quieted, the multiplicity of things disappears."[54] Simplicity of sentience took my consciousness by the hand and led me. We need to move, but, within the movement, there's a radiant, vacuous center, what just about every religious tradition has given a nod to; the void, the moment of creation, the dark light; hence the claim that the bardo is always present, which it is, the psychological truth of time. We have been trained to not notice it.

What that hospital room taught me, on that Wednesday morning in Baltimore, was this: every space is wild, wild in the sense of untamed, broad, resolute and of solitude. Our small minds constantly tame our spaces, but right there, ever present, is a ground that isn't one. We just need to see more clearly. When we are in the mountains or the great canyons and the stars beam overhead and for a few seconds the world feels impossibly beautiful, just as it is, and we see our smallness with profound sobriety: this is what we mean when we say nature is humbling, or that it "puts us into our place." It's a rather odd turn of phrase, but apt nonetheless, analogous to religious language of "returning to the source" or "resting in god" or "dwelling in the divine." Into our place is *the place* where the world comes and goes, where we unseat the small mind self for a fleeting moment and witness ourselves and the creation of the world alongside us (bardo, moment of creation, etc). It's not a coincidence that every religious tradition puts a premium on this placeless place; it is the transcendent hero with a thousand faces.

What is this place we are put into? Exactly where we are standing.

In the "tame" and cultivated space of a hospital room, I felt the same exact feeling as I did when I stood on the edge of the Grand Canyon or slept on the side of El Capitan. I didn't understand why at the time, but if the student is ready, the great wind blows.

You Can't Ignore Motherhood

You can ignore your mother, but you can't ignore the fact of motherhood.

When I look back at myself, fresh out of college, that boy was thirsty in so many ways. He wasn't dreaming about a place, nor about a person. He was dreaming about intimacy; a relation, as philosopher Gilles Deleuze would phrase it; a becoming landscape of person, a becoming person of landscape. The medium. He was dreaming of Emerson's idea of nature's salve: "I feel that nothing can befall me in life—no disgrace, no calamity, (leaving me my eyes,) which nature cannot repair." The medium as medicine. Young Francis was trying to fix something broken.

And yet, in many ways, I was dreaming of a new zero that was, in a strange way, not a self, because it had to be open in order to be. It had to be porous. Impermanent. I think I got lucky that I chased this zero, as I could have chased an identity that constructed barriers instead.

To be open, to merge, to become the all, to disintegrate—it's an old mystical desire, perhaps the oldest. Perhaps also the most misunderstood.

Throughout history, the status of this relation, of person with landscape, of the finite with the infinite, has gone by many names. Plato might have used the word *participate*—our minds, made of form, participate in the formless form-giving, a quasi-deity of cognition and spirit and cosmic importance. Buddhist thought might describe big waves and small waves and the ethereal flowing of mind containing them. A Hindu would frame it as the interplay between self and Self, small me and our Atman, individuality and that which transcends, yet contains, the most idiosyncratic aspects of human life. A Muslim might describe this act as one of submission, a central tenet of the Islamic faith, and a death of ego so as to be proximate with God. Taoists speak of merging with the Tao, unifying opposites, living with flow. Zen would approach it as an experience with no small mind interference. In each of these, the desire aims for different outcomes—intimacy with God, greater ethical clarity, etc—but the *desire*, on face value, an impulse to escape and return in one and the same movement, fits a pattern. It is, in many ways, one of the great human desires, along, of course, with the desire to kill or love, and it is the basis of what goes by the name of religion, likely of Latin origin, *religare*, to bind, tie, or go back.

* * *

Courtesy of advanced technology and isolated devices needing to talk to each other to work—which will likely not be the case in the future—the metaphor of connection dominates our collective social-psychological psyche. Each epoch assumes the mental images dominating the culture, and these metaphors seep down into our habits, expectations and overall comportment, which is not to say these metaphors are always acting in our favor. Within the concept, and story, of "connecting," we exhume our own mythos.

We connect with others, with communities, with old friends, with our followers online, with nature. "It was good to connect." "Let's connect." It's always positive. We never say we connected with someone if the interaction was toxic; in that case, we say we "didn't connect." In the film *Avatar*, the metaphor takes on a literal aspect when the Na'vi sync up with animals via a literal cord, sort of like a spiritual USB. Connection is literal and existential, as if the one implies the other. The connection lets them feel the animals on a deeper level, tap into their thoughts, become "one" with the animal such that thoughts in the individual can direct the action of the animal.

This is, of course, an ancient mythos redressed. Around the world people have devised creative ways and methods for tapping into animal energy. Often, as with many Indigenous traditions, it might be a costume, such as the wearing of bear claws or feathers, a necklace of teeth, and or a ritual, to get one into an animal's state of mind. The relationship between Indigenous peoples of the Great Plains and horses comes to mind. The horse was sacred, held tremendous strength, and thus to bond with the animal could give the warrior added power. Shamans were often assigned a spirit animal, and they would be bonded to this animal for the entirety of their lives. The pathways for intimacy were never passive, however. It was a becoming-horse of the warrior and a becoming-warrior of the horse. The animals "out there" spoke to the shaman, protected them, and vice versa. The connection to Mother Earth was permanent, taken for granted, and not something you could, or would want to, unplug.

You can ignore your mother, but you can't ignore the fact of motherhood.

Ours being a world of cords, to connect means to be plugged in, digitally or electronically woven together. Data transfer. Power. Wi-Fi connectivity. Things talking to each other. On the one hand, connecting implies a mutually beneficial relation, since connecting implies the two things being connected were designed to be. Food and the body connect; you can't digest rocks. To connect, as in directly, implies a capacity in each of the two discrete entities, because now they have capabilities they didn't before. When you connect your phone to a charger, your phone charges because it has the ability to charge, and the charger realizes itself as a medium of power transfer, utilizing its internal machinery, precisely what it was designed to do, a realization impossible without a phone on the other end. Connection implies compatibility. You can, of course, connect with a stranger, but to actually connect with them, at least in terms of how we use the phrase, implies there's something in the stranger analogous with you, whatever that might be. When it comes to the wild, we, as modern consumers, are increasingly just *meeting* the wild—in the same room as it, nodding and delighting at our company—but not connecting with it. We are simply showing up and expecting the transfer to happen. An analogous assumption would be showing up at your father's deathbed and assuming that just sitting there is healthy grieving. It's not. When *you* show up, you only see what concerns *you*, and to honor a death, you need to get yourself out of the way. We know at a bodily and subconscious level that we are of the same cloth, the wild and us, but in our conscious minds the wild has been stripped of its sacred mythos. The wild has no agency, we think, no wisdom to impart aside from vague positive feelings of pleasure we get from it; the basis of the nature cure, i.e., nature relieves stress, etc. There are assumptions we are making when we think we are "connecting with nature," or going outside to do so, that render the task more difficult, and, on a deeper level, are misguided. What we think we can get out of the wild is a Rorschach between quasi-romanticism and unmasked self-interest, and they are difficult to unbind. We chase tales of being outside ourselves, transcendence in a grand, ancient theater; we pine to participate in beauty, absorb it, be surrounded by it, and have it inspire us. The magic of the non-human is there, baffling us and generating curiosity, and we want to feel the catharsis of awe to satiate our souls. We need separation from the man-made. We do all this not connected to technology, hopefully, hence the assumption we are connecting to non-human entities and forces, such as the charm of a prairie lily or a granite boulder in a clear mountain stream. At other times, we need to get fit and stretch our minds. Nature, we've been told, is good for that. We listen to the wind to check boxes in our minds. We go because we define ourselves as outdoorsy or adventurous.

In urban environments, weather is a backdrop, but in the wild, it is foregrounded. When you hike in the canyonlands of the American Southwest, it is about rain, and, by default, water—when did it last rain, will that spring on the map be dry, will there be a flash flood? In the mountains, it is about the impending clouds and hail, the river that will swell and be hard to cross. And so on. Not one eighteenth-century Romantic painting lacks storm clouds or moody atmospherics; part and parcel of the attraction to nature is its organic moodiness; a cosmic yet earthly drama, emotional landscapes, frothing, dying and decaying—the whole. Harmony and disharmony. Perfection and the shit plant. *Kintsugi*. In the wild, we look up constantly.

We think of nature in terms of messaging and information, even if that information is abstract, fuzzy, or, for some, of the mystical variety. We think nature is communicating, and we just need to listen. But that's misguided. We have the connection part right, but we have failed to understand what's on the other side of the cord.

The German-American theologian Paul Tillich understood theology as a problem of message and translation. God is up there, infinite, eternal and unlimited, and circumscribed by all the omni words (omniscient, omnipresent, etc), and he/she/it is communicating with us, who are all the things god is not: we are finite, temporal, limited, anti-omni in so many ways. Tillich's problem was simple: how can we, who are at the opposite ends of the spectrum, the finite, be expected to understand the infinite?

We have ears, but do we really think God has vocal cords and can utter sentences that our ears can pick up? Our ears are a unique product of evolution and we can only hear vibrations on a certain spectrum. God never had to be subjected to evolutionary processes, so can he hear us? Same with vision. Does God have actual eyeballs with retinas and pupils, and thus can't see at night? And language—we acquired that not long ago. What does God's voice sound like? The monotheisms are especially invested in this problem, since baked into their system is a single (mono), communicating entity (God), typically beyond space and time, but of course dabbling in both, and thus all of their emails and texts to humanity have a God-quality, which means said messages need to be interpreted by humans (with few mystical exceptions). Much, much ink has been spilt, nay, the majority of it, on what god means, hence the phenomenon of prophets, those God-language translators. We might not even have religion as we know it if God just spoke and we just understood. What use would we have for intermediaries—shamans and priests and rabbis?

Fully in a Body

It is forgotten that the experience of being fully in a body is the same as feeling you are outside of one.

As any translator knows, moving words across languages and cultures is a tricky affair prone to grave errors of misunderstanding. But, solutions to the problem of interpretation aside, there's an issue we can hardly catch sight of unless we are being very attentive: we are assuming we need to interpret something, that there is, in fact, something being communicated.

We are under the assumption there is something *out there*, from God, from spirit or Ra, which would be *better* dressed up in human cogitation, as opposed to left naked, in its natural, bio-semiotic attire. Revelation is another word for interpretation, for repackaging the great message and writing it down, yet writing does great violence to the meaning inherent in speech, which is always delivered by a person in a place in a time; religious speech is delivered with sensation, by the voices and the bodies of the person delivering it, and, thus, you can't separate message from messenger. Some luminaries, however, saw the problem early on and didn't write. Socrates, the finest of philosophers, never wrote. Jesus avoided it, preferring to speak to small gatherings, to heal. Mohammad didn't bring quill to parchment. The Buddha also didn't put word to ink. They knew exactly what would happen. Unfortunately, their followers wrote volumes, creating the problem of translation and of interpretative anxiety—that we are never any good at it. As a result of the assumption that we can't listen to naked messages, the monotheisms have set a cultural listening device inside of our minds which, after millennia of us soaking in the way we read and interpret God-signs, makes it hard to get out of the habit of thinking God-talk is a language needing to be deciphered. It's a widespread historical and cultural hang up, and very unfortunate. The rub is this: we apply the same interpretative hoops to nature. God and nature speak, or don't, the same language. Many a nature mystic and nature writer have banged their heads against this problem, Heraclitus included. Nature loves to hide, right?

What is nature trying to tell us?

In that simple, straightforward question, so many assumptions. The problem is akin to someone saying, "Go into that room and count the white things." You go into the room and count the white things—a white tablecloth, a white picture frame, a white ceiling fan. You exit the room and proudly tell the person you found three white things. "Now, how many were blue?" they ask. You have no idea because you were led, from the outset, to look for white things. In nature, as with God, we have been trained to look for white things, but even more important, we have been trained *to look*, to pick apart, to decipher, to activate small mind. We are clouding our perception by looking for certain things. We are allowing concepts, and their besties judgment and interpretation, an intermediate, ultimate and foundational role in our making of the world. When this happens, we become like Heraclitus, wondering why nature is hiding.

All day, unless we have the tools to turn it off, we are looking, looking, looking, unconsciously or otherwise, for what our minds are preoccupied with. This is the essence of an unmoored small mind, just going about, one thing to the next, looking and feeling and judging and perceiving. Small mind, however, is the death knell of deep experience.

In order for the wild to arrive, in the shape and power that it deserves, we need to get ourselves (*our selves*) out of the way, as the latter is the prime agent and locus of interpretation for the small mind, which is also directing our awareness out of its own value system. But how much can we actually peel away from our organism? Some will claim you can only peel away so much, and that, in the end, you will still arrive with a human stamp on your eyes. I mostly agree. The point is not, however, to deny your organism, to deny your flesh—which sadly Christianity has advertised for centuries—but to fully embody it; when it is fully embodied, small mind has no place. The history of philosophy and theology, mysticism too, often makes a grave mistake—it has forgotten that the experience of being fully in a body is the same as feeling you are outside of one. "The supernatural is the natural not yet understood," said the wise Elbert Hubbard. The body isn't the end of the diving board, upon which you leap into the ethereal divine. This mistake grows from a simplification and gross misunderstanding of the body: we think the further we get from the body the nearer we get to the good stuff, like soul or spirit or the divine self, but it's an odd stance to have, since nature, the grand Mother Nature of history, the grounding principle and co-creator of all religious truth, despite religious claims to the contrary it has transcended the world, can only be felt in a body, through our senses.

Ignoring body for spirit is not the quickest way to the latter. In fact, it's the slowest. We find our bodies the fastest, at the deepest level, in the landscapes in which it was conceived, because in them our body is privileged.

When the Whole World Feels Like Leather

When you wear leather on your feet,
the whole world feels like leather.

Place is, in the end, irrelevant, which is not to say all places are equal. As Ram Dass is fond of saying, when you wear leather sandals, the whole world feels like leather. The summer preceding my father's death, I went, along with my family, on a beach vacation. We'd spent a few days with my dad first, who was bedridden, the cancer ever creeping into his bones, then went to the Delaware coast to meet up with cousins, rent a house and do the East Coast beach vacation. Hell to heaven, you could say: from a room smelling of death and dim lamplight and heaviness to sunshine and smiles and ice cream and children chasing waves.

As I went from one place to the other, I noticed something curious: my internal landscape remained unaltered. I found no more joy on the beach with cousins and their children, sitting in the sun and playing in the waves, than when sitting at my dying father's bedside, spending what I knew to be our final hours together, in a concerned, ceremonial silence. Pleasure was there, and sadness was there, perhaps deeper than ever, but it hadn't captured me, hadn't sunk the boat nor lifted the tide. I felt like something was wrong with me, wrong not just for not feeling the highs of being on a wonderful beach vacation, surrounded with so many loved ones, but for not feeling the weight of my father's cancer, for not falling apart, because that's what we are supposed to do in these situations, right, fall apart? With my father, there was solemnity, but no falling apart. At the beach, there was pleasure, but no deep joy.

Something was wrong with me. Part of me wanted to fall apart with him just as a part of me wanted to feel ecstasy at the beach. But neither were possibilities now.

There was a stranger inside of me, or, better put, I was

becoming a stranger. It was, no doubt, a result of all the work I had been doing on myself—well, not on myself, but on letting that self go—all the meditation on death, my ability to say goodbye with honesty, without holding on, sitting in the room and just being so *there*. The fruits of my labor, over decades maybe, had stabilized. I had been nudged off the cliff by my father, yes, but also fortuitous circumstances—I was thus looking for a job and contemplating moving my family across the country; Christy had lost her stepdad and her mother; our remaining local family, had moved out of our town; and I was stubbornly realizing I also needed to start saying goodbye to my mother—her Alzheimer's was progressing. I was starting to lose her. Suffice to say, I didn't have much to lean on.

The losses compounded, and I knew the way out wasn't to indulge the pain or pity myself, but rather, as Nietzsche says, affirm it. In order to affirm it, I needed to let go of Francis a bit. The feelings I was used to having were there, but as if on TV, or a background noise. I felt a tad shocked by it all. At a deep level, I knew this stranger in me wasn't a stranger at all. For a few weeks it felt like I was floating. I was adjusting to a new reality. All the feelings were there, but they were not mine anymore.

The strangeness, however, gave way to something else; the more I embraced it, the more my self-critical voice, anxious about this turn of events, quieted. My new mind started to see the world afresh, and it did this by being in no place other than where I was. In direct proportion to embracing the gritty, impermanent messiness of it all, my days got better; the emptiness accumulated and finally tipped to a full-body sensation of lucidity. I soon found myself saying, bedside with my dying father, what a *fucking wonderful day it is today. Just so beautiful. How lucky am I to be alive*, even though, by previous standards, a wonderful day it was not; rain, final moments, sedentariness. I'd be sitting there and thinking these thoughts and just being flabbergasted I felt that way. Before, I'd count these types of days on one hand per month, typically the result of something unique I'd accomplished, or having been in a beautiful place, typically the mountains, but now the same feeling came: almost bliss, an even bliss. Peace. Calm.

Was this even bliss the fruit of practice? Definitely.

There is indeed an untouchable part in the mind, an alcove in the harbor of consciousness, which, being of the harbor, feels to be not of it. You can see the harbor from this alcove, including the alcove where you are, but the waves don't rock your boat. The waves want to rock your boat, and you feel their gravity, and they are real waves, but they never quite reach you. In the history of religion and philosophy, this alcove is well known. We get whiffs of it in martyrs, saints, prophets, poets and realized beings, notably in their expressions, poetry or lamentations of being untouchable, proclaiming "there's nothing you can do to me." The philosopher's stone of the alchemists. The indifferent Taoist master. The imperturbable Atman of the Hindus. For Muslims, protection in submission. Big mind for Zen. These states of consciousness are not the same, but there's a pattern, to be sure. When the philosopher-protagonist of Nietzsche's *Thus Spoke Zarathustra* proclaims, "One must be a sea, to receive a polluted stream without becoming impure," he is talking about expanding into big mind, which, like a pot holding a stew, contains all the variations of small mind—those little morsels of meat, such as jealous states, anger states and lust states—without, however, being identified or polluted by them. This was happening to me. The tragedy of my father wasn't reaching me. The beauty of the beach, the same. But the irony is this: the power of the place, on the hot sand with my children, in the room with my dad, became more poignant, more powerful, a more delicious *sensatio*, as a result of being less attached to it.

You might feel untouchable—and I wasn't quite that—but this in no way means you are not being touched. The listener zero had haunted me my whole life, and now, here, it was oddly saying hello to me, except with a twist.

A month after I got home from the beach, living across the country from my father, I got challenged on my assumption. Which is as it should be. Just when you think you've gotten somewhere regarding place, you feel out of it. Out of place, that is.

Why is it that I felt so out of place *here*, in Colorado, while he was *there*, in Baltimore?

Hadn't I done that work, the fruit of which I just described?

On the one hand, I was having one of our most primal attachments to life—our parents—peeled away from me, and I can only presume that to be in proximity to them would have been advantageous to the grieving process. When you live, you create bonds with and through people. These bonds form the texture of you, and color how you view the world. It's nice to be in the presence of the person when those bonds are being broken, so you can, at any rate, witness the bonds being disintegrated. As I looked deeper, it was a question not just of what binds us, but of the ultimate value of those bonds in my quest to learn as much about the mind as I can, to find freedom in it and from it, to master it, in a sense, to be surprised no more. Part of that quest I'd learn involves engaging in the deepest way possible with the role of place, as vague and uneventful that word is. For me, place has always been associated with landscape. The Rocky Mountains. The Jordanian desert. The Okavango in Botswana. The Kalahari in Namibia. The Burmese Highlands. All places I sought. But I wasn't looking close enough. Place is also Ocean City, MD, on the boardwalk, stuffing my face with cotton candy and funnel cake. Place is family, home. And I was losing that in spades.

On the other hand, I knew that, for many traditions, leaving place—oftentimes the home and family—and becoming supremely detached from all places, is highly recommended, if not a prerequisite, for higher understanding. In India, it is common practice, and idealized, to leave one's family after all your duties are complete, such as raising children and working, to spend your final years wandering, mendicant bowl in hand, on the shore of the Ganges in meditation, trying to crack life's code. Native American shamans used solitude to listen in to the voice of the creator, and they often lived, physically and symbolically, on the outskirts of the village. Zen monasteries, like Christian monasteries are often in remote places, physically and symbolically distant from the goings on about town. In China, as in Tibet and other cultures, there's a deep history of the mountain sage, whom, equal parts poet and prophet, has leveraged their indifference to place and people so as to pluck one of life's sweetest fruits: unwavering, unshakable truth. Even today, you will find holy men and women in caves, sitting and praying and thinking and not thinking, coming down now and again to serve up lessons to the great unwashed. The notion of leaving seemed obvious and common sense. In order to be free, you need to be free of attachment to place, because the latter has an extremely strong hold on our psyche, pulling us to earth when we are trying to be birds. For a long time, I felt the life I had chosen—kids, family, job, etc.—just didn't set me up the best to know my mind, at least with the depth I expected. But that was just a story I was telling myself. In many ways, leaving can be a form of escapism.

But are we supposed to be birds? And don't birds still need the cool water of a bird bath?

For these very same traditions, their on-the-record theological abhorrence of place was expressed in odd ways—gilded palaces, silver chalices, ornately carved wood. It's worth repeating: at one and the same time the main teaching of so many world religions—to focus on the spirit, the immaterial, to forget the body and the world—found itself expressed fully in all the trappings of luxury, pomp and things that seem in common sense to be totally irrelevant to the spirit.

A contradiction? Maybe. Just a fact of embodiment? Likely. A basic and systemic failure on the part of nearly every world religion? I think so. Something inside of me was thrusting forward, unable to let this question just idle. The problem, as you can imagine, was inextricable to the "problem" of the wild, just as it was to my parents, truth and freedom.

* * *

In late August, a month after the beach trip, I got a call. My father said I should come home, a request he hadn't made yet. His kidneys had failed. Darkness was drawing near. I could hear it in his voice, the adamant yet calm tone of someone knowing they are dying and wanting to see their child for a last time. "Sure dad," I said, "I'll be there tomorrow." It was time for a final goodbye. But there was a problem. My sister was there. My sister and I had a very strained relationship. It had been eight years since we had seen each other or even spoken. It wasn't just distance. It was hard feelings. As soon as I heard she was going to be there my body tensed, my mind raced. My father was dying and in great pain—that's hard enough, to be in the room and be centered for him, to not bring in the pain of my impending loss and give it to him. He didn't need that. Just to be there, for a full few seconds, in the room with a dying person is extremely difficult. But, on top of that, I had to be in the same room as someone whose existence I wanted to avoid and who, I'm sure, felt the same way about me. How was I to mourn my father, front and center, with this other thing front and center—the hard feelings, the awkwardness, the pressures to make small talk, or, even worse, reconciliations, which would have felt cheap and opportunistic. It felt unfair to me. I felt robbed of an experience I needed and wanted.

But there it was, the shit plant up my nostrils. Nice to meet you, old friend.

I wanted a perfect mourning experience: to be there in silence, hold my father's hand, talk to him. Nothing extravagant, mind you, just no distractions. I was mad. My father and I had been close all of our lives; he and my sister had not. But I also wanted my sister to have time with him as well. She deserved that. I didn't want to get in her way, and I didn't want her in mine. I didn't sleep that night.

The following morning, I drove the four hours to the Denver airport. On the drive, I imagined the room he was dying in, with me and my sister in it, and I couldn't make sense of the situation. Small mind was doing this, as it is trained, to get a future sense, learn something of the situation I was about to be in, and try to make it predictable. In climbing, the practice of visualizing a route is a powerful tool to work through the emotions you will encounter on a climb; when you visualize properly and then later confront the thing you have visualized, the experience feels more uncannily predictable, familiar even. This is what the mind does, one of its biological imperatives—think ahead, read ahead. Prediction is a form of ensuring survival. I was imagining my father's living room—his bed set up, paintings on the wall, white crown molding, silverware on the table—and in that room was a very uncomfortable energy. Place was really the constraining element, as in proximity, since it would have been fine if my sister stayed at a hotel and we visited at different times. But the two of us in the same place—that was the problem for me. I just couldn't visualize how the moment could be packed with such incongruity.

Nonetheless, I needed to work inside this vulnerability. I needed to see it more clearly. I needed more capacity, more big mind.

I had a layover in Tampa. As fate would have it, Hurricane Idalia was four hours from making landfall, its outer orbit just now creeping to the edge of the terminal I was sitting in. It had charted a path from the western edge of Cuba, straight north and a tad east, then toward Tampa, and then, as if by divine ordinance, to me, waiting to board a flight so I could see my father before he passed. Every minute counted. My sister was there, and I was so mad at that fact. The hurricane was scheduled to make landfall at 11 that night, and my flight was supposed to leave at 7pm. Winds outside the terminal's bay windows were whipping up, more so each minute, and flights were already delayed on the boards. The entire airport suffered from collective anxiety. Miraculously, we got the cue to board. The rain was angry and horizontal. The plane taxied for a bit then pulled to the side and ground to a halt. Yep. Bye dad. Sorry I couldn't be there. I tried. The pilot came on to let us know that things were "in flux. Hold tight." That was an understatement. I imagined going back to the terminal, eating McDonalds, and getting the call. My sister, on the other hand, got to be there, in the *place* I wanted to be. It was unfair. This was not the experience I wanted.

Like the hurricane, she still held tremendous power over me. The energy in my body was rising to a fever pitch.

Then, just like that, as if out of a book, while sitting in an uncomfortable middle seat, the plane idling, the hurricane bearing down, my father taking his last oxygen, the proverbial clouds parted. The sunshine, up there, so high above the clouds, whispered from a quiet place: she has no power over you. *You are not that person anymore.*

The alcove. The voice of big mind. And it was right.

My sister did have the ability to affect me, but only because, up to that point, I had given her the power to do so. But enough of that; I was reclaiming my mind. In order to take it away, I had to step away from Francis a little more and develop a capacity to see him in his fullness. He was too caught in the story. The less it was about him, the less it could affect "me," whatever this "me" was.

And that was the moment. I readjusted my arms on my uncomfortable middle seat, wiped some tears from my eyes and smiled. I have not been the same person since.

The tension in the room I had obsessed and fantasized so much about, the one with me and her and my dad in it, with all its noise and hard feelings and chaos, dissolved and turned to dust. I was now prepared. That moment marked a true turning point in my life, as much as the birth of my children. The place I was walking into no longer mattered. It stopped being place, as I had known it before, and it became something else. It would become an occasion for practice; it would be filled with sensatio. Everything, everywhere I went thereafter, stopped being place, an "abstract position," as it is defined; generic place became filled with specificity. Two years later, it would remain the case. The room ceased to be filled with my fears, my concerns, my worries, and, as a result, I could enter the actual room, the one with my father's dying hands hanging over his bed, the man to whom I needed to say goodbye and the estranged sister I had to be in the presence of—and I could see what was in the room, no longer shackled to what my fears and projections saw. The room had trees; a small stream ran through the kitchen, snowmelt I think, and it smelled as fresh and clean as a newborn. The room was so, so beautiful. I wanted to be there now, in that place, a complete reversal. The plane took off in the worst weather I have ever seen. When I physically entered the room a few hours later, there was nothing but peace and serenity and clarity on my end. A chapter, of decades of hard feelings and avoidance of my sister, had come to a close. My father passed within a few weeks of this visit. I took this valuable lesson right into the slow death of my mother, which would begin about six months after my father took his last breath. When with her, I knew I had to look hard, look often and look courageously. I had to disintegrate along with her disintegration. I had to let my body guide me, allow the sensations and feeling to run deep, all the while not letting them steer the ship. The pain and the grief had to cut as much as they could, because only then could I learn from them. This tactic might not be for everyone, but I can say for sure it saved my life.

Microtopia

When you can't see the shit plant,
assume you are not seeing clearly.

When I came home from that trip, utterly vacated emotionally and physically, I learned I'd have guests at my house. No peace to be had there. While I prepared the eulogy, I felt pangs of frustration. I didn't want to write anything, or talk, during my dad's funeral. I didn't want to do a good job. I wanted to sit and be with my family, just another person in the pews, not having to print out a talk, make edits, deliver something of value. But none of that is possible. Life didn't give me what I wanted. And the more I looked at the cause of the frustration, the more I found I was in denial of the building blocks of experience which can be summed up thus: life presents no situation that does not contain the *shit plant*. It's just how it is.

The shit plant, despite all desires for it to be otherwise, is the norm for the experiential moment. Which is to say, when you can't see the plant, either in front of you or around the corner, assume you are not seeing clearly. Be glad you see it. It is there in each moment. Mind is *the inescapable*. Awareness knows no bounds, and it fills all things. This is its basic nature: illumination. I think the multiplicity of the moment—the fact that experience is a composure of harmonies and disharmonies—was first impressed upon me during the beach trip that summer, when I was neither at the beach nor my father's bedside. In other words, I had expected to be on the beach, with joy, and then be with my father, in sadness, but neither came to be. Both, poised in my mind, with such clarity ... and then one.

This is not to say, however, that pleasure can't get us closer to the goal of happiness. It can, kinda. Island vacations and solo trips into the redwood forests do move the dial. But the debate is rigged, and we forget the real question. The question isn't, "what can pleasure do for our happiness?" but, "can pleasure help us understand the nature of big mind?" and by "big mind" I mean the essential nature of the thing—what a Buddhist would call our essential nature, or Buddha nature. The open. The inescapable. The perfect shit plant. Yin and yang. Pleasure can help us understand mind, just as sadness can, but, ironically, they are helpful only when they lose their power over us.

This is what the perennially confounding "union of opposites" means, at least at the practical experiential level of living in non-dualist thought. When we succumb, we are neither pushing away the bad nor chasing the good; multiplicities are embraced without judgment, and without judgment they have no power. Just to be in that position is not to be in one. When theologians talk about spirit-transcending opposites, they are merely putting a label on energies available to us that feel otherworldly (but aren't) and logging a basic observation of small mind: it judges and values things, but true reality as witnessed without small mind has no value. Therefore, according to theology, divine essence must be beyond judgment, beyond good and evil. The purveyors of the beyond opposites are, as one might expect, quickly branded as outcasts or mystics, since the latter have effectively challenged the working assumptions of common sense experience, and with that, the foundations of communication and civilization itself, requiring as it does agreements on good things and bad things, the belief that such agreements are unalterable, and then the putting of those agreements into concept and language, a process further reinforcing the self-importance of the organism who created them.

But back to pleasure. The role of pleasure in happiness is

not a new topic. Of course, many feel that happiness is the goal of life. Even the Dalai Lama will say such things, but he doesn't mean happiness in the way we use the word. We understand the word more in a vacation-psychology sense, not as a deep-seated contentment, which is what he means. The problem with the "happiness is the goal of life" position is that happiness comes and goes, and unless you have enough time and money to wrap happy things around your life 24/7, you are going to come down from the high, and thus you are going to spend a lot of time and effort to get back there, because the goal is to be up and you are intolerant of the lows. This is what 99 percent of people do—fill the lows with the search for the next high. As it goes with food supply in winter, it's better to find a more stable source.

There are hundreds of theories, opinions and research papers on pleasure, some of which go back to the origins of philosophy in ancient Greece, many of them quite convincing, but when I follow pleasure to the end, I still find *the inescapable*, the shit plant. It's just not possible to focus on the happy thing, or happy moment, to the detriment of all else. You can for moments, sure, but the clouds of discontent will always block your sun. You can try, but you *have to try*, and the fact of trying, of this effort, is avoidance, and something inside of you knows you are avoiding, and so a tension is created between trying to avoid the avoidance—because that comes with sadness and letting oneself down—and cradling yourself in the happy thing. On the one hand, you are avoiding the avoidance, and on the other hand, you are attempting to prove to yourself that you are not doing the former and so you attempt, with gusto, to be in the happy moment.

Each requires self-deception and exaggerated response. Each leads to failure.

All of this is deeply personal and problematic because, for me, the wild is pure pleasure. Wild pleasure. Historically, that is, growing up, I found very few shit plants in the wild. What

Walt Whitman said—"I am mad for it to be in contact with me." When I went running in the mountains, I got the dopamine drip. My eyes rested on distant hills. My mind slowed down. I was in heaven. I was high. I was alone. I was a part of something. I was listening. I was out of my body. Trees talked to me. Poems formed without effort. I was a poster child for the nature cure. I was becoming the zero I had always wanted to be, or at least I was on the path. I was utterly in love with the world.

No one has ever surpassed this feeling, I told myself. What else could there be? Muir, Basho, Whitman, Black Elk—they were all there, in me.

But, upon arriving back to the trailhead, I'd be thinking about work on Monday. The good feelings would continue, of course, yet still, on the drive back, I'd think about emails I had to write, meetings I had to tend to and when I could return to the mountains. That was a problem, but why was it a problem? The joy was unstable.

Impersonal Forces

The wisdom to navigate any block of experience is found in holding all of the competing forces lightly in your mind, without contradiction, conflict, or even expectation of harmony.

Going home, or coming down, is also the problem of psychedelics. In high school, I did a lot of the latter. I had discovered the Zen poets and Emerson and Thoreau at age fifteen, then, about a year later, I discovered magic mushrooms and LSD. They brought it all together for a while. My mind undoubtedly grew. I would skip school and trip in the forest, *The Doors of Perception* in my back pocket, and climb to the tops of trees with my friend Pete in a thunderstorm, like Lieutenant Dan in *Forrest Gump* on top of the sailing mast, yelling at God in the rain. Whereas Lieutenant Dan exercised his anger, I explored my joy. Both of us posed the same question to the earth—what else do you have for me? I came down late in high school. I didn't like to come down. My readings in mysticism, however, quietly made their point: what you find, if it's real, shouldn't *go away*. The ecstasy of drugs went away. The good stuff, the stable drug, could only be found in the mind itself. It took a long time for the idea to impress itself upon me, but finally, one night in college, it did. And just like that, sometime in my sophomore year in college, I stopped getting high and never looked back. What I didn't know was that I might have to quit nature in the same manner.

That infamous skinny-dipping night, I had gone on a literal night run, with a literal headlamp, chasing an image of myself in this place, a ground zero of intimacy with the wild. Chasing peace, solitude, poise and wisdom. Chasing a place I thought would solve what was going on in my heart: a general unease, a feeling of alienation, the sense that I had stopped growing, the return of the bad feelings of being cheated on and losing my childhood friends, which is everything to a teenager. I finally realized what I was running from, and what I was running to.

Not long after, at age thirty-four, I invited in the unthinkable. I invited in the thought that perhaps the wild had moved on from me. I invited in the thought that I might be a failure, or at least, had failed for a long time. I invited in the thought that I didn't know what I wanted anymore, nor how to find what I wanted in the first place. I invited in the thought that my best efforts to listen to the earth had failed. I was crushed.

Trying gets in the way of the right effort.

Sutton spent millions to turn a dilapidated island into a multi-million-dollar nature retreat, which is odd because nature gets no more beautiful the more money you throw at it. I spent years building up a body (climber zero) and mind (a PhD; listener zero) that I thought would deliver the same result, which is again odd because nature gets no more beautiful the stronger the body you throw at it. And nature gets no lovelier the more PhDs you arrive to the trailhead with. You can be the foremost art critic on beauty, but this in no way means you appreciate a mountain stream more than an average eight-year-old.

On the other hand, we would be remiss to believe such things are irrelevant, that a mountain runner doesn't have a unique—which isn't the same as privileged—relation to the wild, born of familiarity and intimacy and muscles and sinews adapted to the hills. There's a unique freedom in being able to go deep into the wild. There's a singularity to the climber's arms, which ache for rock, to the runner's quads, which desire the trail. I know this first hand. My muscles dream. They nag at me. They are part of me now, like little intelligences on my limbs, whispering this and that, desirous in their own little way to be exercised in the manner of their intelligence. The bodies we build in life come to have a life of their own.

The lure of the endurance athlete, for instance, is to travel further, to fight the entropy of the body, and, with that *further*, go deeper into *the* experience. The Greek Gods were often depicted with muscles. This was because the human body got tired, a slave to its own mortality, but the Gods never tired, their muscles symbolic of not getting exhausted. This primal whisper motivates athletes to keep building a body in the hopes the experience will arrive. In fact, the official Olympic motto is "faster, higher, stronger." But of course, faster, higher, stronger in service of an ideal: an ideal experience awaiting the athlete. But always, after those mystical moments in the hills, we are stiff the next day. Our bodies hurt. We think about emails. Tendonitis squats in the parlor where exuberance just was. The experience fades and turns into hopes for the next one. Our mortality comes crashing down. *Mono no aware*, the Japanese say, the sadness in the passing of things. Nothing is as humbling as the body. With exercise, as with drugs, you have to come down.

Sutton didn't build a body. He built a luxury retreat.

What gives then? Does having a fit body, or having a luxury island, matter? Does any of it matter? Billion-dollar industries, such as luxury, or luxury travel, testify to the opposite, not to mention the fine items found in virtually all sacred spaces the world around.

Sutton's ground zero was the island *not* as it was when he first saw it, but a vision of it *after*. My ground zero was to be in a place where I could prove to myself I was still in touch with the wild; I was like an abandoned child who knows who their mother is, and has to drive by her house once in a while to get a sight of her, to remind them of the basic truth of their origins. I didn't know at the time I had been merely driving by, removed from the wild in the safety of a car, behind the glass of expectation. I had been transitory with the wild. I visited often, for hours and hours per week—but time *at* a place never, ever, means time *in* a place. Just as I wanted in, the wild was slipping through my mind like sand through an hourglass. Nature and I had relationship problems. I tried to rehabilitate our failings by doing instrumental things with nature, like an estranged couple cleaning out the garage together. Cutting the vegetables in uninspired silence. Getting naked and swimming at midnight … those kinds of things.

Decent ideas, with the right intention, just not the right intelligence or right action. The wild had a lesson for me, but I had to be ready for it. And I wasn't.

One aspect of the wild that does matter, perhaps rendering it superior to other types of landscape, such as a city block or an art museum, for instance, is that it lacks human intention or design.[55] A sign on the street can be as lovely as a rose petal, without question, but someone made the sign, and our minds know this on a very deep level; we know this fact, of it being man-made, and this awareness changes experience. It changes it because our minds default, largely on an unconscious level, to an interpretative mindset. We are back into mind because we seek intention, aka, someone else's mind. In psychology, it's called *agency detection*: "Agency detection is an evolutionarily-based psychological capacity to see an event to be motivated by an action tendency."[56] In short, when we see something we often are looking at what or who made it the way it is. This is just what the mind does, and, as such, it can't relax, can't shut off. Yes, our man-made environments are things of great beauty, same with music and art, but art cannot recreate the mountain vista; these experiences operate in different areas of the brain. How many people look at sidewalk gum and become transfixed the same way we view a glistening river cobble in the sunlight? Very, very few. It's biological. It should be possible, and it is, and in truth we should aspire to such convalescence, but we bring perception and concept. We bring judgment.

Judgments are patterns in the mind, and are extremely difficult to dislodge; prior to judgment is *judging*, one of the deepest functions of our brain. Like muscle memory, concepts are mind memories we bring to life through our judgments. From William James, a founder of modern psychology: "ideas, and others equally abstract, form the background for all our facts, the fountain-head of all the possibilities we conceive of. They give its "nature," as we call it, to every special thing. Everything we know is "what" it is by sharing in the nature of one of these abstractions."

Imagine trying to forget how to ride a bike. You can convince yourself all day you don't know how to ride a bike, but the second you get on a bike you know how to pedal, balance and steer. Though not exactly the same, concepts are like the muscle memories of our brain, informing us on how to do things, how things work, who is what, and who is going to do what. Concepts are so prevalent in our mind the most influential philosopher in the Western world, Plato, contended that the Forms, also referred to as the Ideas, dominated every aspect of the human mind; the Ideas were the concept of concepts. For him, the Ideas were quasi-mystical entities, of the ether but guiding the world at the mind's inception, cosmically and practically. In later religious and philosophical systems, the Ideas would influence how we think about God—God being the formless giver of forms—but, more importantly, and what the Christians missed entirely, was that Plato was onto something. He was searching for the deep structure of mind, a solution which would unlock all subsequent ideas and habits and behaviors. Whereas theology largely took over as the main form of thought, at least until the Enlightenment, Zen and a lot of Asian meditative traditions never took their eye off the prize—understanding the concept is central to becoming awake.

Just as our lungs pull air in and out all day, most of the time without us knowing it, our mind is using concepts: protecting old ones, trading old ones for new ones, or creating new ones when it stumbles to understand. The desire to conceive is a reflex, no different from your body pulling its arm away from a flame. Conception; to conceive; concept. They are partners. To resist conception is therefore to resist a basic act of mind. One could even say that concept and small mind need each other to survive. We want something—this simple act requires a concept of ourselves, a concept of a thing, perhaps a feeling of covetousness association, the concept that having it will be of benefit. The idea of benefit, too, is a concept.

Concepts are efficiencies geared toward survival. Imagine how difficult it would be to have to relearn to ride a bike, as if you never had seen one before, every time you wanted to ride a bike. It would be ridiculous and a total waste of time. We'd never do it. But, without conscious effort, the mind accumulates data on the act and stores it; it does this with such insistence we can't convince it to do otherwise. Neural patterns are set in no time. It knows what a bike is, where our feet go, what it's good for. Concepts are, indeed, products of pattern matching. In our evolutionary history, it's not hard to imagine a scenario where the ability to know a tiger is dangerous would be advantageous to your survival.[57] The individuals who could make the connection quicker passed on traits of the mind to their kin, having not been eaten, and thus the mind-trait of judging became passed on in the gene pool. Surely, there are nuances. Worms recoil in hot sunlight. They are not judging, they are reacting, and yet, as consciousness becomes more complex and self-aware "higher" up the chain of organisms, creatures such as ourselves understand the why of our aversion, so too with our attraction. Concepts are not evil, just foundational, and because they are foundational, they are front and center on the path to being free.

Some concepts are, of course, stickier than others.

Our judgments are dense in *un*natural places, but when we are in nature, the concept-judgment machine quiets, calms down. We go out in public and judge this or that person as ugly or pretentious, rich or poor, or a space as dirty or clean, and we feel disgust or pride as a result, and yet, when we stroll in the forest, we see a mangled tree with scraggly moss at its base and feel no disgust. In fact, we likely think it is more beautiful on account of its disharmony. Why is this? When we perceive, it is predominantly through the lens of small mind. Small mind is in service of self, and self needs to be protected. The primal function of judgment is to protect, hence judgment being the default; our agency detection is constantly on the lookout as to what others are trying to do to us. About 99.9 percent of the time, we see only what our small minds are working through—fears, insecurities, desires for this or that. Recent studies have upended an old assumption about perception, namely, that perception is first and judgment second.[58] Now we know that our values inform and constrain our perception prior to any sense input, a process prioritizing the personal and judgment-guided traits of small mind. The emotions and beliefs we have inside of us literally determine what we experience. The wild, on the contrary, has a built-in propensity to loosen self-centered perception. The wild unmoors Protagoras's statement of mankind as "the measure of all things," which, literally, found its way into DaVinci's Vitruvian man, and, later, the assumption that the wild is here *for us*, either for extraction or recreation or appreciation, all of which are forms of consumption. It is for neither. It is akin to saying chocolate realizes the ultimate nature of the cacao bean. It doesn't; but it might *for us.*

When neuroscientists say the mind is primarily a pattern-recognition machine, we have to qualify the statement.

The wild has often seduced the romantics in history because it enables a small space in the mind to be open to the non-human, which isn't so much an activation of said space, but rather a *deactivation* of the concept-mind; because we don't see people behind the architecture of the wild, our agency detection is dampened. There's truth here. It is in this vein that Christianity advises we become like children, because children are notorious for being non-judgmental. "Truly I tell you, unless you change and become like little children, you will never enter the kingdom of heaven." And from Seng Ts'an, in the *Third Chinese Patriarch of Zen*, "Do not search for the truth; only cease to cherish opinions." The nature of mind isn't encompassed by concept-mind (small mind), but quite the opposite. Concept-mind is contained by mind (big mind). The nature of nature might just be that it unteaches us.

Buddhism has a word for when a teacher uses just the right tactic to reach a student, a tactic tailored to their understanding, and or lack thereof. Something to meet them, at that moment, perfectly.

It's called skillful means.

Skillful Means

A cheating spouse is not your suffering.
The new car is not your happiness.

For so many years, I lacked skillful means for my self-understanding. The skill can come from out there, but it can also come from within. Big mind is always trying to correct small mind; the latter is petulant, devious and likes to take control—as it is designed to be; the former is none of these things. Nature is skillful, arguably the most of all, for a few reasons: first, we let our guards down; because of the dearth of human intention, we can see the human with more starkness, against a darker background, as it were. It doesn't judge us, we don't judge it. Meditation functions like this. Second, there's nothing it does not contain, at least in the sense that its associations for symbolic learning, *inner learning*, are endless; concretely, the associations we get are in the wind, moving water, trees, acorns, juxtaposition, interaction. Because it contains no thing in its essential nature, it has, with the right perception, a bit of everything. The all. And because it is the all, it has no conceptual constraint. Our minds rest when they are not looking for the trace of others.

There is a story of Vietnamese Zen master Thich Nhat Hanh overseeing a Zen tea ceremony. He was helping a novice monk learn the art of tea, a formal affair in Japan, with complicated rules on where the server should stand in relation to the invitees' line of sight, bowing to the host at certain times, eating your sweet before sipping the tea. The rules are dependent on the season, time of day, and so on. It is more a choreographed aristocratic dinner than anything else. Think *Downton Abbey*, but in Japan. During one training session, Hanh noticed a monk was too caught in the rules of the tea ceremony, in the purity of it all, and lost the forest for the trees. Rule following, however imperceptible, had taken hold of the monk, and nothing irritates Zen more than attachment to rules; one must hold everything lightly. On one occasion, as the young monk poured a cup of tea, Hanh dipped his finger into the cup, making sure the young monk saw him. The young novice was shocked. Aghast. Tea was sacred, pouring it ever more so. Purity was paramount. Sticking your finger in it was like burning a portrait of the Pope. He was incredulous.

Hanh had deployed skillful means.

Why did Hanh do that? The novice had thought going through the motions was the point, that purity was in *execution*, but he missed the point. The student had mistaken ends and means. He had mistaken *being-in-execution*, being there in the ceremony, performing the rite, surrounded by all the accouterments, with the *end*, when in fact it was the means to the moment. To mistake one for the other is to mistake the finger point at the moon for the moon, LSD for the high you need. I had done the exact same thing with being-in-the-wild.

As such, we not only set up false idols out there but an idol worshipper inside us. I'm with Nietzsche, however, in that we need to destroy both: "Not in shattering idols, But in shattering the idol-worshipper in thee, Consisted thy valour."

Another example, told a few ways in the Zen traditions: it's midnight at the monastery. The students are serious, very serious, and hang onto the master's every word. They are earnestly doing their nightly meditations, or, if it's very late, are unfurled on their bamboo mats, lined like sardines, and asleep. But in comes the master in the middle of the night. He is drunk. He clambers and moans and shouts down the monastery corridors, making a racket. The students are scandalized … alcohol is forbidden. And the master must never lack discipline. They have no idea what to do. But this is the master's point, to bring forth *their* scandal, not his. The students have turned the master into an idol. They are just rule followers, idol worshipers. The master needs to rid them of guru worship. Coming in drunk typically does the trick. You can never see your teacher, much less the teachings, if all you are doing is going through the motions. The master deployed skillful means.

A last one, this one known the world over, is the parable of the butcher. It reads, "A good carver changes his knife once a year; by which time the blade is dented. An ordinary carver changes it once a month; by which time it is broken. I have used my present knife for nineteen years, and during that time have carved several thousand bulls. But the blade still looks as though it had just come out of the mold. Where part meets part there is always space, and a knife-blade has no thickness. Insert an instrument that has no thickness into a structure that is amply spaced, and surely it cannot fail to have plenty of room. That is why I can use a blade for nineteen years, and yet it still looks as though it were fresh from the forger's mound."

The butcher is skillful; he is not willing his way through the animal, but, without being guided by the self, and armed with the Tao, he can see the whole and has the humility to move just so in the metaphorical medium of the carcass. He thrives in the world because he lives in the alcove. It is the space that is a place.

Skillful means is not exotic, nor Buddhist. In 2018, James MacDonald disguised himself as a homeless man and sat out front an American church, where he was the pastor. He was trying to see if people acknowledged him. Few did. Too few. Minutes later, he revealed himself on the pulpit to the shock of his congregation. He made his point. He deployed skillful means. When a poor Nazarene got himself onto a wooden cross to highlight injustice, he deployed skillful means. When Martin Luther King advised protesters to practice nonviolence while violence was being done to them, to mirror to the world the unjust rawness of racism and violence, he was being skillful.

Skillful means can come from a person, with intention, or from the wild. When you build a multi-million-dollar home on a private island and stand there and nothing happens, the great thoughts do not arrive, or if the wild rebuffs your advances and refuses to give what you seek, you can either get back on the treadmill and keep searching or you can stand there, or float in my case, and have a think about what the world is telling you.

Skillful means is just a concept attempting to explain a set of circumstances. An understanding is stuck then becomes unstuck; truth, or enlightenment, as subtraction. Skillful means is defined by small mind's unraveling.

But it's all skillful means, isn't it? It *is* here, everywhere, coming at us ceaselessly … if we only look.

In what way could something ***not be skillful?*** Such a thing, or scenario, or person, couldn't exist: meaning is contextual to each individual, and thus no principle could exclude meaning from any thing or person or moment. Art is truly a testament to this fact—the Oppenheim's furry teacup, Warhol's soup can, Ansel Adam's clouds, a photo of a teenage girl walking on the sidewalk. The field is infinite. Our minds have the ability to create meaning from nothing, *ex nihilo*, and this fact reveals a curious, and seldom acknowledged, trait about the human mind: no thing, person or act can be robbed of the symbolic with the right perspective, the right intentionality and an openness to skillful means at all times and places. Intention activates small mind, concept mind, and it is in the realm of concepts where meaning often plants its flag. But meaning narrows, because when you have one meaning in your mind it is extremely difficult to see another, and it is in the nature of the world, of the earth's rivers and tides, to not have one meaning.

Just yesterday I saw a praying mantis while running down a gravel road. The insect isn't particularly rare in my area, nor particularly common. It was there on the hot, dry road, apparently waiting to get run over. I'm not sure how I noticed it either. Nonetheless, I instantaneously thought of my father. I mean, there was no other meaning to it. He was saying hello to me in the mantis. I've never had a superstition for insects, or reincarnation, but my mind made meaning immediately out of the little green insect, without a sliver of conscious intervention, and, for a few minutes, I was comforted that my father was ok. Hey dad. Thanks for the hello. It got me thinking, however—in this simple observation could be the germ of why mystics throughout history have claimed we do not need to rely on the world for anything, why a jail cell robs us of nothing, and why tragedy is of no consequence to our inner poise. Meaning is everywhere, skillful means everywhere, and these mystics have simply removed the blockages most are ensnared in.

Our ability to find meaning isn't just a talent of the mind, but it is why the human mind is so fantastically unique and beautiful and profound, the font of our music, art, complex social relationships and Stephen King novels. But it might also be our greatest weakness, the reason we are such tortured animals, our tribalism so rampant, why we classify people and places into friends and foes and nations and rivals; to and fro; approach and avoid. It may be the cause of our failure, after so many thousands of years with complex brains, to unmoor ourselves from base instincts of hoarding, greed, and fear.

What I extracted from the praying mantis is this: judgment functions with distinction, beginning with me noticing the insect: sensation. My consciousness focused. I determined that there was, indeed, an animal; and this determination was no doubt fueled by the loss of my father and my unconscious wish to find him, connect with him in any way I could. Armed with this deep intentionality, the wild stepped in. I was not taken in, as a three-year-old might be, by the look and shape of it. I had seen one before and I wasn't wooed. Pattern structures in the mind, such as a concept, aid the process; emotions can germinate as well at this point, depending. Ideation ensues; the moment of ideation is the moment when concept arises. When a concept arises, and it becomes personalized, which not all do, it creates the potential for meaning—sensatio. This was the moment my father was associated with the insect. When the thought carrying the concept attaches itself to self, with the halo of awareness, it creates actual meaning; emotion can express as feeling once ego has time to create a concept of self-understanding around the emotion. This is, however, a wholly inadequate sketch, and we have only just begun to understand the machinery of the mind. Just as we are finding quarks centuries after gravity was discovered, centuries from now we will continue to map the biological, evolutionary and psychological nuances of our brains. But brain is not mind, and the research will be difficult to apply. If you don't believe me, go read a paper on memory in the *Journal of Neuroscience* and see if you can apply it to your life today. All the more reason for us to study our minds as experienced *by us*. The task is on us. AI will no more teach us about ourselves than understanding how gravity works helps us kick a football.

To understand the nature of mind isn't just to know, intellectually, that the mind creates meaning. That's an easy prize. The ultimate goal is to see meaning being created in your mind at each level of construction, in real time; the lower you go, however, the harder it is to "see", since the very machinery we rely on to analyze is what we are trying to analyze. Science can show us this with sophisticated machinery, but unless we can see it ourselves it will be someone else's knowledge. There is sensation and there is ideation as bookends; sensation is initial, and informed by value, and ideation is the realm of good or bad, which produces a final expression, a judgment, of our unconscious values. It is possible for ideation to be without judgment, but it's rare. In a lot of cases, judgment is a tool of exile, an exile born of a misunderstanding and a runaway mind—the misunderstanding that sensation ought to be judged, and that, being judged, it has a greater value, an inherent value.

The praying mantis was, of course, not *my* father. I made that association. But it gets more complex. A new car is not *your* happiness. The death of your parents is not *your* suffering. The association of inside states of mind with exterior states of material is partly the brilliance of our mind. This pairing has allowed us to imagine greener pastures, get out of bad relationships and move toward pleasure and away from pain. But it has also fueled all our ground zeros, reliant as they are on consuming, purchasing, owning. The more you are attached to the external thing, any change in it—whether good or bad—will have an equal effect on the state of your self. As Yongey Mingyur Rinpoche observes, "Misunderstandings about the source of sensation occur because the perception and the interpretation arise almost simultaneously, so close together that the strong but incorrect impression is created that the interpretive reality—good-bad, attractive-aversive—is lodged within the object itself and not in the mind. It can be very difficult to accept that the source of what we like or do not like arises in our mind … When we relate to the world with a mind full of preconceptions, we erect a barrier between us and reality as-it-is." Key words are *incorrect impression* and *barrier.* We are duped into thinking a person or a thing, or the place where the object is, contains the value we give to it. Because of this innate function of mind, a barrier is created between us and reality—skillful means is a breakdown of this barrier and enlightenment is the ability to see every facet of this barrier. The wild is the original deployer of the tactic.

The Ground Zero Fallacy

A state of being is not who we want to become,
but the inner life of the "who."

As Mike Tyson is fond of saying, "God punishes you by giving you everything you want."

Sutton fascinates me, because he and I are no different. We fell victim to the ground-zero fallacy, a turn of experiential logic outlining, in unequivocal fashion, the cat-and-mouse dance of expectation and reality. Sutton and I both got dressed up for the ball, a party of our own design … though in my case I technically got undressed.

We got what we wanted. But the banquet hall was empty. The emperor had no clothes. The shoe didn't fit. And so on.

Sutton standing on the shores of Columbia Island, me on the waterfront on an unforgettable Tuesday night, you in your life chasing your micro, or microtropia, the coming weekend—it's the same dynamic, and endless until the day you die, unless you put an end to it. The night runs we take are big and small. They are ceaseless and exhausting. Running beneath it all is an inalterable quiet, as thick and viscous as a cold wind in the summer coming from lands unknown. Our minds need to feel that wind.

* * *

Ground zeros are places we imagine, with an idealized version of ourselves in said place, yes, but they are really *states of being* we want to inhabit—a state of being is *not* who we want to become, but the *inner life* of the "who" embedded in a specific landscape, urban or otherwise. The problem: our minds confuse inner life and landscape. We get confused because rather than chase a state of being, we become directors of our personas in these scenes, effectively becoming obsessed with set design rather state of mind, which, ironically, you can't design, only undesign. As Norman Fisher has observed, "The truth is, what we call "materialism" isn't really materialistic—it is idealistic. In other words, it is not the objects that we are after in our consuming—it is what those objects mean to us and the people in our world." What they mean to us is… *us*.

Mind design and set design—we should not confuse the two. Often, and this is the fallacy in ground-zero, we expect our inner lives to travel, or level up, once we inhabit the scenes we've designed. When we get that job requiring confident leadership, we will become a confident person. When we build that peaceful, luxury home on the water's shore, we will find peace. When we arrive on the water's shore at midnight, the wild will embrace us. The essence of expectation resides within this chasing, this waiting for mind to follow design.

Though forgivable, the fallacy is a psychosomatic carrot on a stick. Of course, many people rely on these versions of future-selves to motivate their today-selves. They run a marathon as a result. Their zero motivates them. Drives them forward. We lose weight imagining our future self. We become better parents. But these zeros are shells of selfhood, life as performance art really, and the mistake is believing, as we do with things, that value lies inherent in these scenes. You are leveraging your self-worth on an unknown. That is risky business.

Lounging on a beach in Hawaii, or building your dream house, *will* have a positive effect on your psychology. But only for so long. The reason your dream will always return is because the deep source of all dreams is discontent. Life is not suffering, life contains suffering, Siddhartha said. Suffering is innate. Out of discontent the seeds of fantasy arise. The mind just does it. There is a reason why contemporary neuroscientists and fifth-century BC Buddhists and Hindu mystics refer to the contents of our memories, projections or fantasies in visual terms. In ancient and modern literature, you hear the phrase "mental images" a lot, or "mental representations," or "re-presentations," and varieties thereof. We remember and process visually as we live; this is a bias of our biology. In the bio-psychological thrust to adapt to changing environments, a hallmark of our intelligence, which our species is adept at, we generate an actual vision of ourselves, and this vision entails all the things real vision has, such as smells, sights, things in landscape. Our inner visions might even have personality traits. These traits lure us, seduce us. My ground zero was of someone able to appreciate the wild with profound depth; thus I chased the wild. Who wouldn't?

Visual preference has a neurological bias in our brains, the product of evolutionary constraints acting on our biology. Our brains devote roughly 50 percent of their processing power to vision.[59] Our body's emphasis on vision has been selected by evolution, and thus deemed essential to our organism's fitness. It could have been different, and our organism could have had more emphasis placed on sound, like a dolphin, or smell, like a vulture, but it didn't end up that way. As such, we have designed our world around vision. More proof of our brain's profound talent for not just seeing, but relying on seeing, and having a bias toward it, was uncovered by researchers at MIT when it was found we have the ability to identify images in only thirteen milliseconds.[60] The remarkable speed of this ability says a few things, namely, our brains are simply hardwired for visual perception, but it also connects the facility of pattern matching in our eyes with how our minds are using vision for concept formation. When Yongey Mingyur Rinpoche observed that "misunderstandings about the source of sensation occur because the perception and the interpretation arise almost simultaneously," he was not off. Turns out it is close to thirteen milliseconds, just about "simultaneous," a fact illuminating how difficult the struggle is to unlink perception and judgment. In short, to do so, you have to rewire your brain. "The fact that you can do that at these high speeds indicates to us that what vision does is find concepts," said Mary Potter, the lead researcher on the MIT study. Vision is central to reading faces, and, as such, essential to navigating social life. Studies have shown we can identify emotions in other people in under 100 milliseconds, simply by reading their faces.[61] When applied to determining another person's emotions, a concept is the feeling, conscious or not, that "Mary is angry," the fodder of which is determining which facial expressions represent certain emotions.

We apply this rapid-fire, concept-formation to places we visit and even, I contend, places we haven't visited yet, since our fantasies are us trying out future experiences in our minds to see how they might or might not pan out.

This is why, in many traditions, it is recommended people close their eyes when they meditate. Why? Our minds are so hardwired to process vision it is extremely difficult to convince itself otherwise, like trying to convince a pack of wolves not to consume the deer carcass they just stumbled upon. Closing the eyes facilitates the closing down of sensation, which quiets a large part of the mind's triggers, which, eventually, quiets concept formation. And when you dampen concept formation, you are starting to tap into non-dualist thinking, the onramp for a different life. A free mind.

Why is this important? Because we receive visually, often with impairment, we project visually, out of this impairment—this is the essence of the ground zero.

Hidden Assumptions in Buddhism

Mental health is the absence of a mind-splinter—
the lack of a deep, and shallow, sense of offness.

The human mind is a lot of things, but, courtesy of evolution, it is first and foremost a problem solver: at first solving survival and mating problems, then social problems, math problems, Instagram problems.

The ground zero, in many ways, is a solution to a problem—the problem of discontent. If memory is a re-presentation of an original, a time and place where an experience occurred, a ground zero is a creative *re*-presentation of the present, existing in the future, except it is not presenting anything actual, but rather it is solutioning our current discontent with a psychosomatic scene (set design), just as it does when we remember (itself often a solution to a problem). Like memories, ground zeros are reminding us of something.

Discontent is, in a sense, another word for suffering, the first noble truth of Buddhism. That Buddhism landed on suffering as its first truth is interesting. It had many options. It could have started with "happiness is possible", and backed up from there. But it didn't. It landed on one irrefutable observation—life involves suffering. Life involves happiness too, but not many consider that a problem. That life contains suffering is a problem. From this simple first truth all things flow. The second noble truth is: suffering is caused by desire. It's a statement about the mechanism of suffering. The kicker, however, comes with the third noble truth—rid yourself of desire and you rid yourself of suffering. This is the real Buddhist revolution, its real psychological entrepreneurship in action. The first and second are good, and not altogether original, but the third is the meat. The third is a thesis on the ground zero, on selfhood, on the deep solution to suffering.

When discontent squats, our mind wants to get rid of it. It's not normal to walk around with a splinter in your foot and, first, not notice it, and then second, not want to remove it. Our minds notice a splinter without having to try, and we'd likely consider someone completely pathological if they walked around for years with a really painful and easy to remove splinter, but never made any effort to remove it. It would strike us as odd. We'd think something was wrong with the person: "How could you not notice you had a splinter in your foot?" The same goes for the presence of malaise in our minds, except the lot of us don't know it's possible to remove it. Discontent, or suffering, or whatever it is we call it, bugs us. Gets our attention. Something isn't right. Between noble truth one and noble truth two, we are, however, missing a step. What we are missing is the *reason* we care in the first place. Without it, Buddhism is incomplete. It's not groundbreaking to conclude that life contains suffering, nor that craving is a huge cause. But the hidden assumption of the Buddhist system is this: we shouldn't settle with this observation. More is out there. Mind can be free. We can do better. The second hidden assumption is this: the presence of suffering is a pretty big deal, arguably the biggest. We shouldn't just believe, academically, we can get better; we need to know getting rid of suffering is an optimum state in our psychosomatic biology.

Writ large, mental health is the absence of a mind-splinter—the lack of a deep, and shallow, sense of offness. Zen showed me my mind splinter, and it also showed me how to pull it out.

All my life I thought happiness was the result of something you *added* to your life, whether to make up for a lack of confidence (a new job to fill you with pride); fill a loneliness pit in your stomach (a new lover to show to ourselves our self-worth); or fix the pothole of failure (a new car or nice things to show the world we've made it). I've been adding my whole life. We all have. We add because we chase. We add because we think a future emotion (a value) exists in the thing or person we are aiming to be. But Freud, whom I think is right on this topic, turned all that on its head. For him, happiness—he called it pleasure—was a *release* of tension in our bodies and minds, not an addition. In other words, it was the subtraction of a tension, not the addition of a thing.

I remember when I first read Freud's theory of pleasure—or at least one of them, as his views shifted over the years. At the time, I was living in Syracuse, NY, where I'd eventually earn a PhD in the Philosophy of Religion. Syracuse was a cold place, with long, seven-month winters and a snowpack more natural at 10,000 feet in the Rocky Mountains than a few hours' drive from Wall Street. The town was vintage Americana, with well-loved local restaurants and deep community. I had a fire one night, which wasn't uncommon. I'd have a fire virtually every night for three to four months. We lived on the second floor of an old Victorian, the entrance on the left, by the driveway; in the winter, icicles from the second story gutters formed pillars to the ground. Once inside, you wound up two flights of stairs on creaky wooden boards, the handrails wobbly. The house could only be described as tired yet undefeated, definitely not in the prime of its life, but not the sunset either. When I would have a fire, the house relaxed after twenty minutes or so, breathed outward, just as I did when sitting in front of it. The frigid wood in the attic and walls would unfreeze, and the cracks in the plaster would grow and widen like mud in the sun.

This one night, I sat on our thick rug in front of the fire and read Freud's theory—pleasure is a release of tension. The premise is that we become blocked. The feeling of being blocked is not pleasurable. Pleasure is felt when the block is removed. Subtraction.

The idea felt scandalous.

It was scandalous because I always felt pleasure was the result of something *added* to your life. Of course, additions don't last long, but then, of course, you went and sought another thing. Rinse and repeat. Nothing controversial there. Craving a certain food. You get the food. You feel satiated. Want a new jacket. Get the jacket. Tomorrow is a new day. This is just how life works and how millions of us function. You exist, existence lacks a few things, and you make up for it by buying, consuming, traveling, experiencing or what not.

But this wasn't what Freud was saying at all. Just as darkness is the absence of light, pleasure is the absence of tension, and the acute serotonin flush of getting a thing is but another word for the tension's release. Pleasure is a *return* to homeostasis—our biological, and hence psychological, balance. When we are out of balance, when our homeostasis is off, we tense up, seek spikes on the "high" side of pleasure to counteract the low side of discontent, the latter going by, and expressed in, many names: suffering, boredom, depression, pain, anger; the very ailments growing in our world. Pleasure adds nothing, but merely counteracts. Pleasure corrects a defect. Remove the defect, remove the need for pleasure. *Holy shit*, I thought. Remember the first two truths of Buddhist philosophy? Life contains suffering; the cause of this suffering is desire (or craving). See the connection? Desire appears in our organism when we are out of balance.

But doesn't that mean the vast majority of those living on earth, all of whom experience desire on a daily, if not hourly basis, are out of balance? Yes, that is exactly what it means. But isn't having desire a natural side effect of being in a body? Yes, it is. And aren't we hardwired to survive, hence we are hardwired to desire food and sex? Yes we are. But we are talking about much more than desiring food; we are talking about feeding our ground zeros, which is where this desire ends up eventually. We are talking about becoming the best possible version of a human being.

As I sat on my rug, the fire crackled before me. The house relaxed. A light snow rested on every leaf and branch. I tossed another log into the fire. The log splintered. Sparks flew out and extinguished themselves on the rug. I watched their embers turn black, singeing the yarns. I did nothing.

An image entered my mind of the human as a balloon, symbolic of our psychic landscape. We live our lives in relative homeostasis until we get a mind-splinter: a problem with the boss, a nasty email, anxiety over a presentation at work, boredom, forced confrontation with a family member while your father is dying. We find a quick solution and deflate. Tension abated. But, as sure as the sun rises, the balloon grows again. That the balloon grows, again, and we seek a solution, again, as unwise as before, is the essence of samara, which keeps us in the cycle of ignorance.

We live our lives in shifting, dynamic conditions on the inside and out; life is a medium, and movement never stops. Pure homeostasis is a fantasy. As it is said in the Ts'ai-ken t'an, "Water which is too pure has no fish." Fish are good. We want fish. We want rich inner lives. We need a sharp stone to sharpen the sword. Tension builds. The balloon inflates. The way out, however, is seeing the cycle with clarity, vigor and bravery. Big mind is needed for that.

When tension appears, fantasy mobilizes, a form of creative prediction and problem solving. Our creativity imagines ourselves otherwise. Enter the ground zero. We fantasize about a ground zero because pleasure and pain are also ground-zero oriented; they are always visualized as a body in a place with those delicious, pleasurable things (attraction), and or the lack of the things afflicting us at the moment of fantasy inception (avoidance). If you pay close attention to your mind, you will see this happening on an hourly basis. We then chase the fantasy, fueled by desire. What we are really chasing is a state of mind, where and when we are free. The ground zero is an *aesthetic of homeostasis*, and thus a more complete picture of who we are; this is why the ground zero is an updated version of Buddhist selfhood, since the latter is rather dry. To a textureless and colorless notion of self, the ground zero adds things, states of mind, objects of desire—the true building blocks of self. Neuroscientist Bruce Lipton believes the purpose of consciousness is to create the neuro-chemical mapping to align with the thoughts you are having now with a future state; thus through the mapping and visualization our ground zeros are potentialities wherein that future state can be realized.[62]

If the tension is small, we rarely notice the squatter. Quietly, it sets up shop, perhaps near our confidence, on top of our depression, or tries to seduce our inner (and irresponsible) child toward some chaotic fun, or might even be welcomed in (the *welcoming* the result of an already-existing tension). From the tension comes a want, a need, a craving, sometimes in the guise of an impulse, sometimes a hybrid feeling. These things are hard to let go. "Sticky" is the word. The balloon inflates. We become filled with excitation. A second urge perhaps rears up. An impulse. If unresolved, the balloon continues to grow, manifesting with an *offness* in our psychosomatic landscape. We become compelled, sometimes obsessed. The next step is often unclear … perhaps an idea attaches itself to a solution, and the two become implicated together. Like a ground zero writ small, the idea is embodied, a narrative draft of us doing something to ameliorate the tension, such as quitting our jobs, telling our boss to go f-themself, building a dream house, or going for a cathartic run at midnight. We imagine, or more precisely, it is the purpose of imagination to visualize a future state, a vital practice, perhaps unique to the human mind. Part of our identity today, as we conceive ourselves in the moment, is therefore disproportionately based off of what we want to be in the future. Hence why more than a few religious traditions have made one simple request—to be who you are in your *natural* state. A request as shocking as it is "unnatural", strictly speaking.

I like the balloon metaphor because it has the aesthetic of a tumor growing in a place where it doesn't belong. The balloon extends to all parts of our body, which manifest discord under tension. Our hands shake when we get nervy. Our palms sweat. Our breath tightens. We stiffen when we move. Distraction, the giving of attention, is a universal trait of tension, which is to say, tension steals attention. Tension is the mark of a mind at ill-ease, just as a tense body marks a nervous athlete. Negative emotions are the most common biomarker of homeostasis out of whack.

We rarely see with clarity the inner dynamics of all our autonomous psychological machinations, as we are typically relegated to chasing the solution, and that's efficiency at its finest—put out the fire in front of you. We seek the solution by trying to add to our system, seeking a new experience to replace the one we are having (offness). We add, thinking we are removing. It's an obvious solution, but ineffective. You don't cure hoarder's disease by hoarding more.

In reality, any type of addition is just inflating the balloon.

As I was saying, I was lounging on my rug, in Syracuse, in winter, beside our fireplace, when I read Freud's theory. Very romantic. The house was cold. The wood creaking. Outside our screened-in porch, plump snowflakes wobbled downward in the still night air. A lone streetlight, long the object of my delight on nights like these, stood opposite the street: yellowish, sickly light, but gorgeous, like an inverse flower, its beauty earth-facing. I wasn't immediately aware of the connection between the balloon image and the fact that the fire was literally filling my house with hot air in the manner of a balloon, but that is just how our minds are always working, either when we are creating, remembering, plotting the future, thinking. The cues of our environment are entering and being digested by our minds at all levels.

To further confuse you, an upside-down balloon looks like a hungry ghost. Well known in the roster of Asian spiritual traditions, especially in Buddhist art and murals, a hungry ghost has a thin neck and huge stomach. It is always hungry, but because it has such a thin neck, it is never satiated, and thus is condemned to a life of dissatisfaction. The hungry ghost is not beautiful. It is ugly, drooping, ravenous, slovenly. It is a form of living hell. When we inflate, we think the problem is out *there*, which is why we chase the solution *out there*, but the problem is in us as much as it is in the balloon. The hungry ghost is portly because it is consuming all the time. The hungry ghost is filled with tension, unease, offness, and it consumes "food" on account of never getting enough of it. It is fat because the things you add never go away. It is fat because it seeks outside what is needed on the inside. What we need to know, and must never forget, is that it's possible to reach a point, an alcove in our mind, when we are not beholden to the ceaseless desire for more.

Freud elucidated this: the problem is in *here*, in us, and any attempt to experience-add—which, to be frank, I had been doing with athletics and the wild *all my freakin' life*, and which millions like me are still doing—you are just trying to remove the balloon by stacking experience on top or around it, hoping it deflates. Sometimes, tension does get released, especially singular tensions of the body, such as hunger, libido, etc. Those emails at work just nagging at you? A long hike on a Saturday does the trick. But the emails await on Monday. The same panic returns. We drink or try to dodge. We plot the next weekend. We imagine what the future is going to bring us then, and, in doing so, the imagining itself is pleasurable. It is pleasurable because evolution has designed it thus, just like it designed sex to be pleasurable so people would do it. But it is also pleasurable because the anticipatory thought is effective in releasing tension on account of the fantasy, which, as we all know, hasn't happened yet. In short, the simple act of dreaming, of creating, is itself pleasing, and it is so because evolution deemed the trait beneficial to our survival. We will likely never know, but I do wonder if landscape itself is the deep source of our creativity, of running out of game and risking a new life in a new valley, one we can see with our eyes, from a hilltop, as we feel the pressure to survive, seducing us to move and adapt. Our creativity is the marketing of a new life, a component of adaptation. Our modern problems are not of survival, but we are working with the same basic software.

Awareness is the pry bar allowing us to unmoor ourselves from the heaviness of demands. Awareness provides the gem of *kintsugi* and is the lacquer holding the pottery together. But we get lost in the word "awareness." It is a base word, undefined and crude.

Being aware means something has lost its power; being aware marks a shift. We think of the term as a light switch of consciousness, on and off. One is aware or they are not. Just as it is with light, however, there are levels and tonalites to awareness. To be aware means to come to light from the darkness. Sometimes, you can make the outlines of something, and that's all. At other times, it's before you, obvious—an emotion, fear, anxiety, love. If someone is aware, it's implied that another isn't, that not being aware is a possibility, and so, to be aware means to no longer be in the clutch of darkness. Small mind is awareness in place, in time, born of our self. Big awareness, big mind, is a state of being with no place, because, at the end truth, it contains everything, because the more awareness is attached to a place, and a body, the more it is circumscribed (small mind); like a prism, big mind is reflected in a body, but it's light is of a different source. Awareness is more or less, and the freedom we experience from more of it, i.e., nonattachment to small mind, is only an effect of the lack of attachment to a *type* of awareness; conversely, attachment to a type of awareness, as evinced in the word myopic, makes us feel the opposite—the barrier or the blockage.

Studies have shown that if a normal person hears a bell, or any sound, and then receives an electric shock seconds later, their brains will pair the two: bell means pain. The researchers found that next time the individual hears the bell, their brains light up in fear and expectation, and, in essence, they experience a phantom pseudo-electric shock, as if it already happened. In other words, the expectation itself turns into a negative experience in the present. But the researchers ran the same experiment with veteran meditators and found that when the bell was rung, nothing happened in the brain; it didn't light up with fearful anticipation. When the shock came, their brains did light up but quieted down very quickly and found homeostasis fast; in contrast, after the shock, a normal person's brain continued to light up, extending the negative experience. The monks have retrained their stimulus-response system, basic to the organism. Their homeostasis was harder to penetrate, prior and post a stimulus, and easier to recover. They were more immune to the whims of small mind.

Meditation allows you to "see" your thoughts or judgments or concepts. When you can see them, you have "distance" from them. Distance from them means they have less hold on you, which isn't to say less intensity. In my own experience, the more free I am in an experience, the deeper I feel it, and this is so because the psychological elements in myself, which are trying to suppress or color the experience, are no longer active, and so the experience can arrive with greater purity. The more awareness we have, the freer we are to experience. As the study showed, it is so with pain and expectation, but it is also with pleasure and the perceived gain in pleasure as a result of something we will get. I guarantee, as I see it in myself, that the brain of the person whose mind is free—this can be anyone, not just someone who meditates—will also unlink the pleasurable thing with the brain centers that light up during pleasure. Just as the shit plant is there, so too is the gem in the bad experience. You can't have the ying without the yang. If you want to rid yourself of the negativity, there is a certain type of positivity you must rid yourself of as well. You must stop the mind from feeling the anticipatory pleasure from the thing you believe is pleasurable. This shift, however weighty, implies a mark of freedom for the person who moves into this alcove. Because we are talking about consciousness, the mechanism is this—in the throes of conceptual morass most of the time, freedom of mind is developed as one removes themself from concept; concept is tied to self's survival via judgment; it's in our DNA, and so we "experience" the thrill of unyoking. Because the mind's original nature wants to be free, any steps in that direction release tension.

Manicured Lawns in the Amazon

Logic is a little field we cultivate in the void.

It's a funny thing that we can use the word landscape to describe our inner and outer worlds.

My mind has a unique contour like the scene outside my window, always in flux, with odd things growing in the sidewalks, some flowers and flourishing weeds, a light breeze, scavengers, moldy piles of leaves. Some memories rot in my brain, while new ones are getting watered constantly and thus bear fruit. There are mountains in my mind, some which are hard to climb and are imposing, like the death of my father and mother, and valleys too, where I go to enjoy myself and relax. When something happens to me, say thinking of my best friend in high school who slept with my girlfriend at the time, that stone is like a trundled piece of granite unmoored from a foreboding peak—I don't always know where it will land. It might land on my self-consciousness, exacerbating it, or on the stone of jealousy, activating it anew. Often, it waters the tree of my insecurity, which heightens my distrustfulness of people close to me. Such was the case for years. Our inner worlds are full of movements, intensities, twists, turns—just like natural landscapes. There is no logic to our inner system, to mind, just patterns born of biology, trajectories of behavior generated thereof, shaped by culture, childhood, informed by evolution, and so on, with bewildering complexity.

Our rationality, in contrast, is a tidy patch of manicured lawn in the Amazon, just sitting there, historical and born in a time and place with specific conditions, and everyone is playing soccer, eating lunch and playing on this field as if that's it, as if the darkness of the wild isn't right there, at the fringes. But it is. The jungle is right there, always creeping. It's daunting to get to know your mind. It requires bravery. And you won't always like what you find.

* * *

The word "landscape" came to us in the sixteenth century, originally *landschap* in Dutch, translating roughly to *region*, but migrating into the visual arts in the seventeenth-century trend of painting the land. Landscape painting. Artists throughout history have been painting the land, but what was unique about landscape painters was the focal point of the painting: the land not as wallpaper or backdrop, but the central character.

Just saying the phrase, "it's a lovely landscape," implies we can see the whole of it. When it comes to physical landscapes, doing so is rather easy. Get out of the car and look. Take that picture. Instinctively, we value such views of land, testified by the hundreds of pull-offs across the world when a road turns and a stunning view presents itself. We just have to stop and see. There might even be an evolutionary reason for liking vistas, courtesy of Jay Appleton's *prospect refuge theory*, which claims our species likes places where we can simultaneously scan for potential dangers and yet have refuge from those dangers. Approach or avoid? This is the question of the vista.[63] While not all vistas have refuge, a vista is pretty much defined by a sudden opening of distance, and so implies being on the border. Biologically, our minds are drawn to borders because they can exercise themselves there—foresight, planning—and it can do this with its dominant organ: vision.

When it comes to inner landscapes, however, we are talking about the holy grail of self-knowledge. Often, this means knowledge of ourselves, and we must start there, but we must also finish in knowledge of the self; the former is personal (how my mind works), the second is architectural (how the mind works). In Buddhism, there's a nice word, or, I should say, there are a lot of words, for our inner landscapes. A fundamental one is *sarvabijaka*, or store consciousness. Framed in agricultural terms, store consciousness contains the totality of the seeds in our mind, *bija*, and is, in many ways, another word for the deep potentiality of consciousness. What it adds to our typical Western understanding of consciousness is the agrarian aspect, namely, the nature of things coming and going (impermanence), things nestling into our inner soils, hibernating there, getting watered, sprouting later or not (our anger, jealousies, etc) all things which constitute our karma, the latter influencing our daily actions and reactions. This ground has no identity apart from the stuff on it.

Store consciousness isn't determinative of daily consciousness or even subconsciousness, but is epi-phenomenal. Environment plays a role, environment being the upper layers of the soil, and even so all the way "up" to how the feelings are deployed in the world and how those feelings are received, and then recycled back into the soil. For me, the wild was a seed nestled early in my psyche, and I'd water it, cultivate it and nurture it through my life. Its mere existence would affect who I'd fall in love with; what I did with my free time; which zeros I'd chase; where I'd live.

Just as the mind likes the pull-off the Grand Canyon Road provides, aware of the distance but not in it, so too it likes to be unattached from the growths on its store consciousness. This is because mind's fundamental nature is to be free; only later, via wind and weather and parents and jobs, does it take the shape it does today.

Self as Coin

The self is not a modern invention,
nor an innately bad thing.

Ground zeros are not just versions of personhood, or a form of identity we aim to become. Identity is a word so fraught with philosophical danger it ought to be banished from the religious and philosophical dictionary. It's like running the Grand Canyon in a kayak with holes, or trying to carry water in a wicker basket. When pressed as to what our identity is, or our personhood, or our inner self—all synonyms, really—we default to a vague list of qualities. These qualities are the "who was she?" question we hear answered at funerals, ("kind, generous, playful...") or moral exhortations ("she had a strong sense of family, would do anything for her children...") or memories displaying a slice of her character ("this one time..."). Our identities are grounded in time and place, attached to the awareness therein, since all of these words implicate an acting body (most of the time acting *in relation* to others), and yet, we conceive of "identity" as if it were an abstract concept (unmoored from a body) describing a personal generally, not specifically.

But it's a ruse. There can't be a permanent "generally" for the simple reason that we are changing all the time.

The self is symbolic coin we trade in the marketplace of modern life. It has no value but is accorded value based on the whims of the medium in which it is embedded. The medium is ever changing. Our friends, mothers, fathers, girlfriends and boyfriends are all in the same dynamic world as we are. The sand is shifting beneath our feet, and we are a loosely formed sandcastle on top of it. We are specific acts in places and times all the way down, with strong tendencies, or seeds, which we call traits; traits are really just statistical probabilities in qualitative terms. When Hindus or Buddhists talk about the no-self, and emptiness, this is what they are talking about: empty of deep, essential permanence, but real and expressed, however transitory. It needn't be an exotic concept. As for those shifting sands—in us, around us, physically and psychologically—that's what is called *impermanence*, and it's a central tenet to a lot of religious thinking, though it seems the modern world has granted Buddhism and Hinduism a copyright on the matter. These two traditions have merely put a pin on it, however, and never let us forget about it. Christianity nears no-self philosophy with exhortations to humility, mystical kenosis and the all-practical "turning our cheek," or not indulging self-centered action; Islam's submission to God is a form of it as well, yet Sufism takes it much further. Taoism speaks of aligning small self with Chi energy. The Stoics encouraged putting ourselves in harmony with the logos. Varieties of no-self abound in the world's big and small belief systems. No-self is valued because when you remove self you remove the manners and means in which you traffic, market and display yourself to the world.

Our era has tended to make the self a strawman for the ills of greed, materialism, tribalism, selfishness and political polarization. The argument goes: if we believe in our fixed identities, then it makes it harder to see the *other*, the other side of the political spectrum, the other class, gender or racial identity, and when we can't see the other, we act out of self-interest, feeding our identities more, curating them like fine china in our grandmother's living room; protecting them at all costs, believing their value—our value—lies in their existence.

If we only think and feel from the vantage point of *us*, how can *we* solve problems of inequality, the climate crisis, ideological tribalism? It's not untrue.

The self, however, is not a modern invention, nor an innately bad thing. Instead, we have a poor understanding of it. What we can say is this—it appears to be somewhat of a global phenomenon; different cultures might have had variations on selfhood, how those identities are valued in their respective social and cultural worlds (self as currency), but we don't want to overstate the point. Feet around the world look different, but most have ten toes. It is a trait of our mind to produce something like the self.

Despite its modern lashings and all the outcry against the self, deep in the traditions the self is acknowledged as it needs to be: the self is an idiosyncratic, organic physio-biological expression, often necessary, necessary even to remove itself, and part of the story of human history. This self is a result of being in a body—it can be no other way. Just as our brains are hardwired to seek food, we are equally hardwired to create a self. This is the essence of karmic accumulation, and also the Buddhist notion of *dependent arising*: when one thing arises, such as a body, another thing arises, such as that organism adapting to physical and psychological stimuli. The self is an adaptive solution to the problem of survival and mating.[64]

The self is also absolutely essential for religious traditions. As it often is the case, it is the thing we need to see, then reject, to move higher up the spiritual chain. Satori, or enlightenment, needs the self the way a map needs borders; a map without borders is just an image. Map and border co-define each other. What is missing in all the self-takedowns by so many modern prophets and pseudo-spiritual gurus is how the self was, first and foremost, of evolutionary benefit.

Keep your friends close, but your enemies closer—thus the Godfather instructs deniers of the self.

We can be excused for *generalizing* ourselves and others into identity-concepts like the self; *generalizing* has a lot of aliases—such as finding structure in data, or pattern matching. This act has been heralded by most neuroscientists as the dominant behavior of the mind.[65] Pattern matching allows us to predict danger, find food in a similar spot, avoid things that hurt us before, be drawn to others. We also apply the skill to ourselves: we notice patterns within ourselves, make judgments, and we indulge this basic movement pattern, creating and telling ourselves a story about ourselves, and then moving toward or away from the ground zeros, which are the outcomes of these stories. The more we indulge our self-styled stories, the more we buy into ourselves, and then, the more we believe in ourselves, thus the more we sell ourselves to the world. "Look, here I am, I'm a successful person." The self is designed, first and foremost, to care about the body it is part of. It has a basic allegiance: you. We don't experience another person's hunger in our stomach. It's possible evolution could have produced a physical manifestation of another's need in us, perhaps the way networks of trees feel deficiencies in others, thus sending nutrients to others, even those of a different variety, but it didn't. Our network is the immaterial web of consciousness.

* * *

The historical conditions of the self are insightful on a lot of accounts. The field of evolutionary psychology is in flux and, historically speaking, just getting started. Nonetheless, there seems to be general agreement that the self appeared in history at a certain time and place, in response to a set of social and environmental conditions. According to one paper, "Given the anthropological and biological evidence, the late Pleistocene epoch (inhabited by *Homo erectus*) is an excellent candidate for the time period in which a symbolic self—one that bears content, structural and functional similarities to the modern symbolic self—emerged." The late Pleistocene ran from about 129,000 to 11,700 years ago.

Yes, the self appeared in history, at a time and a place. It hasn't been with us all along. Before that, and we are all speculating, was awareness, action, survival, and a host of other actions from our ancestors ... but nothing like the self we strut around town on a Friday night. What were the conditions of the birth of the self? The paper continues: "It is especially relevant that during this time period (a) the brain exhibited substantial increases in capacity and complexity, (b) hunting apparently became an increasingly important method of food procurement, and (c) humans began to exhibit signs of increasing complexity in social organization." In short, the self emerged at a time of increased hunting, increased social complexity and brain-size development. Just as some animals have multiple hearts—octopuses and squids actually have three—evolution could have bequeathed minds in which four fully functional selves were optimal. I don't know what those conditions would be, but it could have been a scenario. The self may be, according to geneticist and evolutionary biologist Theodosius Dobzhansky, "the chief evolutionary novelty possessed by humans."[66] This isn't to say animal consciousness doesn't contain traits and properties of selfhood. It does. It's a scale, and on the scale of complexity of self, at least as we define it, we are at the top. Top does not equal best. What was once good for us might not be anymore. The self is an adaptation. The self serves. But the self co-arises with another thing—consciousness. And so we have self-consciousness, which we need to tune like a guitar. Too much of it and we are paralyzed to act, overly judgmental of ourselves and others. Too little of it and we are considered ignorant.

On the heels of the self, consciousness, once turned outward, turns inward to our inner landscapes. Neuroscientist Anthony Damasio observes: "Consciousness occurs when mind contents, such as perceptions and thoughts, are spontaneously identified as belonging to a specific organism/owner. Conscious minds are said to have a self that experiences mental events."[67] Consciousness, as we define it today, requires the self the way a brick home requires the existence of red clay; it doesn't just react to sensation, it manages their input. Though potentially germinated in a time of new hunting methods and sociality, the self evolved: it became a regulatory mechanism for our emotional lives, storing and preferring self-relevant information better, and with greater speed, than non-self-relevant information. It tends toward positivity, rather than negativity.[68] The world sells itself to us through the self and through it we sell ourselves.

Not only did the ancient meditative traditions *not* have a sense of the historical provenance of this all-too-human creation, since evolutionary theory hadn't been developed yet, but because they were not aware, the self got largely misconstrued as the main bulwark to enlightenment and spiritual progress, when in reality it is the very thing *making it possible*. Misunderstandings abound. The self is a great achievement, evolutionarily speaking, and thus serves the organism. One cannot study, and remember information, for instance, without the self. One cannot teach, cannot consider others, cannot formulate complex thoughts, the latter required for disseminating religious thought. The irony, however, remains: despite the self being the very thing allowing me to write this, know my children and keep a job, it is nonetheless the very thing standing *between* where the lot of us are today, as fully selfed animals, and our supposed spiritual destination, where we shed the cocoon of civilization and our bodies, and become near to God or Atman or the great creator. As the Hindu's say, no one can become enlightened. Emphasis on *no one*. There's truth there. In short, a person, the self, the thing keeping us myopic and ultimately ignorant, is the very thing preventing you from ultimate realization: realization of *you*. One of the great Hindu masters, Ramana Maharshi, would repeat the same thing over and over for decades: you are not yourself, and you need to realize this basic fact in order to see clearly. So how do we handle this paradox, of having this ancient and necessary center of gravity in our minds while at the same time our wisdom traditions, in near unanimous fashion, consider it to be a defect, unnecessary, the main impediment to greater self understanding?

I'd modify Maharshi's sentiment: we need to thank the self for its service and study it well, but we need it to relinquish control to make room for the richness of wisdom.

The "modern" self is the result of pattern matching when applied to us or others. People become knowable individuals when we "get a sense of them," and they become predictable. We know how they react, how they like their coffee, how to make them laugh, and so on. When applied to us, a sense of self emerges in our development. The path from "self-concept," to use the language of developmental psychology, to a robust sense of self is nuanced, meandering, inconsistent, stalled, hastened, but altogether more predictable the more you leave the weeds. We are born, we learn we are an independent being, then we explore, develop tastes, have children. We develop egos, quasi-stable perspectives on our self as constructed and construed. Forever impatient with the world, it is a mark of our minds to never be settled. Self-improvement is adaptation at work. Finding a spiritual path, which might disparage the self, is often the result of the self sensing its own limitations.

Understanding the self is crucial to understanding the wild, as it is through our self that the wild's value is created and experienced, and it was in the wild where the self was first created. In the folds of the wild, therefore, are the seeds of the self; its deep origin, the process through which our sense organs arrived to us today, as it remains through our sense organs that we perceive our inner worlds just as we use them on the outer world. This is because we can't imagine or visualize our inner selves without embodying them, without our senses re-constructing the self. If we get mad when we look inside ourselves, perhaps because we were short with someone the day before, that madness is felt.

The self served us then and it serves us now, but what if, today, we remain all-too-loyal to the self in the manner of an undying ancient reflex, a reflex which served its purpose well when we were hunters and nascent socialites learning to navigate tribal life, but which doesn't serve us as much today, at least in the cult-of-the-self of it all—the dominance of the ground zero in all modern life. Like in chess, we think the rules of the game are its basic assumptions, but, in fact, the existence of the player is prior. Biologically innate impulses don't always serve modern life. This is obvious in the speed with which some men turn to murderous aggression. A penchant for violence would have been a fine trait if you were aiming to keep your tribe of five alive on the rough savanna, but it does no good in New York City, under Friday-night lights, in 2025. As it turns out, there's a convenient concept describing things we have outsized responses to: supernormal stimuli.

A supernormal stimulus is a type of stimulus, originally found in nature, that elicits a stronger-than-normal response from us.[69] Consider junk food. There was once a time when it was good for the body to crave fatty food, since fat was scarce in Stone-Age times, and fatty food gave us an advantage. Fuel meant calories, which fat has a lot of, and fuel meant a greater chance of survival. Today, however, the irresistible urge for a greasy burger is out of sync with an environment of plenty, where fries and shakes are a short drive away, 24/7. Our brains know this, but our bodies don't, and our urges continue as if it's 10,000 BC. Supernormal stimuli rely on ancient instinct and were biologically germinated in us from proximity with nature and the constraints therein, but, when deployed in modern environments, they outlive their utility (maladaptive). It is the same with the need for stimuli. At one point the brain needed it, and thrived on it, and, as such, in our modern environments we create exaggerated sensate environments because the cheaper variety just isn't sufficing. When religious traditions are scouring the self, it is its maladaptive hangovers they are concerned with.

I think the self is a supernormal stimuli. We are drawn to it. Seduced by it. And yet, tens of thousands of years later, we get hijacked by it day in and day out; we are hijacked by it when we are greedy, when we compete for attention or resources, when all we can see is how a person or situation can benefit us, when we fear social ostracization more than anything else. It's a "what can the world offer me?" attitude, which, of course, narrows our awareness to find only things and people benefitting me. We take this mechanism for granted to such an extreme it's difficult to see clearly.

Consider the opposite—someone who has no sense of self. Even the most selfless and enlightened people on earth have a robust sense of self, of who they are, even if they are not attached to it, which is to say, their egos are quiet. It's hard to imagine how they'd go about their day without a self. I don't think this person has ever existed. Would this person be a total failure, culturally speaking, unable to climb the career ladder, make small talk and find a lover? Surely. In fact, "a weak or unclear sense of self is problematic, associated with personality disorders and other psychiatric conditions, insecure attachment, difficulty with personal and professional relationships, and personal development hitches."[70] If you know anything about theology or mysticism or religious leaders, the irony should be obvious—what the article cites as bad is precisely what the traditions say is good. Nonattachment is good; most relationships are a ruse, since the only true relationship that matters is between you and god; living uniquely outside of the straight and narrow path of personality development is something you should be proud of, since the "ordinary" is what needs to be avoided to achieve the extraordinary.

We need the middle way, as Lao Tzu advises.

A sense of self is the portal through which inner awareness directs itself and is directed. It is, as a result, the thing we are protecting and the thing doing the protecting. Since the mind is a pattern matcher, the self (and a ground zero) being the placeholder where this occurs, our version of ourselves is also a result of pattern matching: "Francis is *this* type of person—you better protect him. He likes *this* type of food—you should eat it. He loves *the wild*—you better feed it to him."

When our habits and tendencies cluster, a personhood arises, an illusional haecceity which contains truth and falsity, depending, but always conceptual illusion. We conform to this self-concept (ego). It's survival, we think, it is our survival. Not long ago, I spent many days in near constant meditation. I needed some time to process my father's sickness. I got a hotel room and meditated that night; I woke up in the middle of the night, and meditated; the next morning, I had coffee then meditated; in the middle of the day, I closed the blinds and meditated. I barely left the room. No alcohol, no TV, etc. I did this for five days or so. After some time, I got to a place where the stickiness of the ego had lost its grip, or so I thought. I was content, at peace, as humble as a nun before God. I wasn't proud of myself for arriving in such a state. I was just in the state. When my time was up, I packed and headed home, and sure enough one of the first thoughts I had was, "You're pretty good, aren't you! Wow, nice job. You're impressive." The self had gone nowhere, and its modern friend, the ego, came back just like a submerged balloon when no longer held underwater. Quite a resilient little phenomenon. I let the thought pass and laughed at it. The self was trying. That's what it does. It puffs us up.

We cannot walk away from the self. The self is good. But it is arguably one of our deepest addictions. The problem of supernormal stimuli is one of moderation, one of weaning ourselves from an addiction and understanding our bio-psychology with clarity. The goal shouldn't be to annihilate the self, as I'm not convinced it's possible while we have a body. Rather, the goal should be to unmoor the self-centric thoughts arising in our minds as a result of our supernormal responses to curate, protect and assuage it.

As it turns out, the wild helps us wean ourselves from our supernormal addiction to our selves, but not in the manner you'd think.

Nature in History

We are people of a land, not in a land.

When you study how Indigenous and pre-monotheistic cultures have addressed the natural world, you find a curious fact: *the natural world means something.* It had meaning in a spiritual register, which is to say, it played a role in a people's understanding of themselves and the world around them. The Great Plains for the indigenous people of North America. The Outback for the Aborigines. The sea for the Norsemen. The jungle for the Yanomami. Mt. Fuji for the Japanese. The desert for the Bushmen of the Kalahari. The West for Americans. The Orient for the early explorers. The textures of these lands, in the form of stories or sacred areas, were seeds in their inner landscapes. "To traditionalist Indigenous Peoples, in contrast, land is not a thing in itself but a social relationship between all living and non-living beings."[71] Land is relationality. It is their medium of life.

Unfortunately, in many modern Western cultures, we perceive ourselves as a people *in* a land, not *of* a land. Being in a land means the land is *out there*, doing its thing, while we are doing ours, *in here*, in our selves, racing to the dentist, posting on socials, going to restaurants, moving meaning around from one event and person to the next, taking this, giving that. Nature, as a summarial concept of animal and plant life, rarely goes deep into our self-perceptions; it did for me, luckily perhaps, in the ground zeros I was cultivating as a teenager. When the wild is a concept, however, you instinctively try to possess it, to own it, because here you are and there land is. It is not a coincidence that, for a lot of us, our primary relationship to land is owning it or not, typically in the form of a house on a piece of property. That we say, "this is my property" says it all. Except the exception always proves the rule. A question, however: what goes through the land I "own" as something I have no ownership over? Nature. "In nature nothing exists alone," wrote Rachel Carson. Because it is never alone, it moves everywhere, can be found everywhere. Thankfully, no country or industry has tried to own the birds in the sky. And yet, the agencies managing the United State's wild places, and some private businesses, are seeing strange lawsuits: Disney World was sued when a bird attacked a woman visiting the park. Around National Parks, trees are falling, injuring campers and hikers, and the parks are getting sued for negligence. In one instance, a wild goat killed a man and a lawsuit was brought against the agency who managed the park.[72] Don't we visit these places to experience the wild, our assumption being that the wild is not owned and managed? It's an odd juxtaposition of phenomena.

We are desirous to engineer the wild out of nature.

Monotheisms, industrialization, classification sciences and, more recently, boutique outdoor fitness regimes have relegated the wild to: god's unfinished handiwork (and of scant importance to divine spirit); an extractive resource, composed of unthinking raw material; the place to exercise our mind's penchant for analysis (concept), whereby we pull a "knowable" item from biological flow courtesy of perceptual boundaries; an arena to "remedy" a sense of the vacuous, void, or to get in shape or "medicalize" our minds with nature therapy. This list is far from exhaustive.

In all these instances, the wild is being leveraged for *our benefit*. But when something is being leveraged for another thing, it is being used. When something is being used, the person using it is failing to see it in its wholeness. When something is not seen in whole, understanding is incomplete. Where our understanding is incomplete, ignorance squats, and in ignorance, violence germinates. That we are violent toward the earth—imposing our will upon it—is an objective fact.

In a historical survey of perspectives toward the wild, what you don't find is irrelevance. Yet this is where we are at today.

Whereas ancient Greeks turned their chins upward in a thunderstorm and believed Zeus was tossing lightning bolts, now we know lightning is an electrical discharge born of a specific combination of atmospheric conditions. We attribute our perspective to modern science, and we rest content with our bias. While some might grant it superstition, lighting has no *meaning*; it just happens. We have been taught this the entirety of our lives and to disbelieve this is about as easy as unlearning to ride a bike, not that I'm saying we need to return to Zeus. We can't and shouldn't. A bad harvest is not a sign of a disgruntled god, as far as I know, and not a sign your prayers have gone unheard, but rather bad luck when it comes to arid conditions. But the loss of a belief system has never boded well for peoples around the globe.

Cultural anthropologists have a name for when one lifeworld is replaced by another; in particular, when one formerly reliant on myth and story is then replaced by a modern scientific one. The term is called *demythologization*, and it happens when your world is stripped of myth, robbed of stories in which your provenance is implicated. Typically, it meant adopting a scientism, like the one the majority of us have in our minds today, and losing a nature-based belief system, where landscape meant something because you and it were co-defined in history, in meaning, in mutual admiration and survival. In the medium. Historically, demythologization has devastated tribal peoples around the world. This loss haunts us today: our basic way of life is decimating the plants and animals of the earth and we feel helpless to do anything about it. Many will say, however, "we are a rich people, filled with stories and histories and thousands of ways of understanding ourselves." That is true, we are rich in a lot of ways, but our minds are poor, our contentment fickle and our discontent large. Is there any other better litmus test?

At one point in my life, I was trying to fill myself up with the richest things I knew of—wild landscapes in the holiest of places. These places meant something to me, in the Indigenous sense, of being central to my self-understanding. How could I go wrong?

Hiking Mount Sinai

Like camels, morality is ultimately a burden on our backs, except we load the burden ourselves.

In 2008, American warplanes were dropping bombs in Iraq, Syria was on the brink, and Israel and Gaza were in violent conflict. Naturally, my wife and I decided it was a good time for a visit to the Middle East. At this point, I had been in graduate school for a while, and was steeped in Holy Land landscape, architecture and mythology. I was enthralled. I needed to visit. It was the next step. The plan was simple—fly into Cairo in early June and get picked up three months later in Istanbul, before graduate classes resumed. We'd travel locally, by bus or taxi or thumb, make no plans in advance, and learn and visit as much as we could. I wanted to go to the Sinai desert, the place God had spoken, and sleep on the sherbert sands of the Jordanian desert. I wanted to go to Petra, Wadi Rum and Cappadocia, where the Christians dug labyrinthine homes into the rock. I wanted to listen.

Arriving in Cairo at midnight, my wife and I felt the political restlessness the way one feels wet grass on their feet. The stare of the crowd on our white skin was sharp, pointed, inquisitive and yet mildly hostile in some neighborhoods. One night, not long after arrival, a demonstration formed on the street below the hostel we were staying. The manager told us to not go outside. "You never know," he said. It was good advice. Turns out the Muslim Brotherhood was congregating in the streets, the same collective that would ignite the fire of the Arab Spring.

Hiking Mount Sinai, or what they call Jabal Mousa in Arabic, was a dream of mine. I mean, Moses climbed it. I remember arriving late at accommodation in a nearby village. The owner, a soft-spoken Arab man with high cheek bones and a manicured black beard, greeted us by headlight. We told him our plans. "Too hot to hike during day," he said, shaking his head. "I can help arrange to hike for sunrise. Very nice." We insisted. "We are mountain climbers," we told him. It would indeed be hot, about 100 degrees in the shade. The Sinai sun a killer. It would feel like 115. We insisted. He shook his head. "Americans!"

After a lazy morning, we decided to go for it. He was right. It was insultingly hot. But the benefit of bad conditions is you often have the place to yourself. You'll know this if you hike in the rain. Very few people hike in the rain. But it's the best time to hike. The same goes for the Sinai, in the summer, during the hottest part of day. Common sense clears the trail.

It was slow, hot going, but in all honesty not as bad as we thought. Before we got to the summit, we came across a pilgrim's way station, like a mountain hut, walls made of sun-burnt wood, a ramshackle roof, clearly built by hand. During the day, travelers could get a snack and a bottle of water here, but now, it was quiet. Who'd be hiking now??!! They must have heard us, as a few Bedouins came out and looked at us strangely. I think they were having a siesta. One had bed head. Christy and I made it to the summit and hung out until sunset, absorbing the ancient theater of granite, not unlike the American Southwest, a land scorched by relentless sun and crushing heat, a land of stone, a land still gracious to life in the most generous way the desert can be. As the sky showed the first sign of darkness, the Bedouins offered us blankets for the night so we could sleep on the summit. I nodded my head *yes* in 1.4 milliseconds. Christy agreed. The two men brought us soup for dinner in pots. I compensated them handsomely. As darkness fell, my eyes were privy to what felt like the closing of an epoch, the stone landscape put to bed by an impenetrable shadow sweeping across an expanse of the highest order. I had never witnessed so many shades of black. Our bedroom was a sloping 10x10-ft slab of beige granite tucked just below the summit. I was incredulous. I didn't want to sleep lest I waste one drop of the experience; it was like seeing the love of your life and knowing in the morning she would get out of bed and leave you for good. I didn't want to let go.

I must have stared for hours and hours at the stars, at the granite undulations, edges softened by the haze of the Sinai night. Sleep insisted but I fought it. I was in the Sinai, on top of Mount Sinai—the back of my eyelids could wait. At some point, my eyes closed by themselves. In and out of dream all night. The morning sun created the world anew. A primitive landscape of gray-brown mountains got their morning blush, the stones regaining sharp features.

And then, a strange thing happened. I heard voices from below. Lots of them. Lots and lots of voices. Chatter. I thought I was hearing things.

This was the first turd in the pearl. The supreme shit plant. Here I was in this ethereal, ungodly landscape, a place of my childhood dreams, just like in *National Geographic*, trying my hardest to squeeze the wildest mysticism from its pores, and I was ready. Ready, like Edward Abbey in the deep quiet of the Canyonlands waiting for the universe to speak; like Ezekiel in the desert, like Lao Tzu on the western edges of the Chinese empire … and then throngs of tourists!! Before I knew it, we were enveloped. I felt like I was in a four-star hotel, just rubbing the sleep from my eyes, and suddenly sixty-five strangers were crowding my bedroom. The moment was ruined. I was mad. Of course, I knew they deserved to be there as well. It was their right as much as mine, but that wasn't enough to shake the feeling of having gotten shortchanged.

Surrounded by the swarm, odd looks aplenty, we sat against the stone, slouched, wrapped in a blanket. After getting their fill of selfies and panoramas, the throngs grumbled and stumbled back down the trail.

Slowly, the summit returned to its natural state, but in doing so, I was shocked again. Dozens and dozens of water bottles now lay discarded, scattered in plain view, like the stands of a soccer area when the game is over. Except this wasn't Manchester. Sure, one or two might have forgotten their water bottle, but the majority couldn't have.

This was the second turd in the pearl, except I am now very happy this happened. Not at the time, of course, but this was the gift I needed. The universe deployed skillful means. I was ready to listen.

I learned something about the wild that morning: Mount Sinai is one of the most sacred mountains in the world, a landmass venerated by millions of people for millennia, a ground zero for millions of people's self-understanding and moral compass, but this in no way means the mountain—the physical mountain—was revered by them in the same way as it was by me. I revered the mountain symbolically, sure, in terms of its history and importance, but I was unable to sever this from the mountain of granite under my feet. The symbolic and physical were indistinguishable. Leaving trash on it was a desecration, but that was clearly not the case for others. Cleanliness and sacred space and tending to the physical place have always, at least in my readings and experience, gone hand in hand. The land on the mountain, the mountain itself, even the earth itself, is a "second skin" to me, to borrow a phrase from the Australian Aboriginals. When I saw trash, I got angry. My heart hurt. Tourists were enthralled and fascinated with the concept of Mount Sinai, and likely a few had powerful experiences on it that morning. We can't deny that. But, for them, the physical manifestation of the symbol, the actual dirt and rock of the mountain, was secondary to the concept of it. It was as if they couldn't look the actual mountain in the face, blinded as they were by the desire to be there, get the photo, tick the spiritual pilgrimage site off their list. But unless you can look at a thing or a person in the face, you can never establish a relationship with them. Their understanding was incomplete.

The truth is in the middle. Love for physicality is good, but not enough. Being in love with an idea isn't bad either, but it occludes the mountain, and the mountain would have likely not been sacred in the first place had it not had a physicality to it, the very same physicality being desecrated each and every morning via throngs of religious bucket listers. Most sacred landscapes, and animals, do have a singularity to them, a uniqueness in shape or character or geology, an oasis in the sand, a column jutting to the sky, which causes their sensations to go deep on account of a sly recognition (sensatio). Devils Tower and Ayers Rock are singularities, as are volcanoes, arches, sweet springs in the desert, big trees, deep caves, the mane of a horse, tortoise shell, etc. Before they were assigned symbolic value, our geology and animals appealed directly to the pre-meaning making aspects of our minds. We were attracted to these abnormalities. Our ancestors oriented a large part of their social and spiritual lives around their interpretation of the earth. They felt the wild and responded accordingly.

Not long after the Mount Sinai debacle, I came to appreciate having my experience shortened and expectations stymied. It was wonderful, the little truth I had been gifted. The tension inside my mind abated. Not here, it said. Look elsewhere. I didn't know *where* to look but the mountain identified my impossible expectations and planted a seed. At Loch Raven, a decade and a half later, that seed blossomed into a life changing experience. I learned a truth about myself too—the demands I put on the mountain were unfair. Unreasonable. I wasn't that different from the tourists, after all. As this insight settled in, I could feel the mountain relaxing as well, like a lover who finally tells you, "I'm not who you want me to be," and then you agree, and think. "But I still love you," you say. They stare at you. At this moment, it's always at this moment, you see them for what feels like the first time. You see *their* face, not the face you wanted and desired, but the face they have. Then you fall in love.

* * *

On that morning on Mount Sinai, there existed a massive disconnect between care for the ecology of the mountain and the love of the symbolic mountain. That group of tourists had little of the former and plenty of the latter. But a conceptual relation is not enough to save the wild. Even the most ideologically devout environmentalist can lack a true embodied relation to the wild. In the same vein, a mountain-top logger in West Virginia can be moved, in a deep way, by the wind and trees, at the same time as he fells acres of timber. In the U.S., we now have a stop-and-shop fast food mentality for consuming nature in our National Parks. Visiting time in the U.S. parks has gone down while internet and car access has gone up.[73] More and more people are visiting the parks, but spending less and less time there, and, while they are there, the man-made is following them. Our parks are falling victim to the convenience of the car, and their very design and character has fallen to the conveniences of laziness and an anti-adventurous spirit.[74] Tourists are chasing their own zeros—snapping a pic of themselves in the landscape is an expression of who they want to be: the turquoise waterfall like that new car or celebrity we stand next to, proud and smiling, advertising our nature-loving self to the world.

* * *

Do not try to become a better person. That is easy.

As for me, I was in between the two worlds most of my life. I was in the wild all the time, physically, mortally, catering to its materiality with intimacy and attention … holding sandstone a certain way, feeling the coldness of the wind, sensing the impending storm, listening to the cracks in ice as I climbed its frozen waterfalls, leveraging it for this or that running or climbing goal, thinking of course I was actually *in the wild* when doing so, which I wasn't. I was in an idea of it, no better than the tourists.

The problem? All my trying.

As a legend goes, a Zen student asked his teacher how long it would take to get enlightened. "Ten years," the teacher said.

Unsatisfied, the student asked, "What if I study twice as much?"

"Twenty years," the master replied.

Because I was in my head, I wasn't in my body. Because I wasn't in my body, I couldn't sense the wild. The body is the prism for the momentary pearls constituting our lives. When you are in your body, in your senses in a deep way, you are not in a concept. But in and out is misleading language; it's a spectrum. At evening, it gets dark slowly, and so it is with the process of becoming awake. The body is the heart of practice, and it is because of it we can practice. As the body purifies, the mind purifies, but not in the sense of the modern cult of the body: it is better to eat out of convenience stores and protect what goes into your mind than it is to eat farm-to-table organic grains every day and allow jealousy and pettiness of mind free reign. Body practice, in terms of engaging what it means to be a body, is mind practice. Right effort is not in finding ways to separate them, but in the means of aligning them such that it's meaningless to say body and mind, a false dualism if there ever was one.

Practice is around us, every day, all day, in our feelings, our shortcomings, our expectations. The hard part is finding it.

When in nature or social settings, our vision is dominated by our unconscious, which is to say, our desires color our complexes; in neuroscience speak—knowledge and memory inhibit perception. When we are starving and walking into a grocery store, we see and seek food. When we are insecure and we go out in public, we seek opportunities to bolster our sense of self-worth or accrue worth by leeching, or taking down, another person; these emotions and desires physically turn our heads in certain directions, *moving us*, and they attune one sense more than another. Our unconscious has drives, and when these drives are unregulated, they drive us. These drives, like bundles of energy in our psychic systems, have "personalities," goading us to do this and that, avoid this, go toward that; they are, in essence, seeds which have been watered. These drives only look out for themselves. At the level of feeling, we call these drives desires. Some of these desires are biological, and some hereditary, but many settle into our inner landscapes as simply the result of living, of having our hearts broken by girlfriends, or boyfriends, of not having a loving mother, of being bullied at school, of growing up poor. This is the stuff of store consciousness. The feelings and emotions born of living are real, but the irony is this: the moment when you can "see" them clearly, from the alcove, is the moment when you feel them most deeply. You are not hiding from them. You are ready for them. This is also the moment when they are the most beautiful, on account of being full, alive with all their intricacies, with no remainder. The person enchained to their drives doesn't have any freedom in their lives other than living them out, and living them out and feeling them are not the same thing. For some seekers, the complexity and competition inside of us forces us to take a stance and pull morality over our minds: morality is the way out, and, ironically, thus their burden: their seeking of the ethical life becomes a drive, a desire. The holy among us are not light, but seek heaviness to prove their lightness, because that's what they've been told to do; to stay on the path, just like the monk in the tea ceremony following every rule with perfection. Remember St. Francis shucking off his clothes. We judge ourselves even more harshly than we judge others, and one easy way out of self-judgment is to follow. Rules, aka judgments, are in reality using the small tools of mind to try to see big mind. It's a strategy destined to fail.

"What is heavy? Thus asks the weight-bearing spirit, thus it kneels down like the camel and wants to be well laden," Nietzsche writes. What do we load ourselves with? The Ten Commandments. Books. Learning. Ritual. Spiritual admonitions. The thou shalts, do's and don'ts. The Four Noble Truths. These concept-burdens are the bedrock of civility, and therefore civilization, the social contract, and so much more … and yet, nothing about the latter makes these foundational or ultimate, because to know mind you need to know foundation, you need to *know* bedrock truth. Do not try to become a better person. That is easy. There are plenty of good lists online to follow. You should aim to become awake.

Ultimate truth is light, not heavy, because you are no longer carrying small mind's burden. Lightness is felt in the person who lives it; lightness is the litmus test. It's not conceptual. It's felt, in the body. It's a dance.

Our inner landscapes are real, but real is only applicable according to the truth you live by. So much of life is worked out on this "karmic" level, karma being the stuff you have been handed at just *the moment before* you realize what karma means, and I say *at just the moment* because seconds after you realize the baggage you have been carrying around is also the moment when your karma changes. Your karma changes because you are starting to see the life you have been given and the seeds you have been watering, and, thus, in direct proportion to seeing it, you are released from it. As Mark Twain rightly noted, "The two most important days in your life are the day you are born and the day you find out why." That night, in Loch Raven, I learned why.

The karma I was given was an early childhood desire to be in the wild. An idolization of it. I was given good parents, an athletic body, a house surrounded by forests. I was an athlete and chased big goals and I achieved big goals. Books, words and mythologies entrenched this desire. For me, it was a faultless quest. A romance, and mystery thriller, of the highest order. I might not arrive, I told myself, but the journey would be worth it. I'd discover Zen and the philosophy of religion. It all worked towards the same goal. All this was my karma. I had diligently watered these seeds, and indulged these drives, ad nauseum, but now, in my late thirties, they had become a weight. These drives drove me. All I can say is the weight first manifested in heartbreak, and then, after an autopsy, in the feeling that what I was doing, my strategy, wasn't working anymore. Defeat, plain and simple. Failure. A real dark night of the soul. There, on the shores of Loch Raven, Francis got presented to me, floating above like a constellation, his seeds like stars, and it was Francis convincing me freedom lay in releasing myself from this karmic burden. Place is everything, and much had to do with the fact that I was home, in Maryland, in the place of my childhood, considering a life there, trying to reconcile my deep ambivalence about it, as it was here where my girlfriend and my best friend had sex in my sister's room and I walked in on it. From here where I'd escape. I ran away. I ran to the mountains to be reborn, and it worked … for about five years. But nature and I struggled, and I had, no doubt, gone to the "bigger" wild the way a heroin addict seeks a more potent cocktail. Reacting isn't freedom. At around age forty-two, precipitated by the sickness of my parents, I knew the game I was playing. And I was tired of playing it.

What is there if you take Francis away? I needed to peel away the onion.

One question I turned over in my mind for years was why it worked this way—why is it the case that the more we can see ourselves from the vantage point of a stranger, the alcove, what the Hindu's call the *witness*, the more we are free from having to be that person?

The answer is where cosmology and evolution butt heads.

Christianity put forward a solution: when we develop consciousness, which later becomes a conscience, we are sharing in God's nature, and it is this way because that's the way he made it. When we share in God's nature, we are granted a vision like his, which makes us feel both alien and of the earth. Cosmology and psychology combine. Ancient Stoicism speaks similarly of a grand Logos, both pervading the universe and ourselves, and so when we tap into it, we tap into the forces that be, and we align with an impersonal energy without personhood. Taoism follows suit with chi energy—it's there and we need to become conduits thereof, but to do so, we need to cease to hold onto opinions and thoughts. "Truth waits for eyes unclouded by longing," Taoist scripture advises. Hindu individual psychology thought is likewise of the belief that our ability to see ourselves is a requisite of the spiritual journey, the result of an innate structure inborn in our consciousness from the first moments of creation. We have big self and small self; big self is our god consciousness, awareness pure and clear untainted by body, and little self is the awareness required to put on shoes, do taxes and snark at coworkers. The main goal of Hinduism is simply reminding us we are the former. Courtesy of Shunryū Suzuki, Buddhism has big mind and small mind; big mind is clear awareness of small mind, with no cosmology wrapped around it. Other traditions might rely on the spirit of the ancestors as to the reason we get called into healing, and or the reason one's traditions are the way they are.

I'm not personally satisfied with any of these answers, if not for the reason most were all conceived in ancient times, and we have learned a lot about the brain since. I'm also not of the school of thought that religious teachings shouldn't change because they were codified 3,000 years ago. The ability to become unchained from ourselves the moment we are able to see it is due not to a cosmological principle, or a creation-given ability; it is just the way the mind works, born of and in our biology, an expression of *that* nature, wild nature, in *our* human nature. The wild is the pure thrust of life, moving in through its flowers and grasses. We seek the same freedom in our spiritual traditions, and it's not a coincidence. The ability is a selected trait, which is to say, evolution found it preferable for our ability to survive in the wild, and in the wild is where we should try to find the *raison d'être* of our ability to turn the lens of awareness toward ourselves.

Going for a run will help answer the question. It helped me.

Puddle Run

Train your eyes to touch, like your fingers.

This past spring I went for a run. It was chilly, around forty degrees, but warm enough for the snow to be melting. Clouds hung low and the air was moist. On the street, on the trails, everywhere—puddles. Deep puddles. Shallow puddles. Hidden puddles. Long and short and irregular puddles. Lodgepole and ponderosa pine hung heavy with wet snow.

I dodged and weaved the puddles as best I could. As soon as I found myself in a rhythm, however, there was a puddle. I'd slow down, move around the puddle, and try to not get my feet wet. It was annoying. Off the sidewalk and to the street, a puddle. Onto the sidewalk, more puddles. Wet feet aren't ideal when running in cold weather. I was aware that annoyance was building, and I was annoyed that I was annoyed, but I kept on stubbornly, with two mind frames—annoyed and annoyed I was annoyed. I tried to run through the annoyance. Then, after twenty or so minutes of this, something happened. I looked down at the puddles. I had seen them, of course, throughout my run, but I had been avoiding them. I hadn't paid attention to them, had made no effort other than avoidance, and avoidance often requires more effort than its opposite.

Nature's loveliness demands to be seen. The more I looked, the more my annoyance abated. Emerson was adamant on this: "To the attentive eye, each moment of the year has its own beauty, and in the same field, it beholds, every hour, a picture which was never seen before, and which shall never be seen again." Indeed. The singularity of colors in each puddle. Of seasons. The singularity and impermanence and lack of attachment nature has for its own limbs. Each miniature reservoir of pooled water had this rich, inner life, as lovely as the turquoise of Lake Tahoe. One puddle took on the exact color of Earl Grey tea; another the color of watered-down pinot noir. Each hue had a *raison d'être*. The Earl Grey pulled from the gray clay earth, recently exposed for the first time in what had been a long winter. Spring had melted the snow and sufficiently warmed the clay, and now the clay was on the move again, which it would be until the ground froze again in the late fall. The pinot color? Of red maple leaves, long dormant since fall and pasted to the frozen earth like an old man's combover. I remember those leaves, and those exact colors from last fall, as it's on my running route and my favorite street in town to run down, lined with no less than thirty maples, each about fifteen or so years old, which bring their crowns down low and cause you to be doused in color when you run under them, each hue a singularity, a vibe of its own. The Gates, the 2005 installation art of Christo Javacheff and Jeanne-Claude in New York's Central park, was composed of 7,500 saffron colored cloth "gates" lining twenty-three miles of sidewalks. The Gates brought to attention the place we walk in every day, what we walk under and through, in nature and not in nature, and how this space is psychologically charged. The colors, at that moment, brought their full karma forth. It was in their nature to do so, automatically. That moment was an expression of their life, who they were, and it needed to be matched with my full being. Fullness to fullness, or emptiness to emptiness. It's the same thing.

I've long been sensitive to the effect physical spaces have on my mind. I think it comes from growing up playing in the woods all the time, like a lot of children, and then as a climber and mountain athlete and the premium these sports put on *seeing with your body*, which is to say, seeing structures and spaces with your physical ability, inside spaces, three dimensionally, with your fingers and feet, with a somatic intelligence, such that you can see and predict with remarkable accuracy how your arms and legs and fingers will perform or react when they are in that situation. These sports leverage the brain's plasticity and literally rewire your circuitry. It's as if my eyes have been trained by my fingers. When I see like a climber, the world does not come back as a concept or disembodied ideology because I am deploying *more than a concept*; rather, I'm inhabiting an experience fully in between landscape and my body; senses over judgment.

A fundamental property of the ground zero is this—you cannot divorce place from the basic properties of mind, either in terms of memory, fantasy, mood, habit. Place is not replaceable. If you don't understand this, abstractly and in your awareness, you are not free. When you are just in a place, you are not of a place.

We go through life largely unaware of the nuance of place, and we go into the wild just the same. As a climber, I'm always shocked by the many hours people spend obsessing over gear, with this or that difference in crampons or ropes, and the zero time they spend on what type of mind they want to bring with them. Typically, when you get shut down on a hard climb it is not because your rope is 12 ounces too heavy. It is because of fear. Panic. Not feeling right. An ill-prepared state of mind. So few people attempt to calibrate their mind in tasks that I have come to the conclusion they have no idea they should do it in the first place. And, stepping back, most of us go through a full eighty years of life living in the same frame of mind, assuming the mind we have, day in and day out, is just the one we will always have. Or the one we should have. The bad news—it isn't.

Buddhists call an unchecked state of mind the monkey mind, as it goes from one thing to the next, almost always at the dictates of desire or frustration or some lack of homeostasis. When I was running on that spring morning, my mind was completely caught up in avoidance and annoyance to such an extent I had occluded all other experiences. But then, my world opened, the filters dimmed, and everything about that moment changed immediately. I didn't see just beautiful things, but beauty as a product of coming forth. I caught it in the act. What caused that?

To Be in a Body

To be in a body is to dance among all the competing forces you are composed of.

To be in a body is to be alive. To be in your senses is to be in your body. To be in a body is to dance, sometimes gracefully, often stumbling, among all the competing forces you are composed of. The body interprets, yes, but is it also in itself an interpretation. When needless filters are dimmed, you feel the world with increased acuity, sensitivity and intimacy, and, because of that, the world will somatically talk to you; in methods and means and accents barely audible at first, you become privy to novel data or information. It takes time because you are rewiring what you are allowing in, and strangers are called strange for a reason.

When you are in the mountains, or just exploring small outcroppings, you get a quirky joy crawling into slots, chasms, chimneys and such. I've seen it with my own children on our various canyoneering trips. It's not a coincidence parks and play landscapes have tunnels to crawl through, compartments to hide in. It's our animal nature, and this is just a small example, yes, but these places have clear emotions attached to them, none the same. Sculptor Richard Serra has made his career of creating spaces—large steel structures, angular and organic and serpentine—that you can walk through and draw out the abstract feelings born from abstract shapes. Serra has brought slot-canyon psychology to the Guggenheim, Moab to New York. Yet he invented nothing—place is a supernormal stimulus, something producing an exaggerated response in us.[75] Like a fish to water, we are attracted to it. He is simply leveraging an old impulse. Positions of the body, whether we put ourselves into them, such as in sacred poses or mudras or chakras in kundalini yoga, or are forced into them, testify to the same phenomenon.

We are attracted to place, just as we are attracted to life and lifelike processes (biophilia), because life is three dimensional; it could have been otherwise, and we could have been attracted to two-dimensional space, but we are not. Our bodies need place to be exercised.

On my run that morning, the colors were momentary in the puddles. The intensity would eventually dissipate. Perhaps later in the day, perhaps a week. I didn't know. I didn't care. What I did know, however, was that my annoyance had turned into curiosity. Wet feet were now irrelevant. Puddles were no longer the enemy of the run, but the point of it. "What's that puddle there?" I'm thinking. So I go out of my way to cross the street and meet the puddle: a dark amber, pulling from the frozen fall leaves. Some puddles lay frozen, and then, of those, some surfaces were as if the top of an ice cube, while others had a grip and texture, and you could run over them unworried.

The hue of the puddles was a shit plant in reverse—when something starts off annoying or uncomfortable or unpleasant then, for one reason or another, you find a pearl in the turd. It is much harder to find a pearl in the turd than it is a turd in the pearl, hence why a fair bit of the world's religious and philosophical systems instruct their flock to contemplate death—the very things our minds want to ignore. Thinking ahead is still thinking, and the mind wants to think.

I didn't go on the run expecting it to be a valuable experience. I just needed to run, get some energy out. Quickly, it got miserable, as I said. Running in cold, wet shoes isn't ideal. But the brilliance of the shit plant, whether in reverse or not, is that within its sensate insistence—given we can attune ourselves to this insistence—we can see our mind instinctively trying to even itself it out. There are always cracks in perfection, in the anticipation energy which often forms the perfection-image in our minds, and you need to see the beauty in that (*kintsugi*). When all you see are cracks and imperfection, or you are annoyed, frustrated, and see no way out, no redeeming value to the predicament you are in, there's always a gem waiting for you (skillful means).

As the saying goes, *it is the mountain's job to fill up the valleys.*

The mountains fill up the valleys because of gravity. Is there a gravity inside of us?

Homeostasis

It is the mind's ultimate job to fill up our valleys.

The mountains fill up the valleys through a centuries-long slog of rain carrying silt, or, conversely, rock fall, mudslides, etc. In dry landscapes, water provides the largest effect, while in wet climates, dryness punches above class. The wild operates best when it operates according to its own will. One philological thesis for the origin of the term "wilderness" is precisely this: self-willed. Wilderness is land which determines itself. Unobstructed. Though just an analogy, the mind is likewise trying to even itself out, to get rid of obstructions and blockages—hence our valuing of truth—so as to return homeostasis to our organism. Truth not in word play, but truth in living.

My mind was doing just that on the puddle run and it changed my life. It made me wonder why, at the most basic level, the mind seeks, and ideally operates, with calmness, inner peace, an unruffled disposition—are these the hallmarks of awareness of itself? Is this just my bias?

I'm going to borrow a term from biology, *homeostasis*, and stretch it a bit, to try to formulate an answer. As that which maintains our stability, homeostasis is a regulating process crucial to the organism's survival, and, as such, has largely been conceived in biological terms. According to biology, "Homeostasis has become the central unifying concept of physiology and is defined as a self-regulating process by which an organism can maintain internal stability while adjusting to changing external conditions … homeostatic regulation is not merely the product of a single negative feedback cycle but reflects the complex interaction of multiple feedback systems that can be modified by higher control centers."[76] At every moment, automatically and without conscious oversight or direction, our bodies are regulating our temperature, hormones, proteins, blood pressure and balance, and so on, all so our organism can thrive in varying stimuli. Homeostasis is in our bodies, as we sit in twenty-first-century chairs, just as it was in ancient organisms. In many ways, the critical survival needs of those ancient organisms are not much different to ours today; the needs of life don't vary too much. Like them, according to neuroscientist Joseph LeDoux, our bodies need to perform five key functions: detect danger, incorporate nutrients, balance fluids, thermoregulate, and reproduce.[77] For us, that means looking out for bad things, eating, having sex, controlling our temperature, drinking enough water … and that's just the basics. Behind the scenes of our consciousness the body continues to work. Homeostasis is the wizard in the basement.

Homeostasis is an odd fellow when it comes to talking about consciousness, because, well, a slug can perform these key five functions, and it doesn't need the ability to understand Shakespeare. The first part of problem is—we know what the body wants. The body wants to survive, get its needs met and reproduce and pass on its genes. The second part of the problem is that we don't know what our consciousness wants. Intelligence wants to solve problems, but consciousness and intelligence are not the same thing. Intelligence uses consciousness, but is not it.

But what if we layered the meditative tradition's insistence that mind is optimized when it has an inner harmony with the biological perspective that the body needs harmony to survive (homeostasis)? When paired, knowing the mind with greater intimacy—aka "spiritual practice" or acute "self-consciousness"—has a biological advantage. Could that be the case?

What we know is this: consciousness is central in determining the inner constitution of our minds. An essential component of that is knowledge of the emotions we are having. Knowing the emotions with higher intimacy and dexterity is, by modern understandings, a "spiritual" discipline, but also another variety of pattern matching and prediction—two pillars of mind. Alongside the birth of the self came the emotions of the self, among other things such as drives and feelings, etc., and, as such, the need arose to manage and regulate and know them; self-consciousness arose, in part, because we are emotional creatures and emotions are data for the organism. Evolutionarily speaking, emotional regulation survived because the individuals who were good at regulating emotions (this includes manipulating their and others' emotions, or suppressing anger to gain an advantage) had better chances of survival; co-operation, for instance, allowed our ancestors to work in groups and share food, and, as is still evinced in local and global politics, co-operation is hard. True homeostasis of mind, of course, requires we are able to manage much more than emotions. Research now proves that balance in mind—as expressed in the concepts of mindfulness or a keen self-awareness of one's inner workings—has a direct relation to physical health. An expansive study on the topic, co-authored by ten medical doctors and PhDs in the field, came to the following conclusion: "The cultivation of mindfulness, involving acceptance and nonjudgment of present-moment experience, often results in transformative health behavior change."[78] Acceptance is non-reactionary, and being non-reactionary is a part of quieting monkey mind. Because the trait of mindfulness has a direct relation to physical health, it follows that homeostasis should be unmoored from a strict biological definition and applied across all of the organism's workings.

* * *

Mysticism is merely a fancy word for seeing the world differently.

But what do the traditions say about homeostasis, philosophical, religious or otherwise?

There's Stoicism and its emphasis on not reacting to emotions, the assumption being that emotions unsettle our inner harmony with all their ups and downs. Emotions rile up our inner nature, wreaking havoc on our ability to be rational and aligned with the Logos, the cosmic and yet personal harmonic energy of the universe; the part needs to harmonize with the whole. There's Christianity on discerning evil intents from pure ones via confession and prayer, the assumption that evil is toxic to our innate good will, the latter harmonized with God but corrupted, depending on which theology you choose, because of original sin. Prayer balances our sinful nature, restoring harmony; the passions are bad. There's new age one love and its mantra of acceptance without judgment, the latter the origin of division and the thing causing a lack of homeostasis. There's Islam and the peace in surrendering to Allah's will. Giving power to Allah offsets the natural way of man and woman, which is to act out of self-interest, which is unharmonious. Taoism uses the language of internal balance outright with its emphasis on the middle way: "Avoiding extremes, the wise gain the experience of the Middle Path which produces insight, calm, and leads to higher knowledge, enlightenment." Hinduism assumes the ultimate nature of reality is of union with God or truth (Atman), and, as such our minds ought to rest in perfect harmony, but our version of it, where our ground zeros dictate so much of our perception, tarnishes our original nature; the goal, therefore, is to rid yourself of attachment and the clinging nature of small self so you can inhabit, and act from, an impersonal larger self. For a Buddhist, desire is the cause of suffering, and even the mere presence of desire, much less the suffering following suit, is a sign of an innate dysfunction and disharmony. We could keep going on like this, and yet, without question, the Buddhist and Hindu meditative traditions—the former growing out of the latter—have explicitly planted the flag of homeostasis, as relative to consciousness, in the vast fields of mind, standing by it for centuries like Roald Amundsen and his Norwegian flag on the first expedition to the South Pole.

If Christianity has trademarked *faith* in the souls of the world as their turnkey, the meditative traditions have trademarked a psychic version of homeostasis. The secret sauce of the Buddhist, and therefore Zen mind, is the cultivation of knowledge of what causes ripples (aka distress or fragmentation) in our mind and store consciousness, the knowledge of which produces not only stability in our mental landscape, but what stability serves. Stability serves adaptation; a stable mind doesn't react, which means various responses can be measured and deployed. Self-consciousness, as the modulator of drives, all of which have their own marketing programs, might just be our main mechanism for adaption.[79] Adaptation requires a freedom to apply a calculated response. A key point is this: despite common misunderstanding, stability is not the absence of passions and emotions in our mind. Stability is the ability to see them with the most sobriety and not be enslaved to them. As long as you have a mind, which everyone reading this does, you can expect disturbance—but you needn't expect to be disturbed.

Back to the puddles again.

In order to even my experience out, to release the tension of frustration—to move toward one thing and away from another—I had to see the beauty in the puddles because they were the very thing causing me consternation. I had expected a lovely run, but the bowl cracked, and it would have remained cracked had my mind not patched it up with the golden lacquer of attention. What did attention do? It broke the chains of concept, the emotional-logical buckets to which we shackle our world, and through which I was judging my activity. But what kind of attention? Attention to the puddles? Attention to the frustrated voice inside of me? Energy, like matter, never disappears. It takes a different form. The energy of frustration morphed into the energy of … delight perhaps, the singularity of a thing, its original face. The water in that moment; me and the water. Nothing mystical, and yet, there is rarely anything mystical about mysticism. Mysticism is a fancy word for seeing the world differently with human eyes. Mystical minds see relevance in all objects in life; LSD experiences do the same. Our wonder, in fact, is there all the time, just turned off. Plato's Symposium outlines how beauty can lead us to the absolute, through a dance of seduction. Kundalini yoga talks about waking up centers of the body, such as sexual desire, but then leveraging said desire for a desire for truth. The essence of tantra isn't sex, but using sensatio as a guide, and origin, for a deeper engagement with the world, a process which must preserve the feeling through the levels. It's akin to the travails of the Alchemist—turning a base element into gold.

I had to go toward the turd to find the pearl. It is a lesson the world keeps offering me … well, not just me apparently.

Sucking the Pus

Move toward the grotesque.

In the vast literature of saints, mystics, weirdos, religiously minded philosophers and theologians, there is a vivacious tradition of confronting, directly and with an intentional manner, the ugly, despicable, toxic, annoying, taboo and repulsive. The things lying in the conceptual graveyards of our minds. The shit plant on steroids.

As a child, I remember the gears in my mind being ground to a halt when I first heard about how Catherine of Siena, a fourteenth-century Catholic mystic, would eat the scabs from the bodies of the sick and dying and suck the pus from leper's wounds when caring for them, exclaiming, "Never in my life have I tasted any food and drink sweeter or more exquisite." What??!!

The seed was planted. I was around twelve.

In my young mind, this had no place in the otherwise dignified pantheon of Christian saints, which, so I thought, should be more like your grandmother or grandfather, draped in white, an upright posture, doing upstanding and dignified things ... in short, not eating scabs and sucking pus from a leprosy patient. And yet, to be honest, I shouldn't have been scandalized by it—on the altar of each church I entered there was a half-naked man in a loin cloth hanging on a wooden torture device, nails driven into his wrists and feet, blood oozing from his side. I was shocked by Catherine because I wasn't looking carefully enough around me. I was a tourist on the top of a mountain seeing only an idea. I didn't see the body. I didn't see what the body, not just the Christ body, meant. I didn't see the obvious—the way to the divine was, somehow, through the body. It wasn't just symbolic flesh. "The wound is the place where the light enters you," said Rumi, the Sufi mystic. Not metaphorically. Literally. The wound is the shadow. The wound of the mind is the shit plant. The wound is what your mind is protecting yourself from, what we are running from, but only in looking at all aspects of mind can you get to know it fully.

Toward or away? Toward.

As for Catherine, I remember being repulsed just by the thought of it, and paintings of Catherine on her knees with Jesus guiding her lips to his side wound for a drink of his blood did nothing to sanitize the matter. More so than others, a sixteenth-century painting by Roman artist Francesco Vanni captures the theological scandal of the moment: Jesus, in a red tunic, his right side bare, pulls Catherine gently to the spear wound on his right side. Blood drips from the horizontal slit in his side. The slit is level with her lip. Her mouth is open. Her right hand is placed on his left hip for balance, the way you'd hold the wall in front of a water fountain to lean in. In a twist, she wears the crown of thorns, not him. She is the bride of Christ, her face in resigned ecstasy. It is sexual. It is intimate. She is the Christ now.

I didn't understand. Pure cognitive dissonance.

Then, years later, around the age of sixteen, when I first started to really engage with the philosophy of religion, I came across stories of Indian sadhus who were known to sleep in cemeteries, eat the flesh of the dead and coat themselves in the ashes of the newly cremated, to name just a few of their dark arts. These sadhus were considered, like their Christian counterparts, to be of the highest spiritual echelon, thought to embody the deepest teachings, the mysteries themselves. Photographs of them mesmerized me. I checked out books of them from my high school library and hid them in my backpack, lest I scandalize my parents. Some sadhus, and especially Aghori sadhus, meditate on dead bodies they have found; and in some areas of Southeast Asia, Buddhists lay out a body and meditate in front of it for days while the flesh rots in the jungle heat. Of course, so do Christians. Some Hindus stare directly at the sun for days, others hold a hand up, for months, until their arm dies. East of India, some Thai monks carry around death cards—images of the dead—to help remind them of where they are headed in life. Tibetans practice sky burial; they chop up the body of the dead on a hill side and leave the flesh for the animals to consume. But in all these examples, which merely scratch the surface, we should not see the grotesque, but rather pedagogy. It is skillful means. It is an old lesson from and of the earth. Today, we try too hard to sanitize our sensations and make them perfect, just as we have tried to remove the wild from the wild.

As the Austrian poet Rainer Maria Rilke has eloquently

stated, "At bottom the only courage that is demanded of us [is] to have courage for the strangest, the most singular and the most inexplicable that we may encounter. That mankind has in this sense been cowardly has done life endless harm; the experiences that are called 'visions,' the whole so-called 'spirit-world,' death, all those things that are so closely akin to us, have by daily parrying been so crowded out of life that the senses with which we could have grasped them are atrophied. To say nothing of God." In summary—the same senses allowing us to see god are the same senses requiring us to confront death. To practice in full is to sense both. Yet we avoid, sanitize. We block out. The senses we used to have, designed to receive the blocked (and the unblocked), are atrophied. We need to rehabilitate our senses to see without judgment and with affirmation. As fourth-century-BC Chinese philosopher Chuang-tzu observed, "Tao exists in the crickets ... in the grasses ... in tiles and bricks ... and in shit and piss." Only small mind avoids.

Many of the early twentieth-century performance artists were Catholic, and it's not a coincidence they used their bodies in art the way the religious traditions used them in every way—as sites of transaction, objects of interpretation, portals to gross and divine energy; the body is made of gross and subtle energy, as Buddhists would say. In many ways, they were channeling millennia old ideologies that spirit and body were intertwined.[80] I think I thought myself parallel as a mountain athlete—I too was training my body for sensations.

Part of the lure of athletics for me at a young age, albeit subconsciously, was the possibility of approaching the mystical, which was for me the wild, with the body. I looked to purify the mind in exhaustion (a real thing), suffer in the wild, take risk in otherworldly landscapes, control my body and make sure it was in sync with nature, train my fingertips to feel and make decisions. I'd come to understand stone in a profound way, how it feels in certain temperatures and conditions, how to adapt myself to it. And so on. It was not an original approach; as I'd later learn the early Christian monks, in solitude and in nature, in some of the wildest places on earth, were referred to as "athletes of god."[81] They had their god, I had Muir or the Buddha's. I thought it was the same.

In the Toxin is the Cure

The only real questions in life showcase the shortcomings of answers. All answers.

I was sufficiently grossed out by the stories of Catherine and the sadhus. Likely on account of my shock, they stuck to my mind like a *koan*, a genre of story, dialogue, anecdote or question used in Zen to test, strengthen and ultimately humble small mind, the mind of thoughts, reactions, wants and desires. In many ways, I'd cut a path of extreme action through life, analogous, or so I thought, to the great seekers.

Typically, *koans* are paradoxical and contradictory. Used in a variety of ways, a master might give a student a *koan* to ruminate on, often for a long period of time. The student "thinks" about it, churns it over, sometimes for days and weeks. Then, when the student feels he has plucked the fruit, the student gives an answer to his *roshi*. If it's not the right answer, a bell might be rung by the *roshi*, the master of the house, as would be the case in some Japanese temples. The student then leaves to go meditate and find the right answer. Typically, the novice tries too hard. They overthink it. They try to craft an answer for their *roshi* to prove they understand. And yet, in all this trying and crafting they are missing the point, which is that there isn't one. There's no answer in the sense of an "answer"—a Logos—because answers are defined by questions; when you ask questions to the world, you are seeking, and the seeking mind is a small mind. A seeking mind will obtain as shallow of an answer as their question. The *koan* isn't so much a question as the encapsulation of an impression from an enlightened mind. Any "answer" to a *koan* must show that what is understood is precisely what the *koan* understands. What a *koan* understands is of the nature of mind. The *koan* is designed *not* to showcase the mind's ability to solve questions of the mind, but to highlight its limitation in doing so, and, in many ways, the ability to not activate intelligence.

Koans are universal seeds, and seeds are present in life all the time.

The *koan* is a seed in life that is ceremonialized in text. The setting for a *koan*, like all good poetry, is life itself, since in the perception thereof, in living and in seeing and touching, the awakened mind draws insight. For some reason, which I now chalk up to philosophical curiosity and the passion to understand, I've always been drawn to *koans*. I am excited by them. I "understand" them ... some of them. I want to know the truth they are communicating, because I know such truth is sweet, like Zarathustra's overflowing honey, but I also know the thrust to understand the seed can manifest in an obsession, a constant churning over a puzzle, an overactive mind, which I have, an attachment to rationale and the undergirding faith that you can reason your way to life's great truths and/or cleverly hide from untruth. Rationality makes a great sidekick, but a horrible leader. You can't outrun ignorance. I tried.

* * *

Koans are a tool of enlightenment. But, if you look hard enough, everything is an opportunity for enlightenment. Everything is a *koan*. Often, in a Zen monastery, the head master will clean the toilets and take out the trash. Why? Because no time is exempt from practice. There is value, perhaps more so, in the act of cleaning a toilet with loving devotion than in seated meditation, in an ancient monastery.

The stories about deviant saints or Indian *sadhus* functioned like *koans* in my mind, little truth grenades lodged in my psyche, the pin pulled but not yet exploded. I'm staring at them, on the inside. On the precipice, always, of exploding. Driving, climbing, hanging out with friends—these stories idled in my mind. For years they loitered. They still do. Little did I know these stories were much more than hooky anecdotal evidence of odd spiritual outcasts, but rather intuitive bodily practices designed to unmoor a "curative" structure inside our minds, one which *protected ourselves from ourselves*, and ourselves from each other, but also alienated us from the wild in profound ways. Then as today.

In the toxin is the cure. In the crack is the perfection. A golden break in the pottery. St. Teresa toward the leper. The same senses that lead us to God are the same senses that lead us to the shadows.

The shit plant is always there. It's not an anomaly. On the contrary, it's the norm. It's not that life is the shit plant, as the latter only arises when we are attached too much to the projection (dependent arising). Experiences in life are the spectrum between the fantasy and the shit plant. The point is not to identify with either too strongly. When we think we don't see the shit plant, we are deceiving ourselves and we have guarded the sanctity of our consciousness (the vault of our dreams and goals and desires) so well our minds are more like a six-course meal dished out by poor servants who we never want to see or interact with. Rather, we need to remove the assumption that experience shouldn't contain the repulsive. Then we will find that, as if by magic, after a long time looking directly into the things we have avoided, their toxin is diluted, their power robbed. This last point, of the toxin turned sweet, is what Catherine was talking about. That is why she became holy. Her journey was rather extreme, and quite dramatic, and while we need to enact all of this in a body, and not just in mind—it is not enough to merely contemplate the shit plant—we don't need to seek out a leper colony. That was her karma. In Buddhism, the peacock is a highly revered animal, as it is able to eat toxic fruits and plants, which would otherwise kill most animals. As a result, it is said to be immune, an immunity symbolic of being protected from the ills, the ups and downs, in the world. The alcove.

As a culture, we have forgotten this spiritual exercise. We have been taught our shadows are defects. Rather, our shadows are what define our light. When we see our shadows, we see more than our shadows, we have the opportunity to see the mechanisms through which shadows are created. This is the key. To see your shadow, you first must acknowledge you have one. A big one. This first and all-important step is rarely taken.

When I went for a run on that cold morning, with all those irritating puddles, my mind was instinctively seeking to confront the thing I was trying to avoid—the puddles. This is a simple example, but I feel more common, and realistic, than going to a hospital and finding people with leprosy and scabs and then … you know what.

Why was my mind doing that? I was aware then, as I am today, that the state of being annoyed is not a desirable state. It's a failure in my opinion. It's monkey mind manifest. I know it to be true, and I believe it is so. As I was running, there was my annoyed self, who was on the surface and reacting in real time, and then there was this pseudo-ground-zero self who imagines himself as the type of person who can smooth out these ruffles, who doesn't get annoyed. The part of me that sought the wild, with its soft edges and celestial peace, its unphased center in the face of drama, had also incorporated the psychological equivalent—like the silent energy in the wild, I sought the dark center in my soul. Unfortunately, or, I should say, fortunately, I'd learn you can't get the latter from the former; the wild isn't transactional. While running, the deep self is insistent on evening out the annoyance. Oftentimes, this insistence creates stubbornness and resistance from the surface self, which is "just trying to do something basic," and doesn't always enjoy being whipped by our better selves, super egos, or whatnot. Small mind abhors being reminded of its inadequacies. But with enough practice, the annoyance loosens its grip and power, and hence dissolves with greater facility and frequency. This loosening, of course, is relevant to more than just puddles, but annoyance in general, annoyance from other people, and so on.

It all comes back to the wild. The wild is the giver of consciousness and the arche-designer of mind, historically and evolutionarily speaking. But mind has since taken flight, or it thinks it has, and thus our brains are like a ship in the middle of the ocean: the original shipbuilder carved the logs, smoothed the decks and trimmed the sails, but after a few years at sea the boat has a new sail made of different cloth and the wood planks are now mahogany, not pine. Decades later, the boat runs ashore and is turned into a shelter—in short, our modern habitats do not reflect the world in which mind was conceived. Thus, as Rilke notes, our senses are atrophied. And thus, as evinced by starry-eyed techno-optimists, we think we are destined for the stars. We are aware of "outgrowing" our cribs. We tell ourselves stories about ourselves. Prometheus stole fire from the gods and gave it to humanity. Fire is a stand-in for civilization. We stole ourselves from nature, the God-world as original nature, to create our own nature. In short, we conceive—courtesy of mind—of ourselves as distinct from an original source. Remember how Adam and Eve got expelled—from knowledge of the nature of knowledge.

But these are all just apocalyptic fantasies concocted in the cauldrons of small mind.

Nature does have a cognitive element, which isn't to say the world is made of consciousness (panpsychism) nor that it isn't (some type of pure materialism), nor that pebbles and leaves contain, innately, mind-stuff, but that these questions are academic and not of the utmost importance for life as it is lived. What we do know is that small mind is moved by beauty, repulsed by ugliness, and that there is no such thing as a thought without a trace of the physical world in it, much the way the mind of the sculptor is preserved, however abstractly, in the sculpture. There's no such thing as an abstract thought; it might feel to be so but, as this sensation of abstractness came from a biological being, it has a biological trace. Cognition is embodied. Memory too is embodied, but not just in the way you are thinking: studies have shown that even in simple memory recall exercises, the place where one is attempting to recall a memory has an effect on what is being recalled, how it is being recalled and the facility (or difficulty) of doing so.[82] Memory champions use place to great effect to solidify the items of memorization.

Embodied memory and cognition, two growing and exciting fields of research, accomplish a few things. They remove the idea that we are disembodied brains scanning an interpreting passive matter or substance. Throughout history, the belief in a disembodied mind, unmoored from physical constraint, dominated much of our intellectual and philosophical history. Descartes, a founder of the mind/body "problem" in the seventeenth-century West, would pen his famous "cogito, ergo sum," translated to "I think, therefore I am," thus solidifying mind and thought as the immaterial controller of the body.

But we have smartened up: modern research places mind, and therefore, the seat of the self, in a complex and ever-changing environment of genetics, biology, culture, and environment; the latter a cipher for place, another word for landscape, itself a generic word for specific places: coastal seawater, dry reservoir beds, rolling hills of sage, juniper and pinyon.

Extended mind theory took the basic premise of embodied cognition and ran with it. What extended mind puts forth is a reframing of what we imagine mind looks like or does. Extended mind picks up where embodied cognition leaves off—stating that it is in the nature of mind to extend itself outward, to make use of tools—iPhones, languages, faces—to exercise mind. We think with our environments. Thinking is relational. Thinking isn't a brainwave in a skull. It is an outwardly reaching phenomenon of consciousness. I'd add that it proves a more basic truth long known to those who study the mind: outward reaching is a fundamental trait of mind.

But really, we are not extending anything. It is already extended. Mind always has been. It couldn't have been any other way. In many ways, extended mind is a subset of the Buddhist notion of interdependence, or interbeing. Zen master Thich Nhat Hanh writes, "If you are a poet, you will see clearly that there is a cloud floating in this sheet of paper. Without a cloud, there will be no rain; without rain, the trees cannot grow: and without trees, we cannot make paper. The cloud is essential for the paper to exist. If the cloud is not here, the sheet of paper cannot be here either. So we can say that the cloud and the paper inter-are."[83] Interdependence is not a small part of reality, isolated from others; it is the whole of it, and, as such, each thing is a condition for the other, and then, because of this, each object or person or event is empty—empty in the sense of not having an isolated existence (impermanence). If you see clearly, consciousness, like the cloud Hanh cites, has the rain within it, the trees. Aware of this, cracks should appear in your small mind. Consciousness has the trees and rain in it: historically, in terms of what evolution has given us and allowed us to sense, and momentarily, in terms of us needing our environment to have thoughts and feelings at each and every moment.

Mono No Aware

Birth and death—in these transitions we find joy and sadness. Joy in joining us, sadness in leaving us.

Nature has, from our perspective, a profound ability to die, or not die, as we see it.

When we itemize nature, it dies, and we have emotions attached to this process, especially for loved ones or pets or even house plants. But this is concept thinking again, which is attached to narrow confines and expressions of life, and thus judges the world on what happens to that narrowness. Small mind sees only small things.

Every life form is, at bottom, a quasi-stable knot of energy slowly transitioning from one form to the next. Awareness, for it to really be aware, needs to follow that movement. Naturally, we struggle with our own mortality and the passing of life from one body to the next. From a God's eye perspective, individual lives are blooming and wilting flowers; this latter observation was, in fact, central to one of India's greatest contributions to civilization—the *Bhagavad Gita*. All will come back. All will return. It's not wrong. We are no exception. Don't get attached to the form. We are all in service of life thrusting forth, and it is not a coincidence we chase this death symbolically in so many ways, to try it out.

When we try to acknowledge this transfer of form, as Plato did, or vow to see someone in heaven, as Christians and Muslims do; or try to live with the thought of death, as many Buddhists and Hindus; or embrace the earth and therefore the spirit of the creator, as some Indigenous traditions do, we are, in essence, trying to square up with the ephemeral of the wild, with its primordial expression, its greatest lesson, with *what we see*. What we see, if we look closely enough, is movement of energy that doesn't care for us, and of which we are in service of, not the other way around.

One of the last things my father said to me as he lay there, his cheeks sunken, his breath sounding as if air from a tube, was, "I'm having trouble letting go." "I'm having a hard time letting go as well," I told him. Francis could relate. "Don't be afraid. It's ok to let go," I told him. What I didn't realize at the time was that one of the main reasons he was having trouble letting go was the person opposite him. It would be the last time he'd see his son. Life for me still contained the future; but for him, the imminence of his death, of potentially seeing no one ever again, for eternity, had a gravity it couldn't have had otherwise. From the stance of small mind, death is final. I can't say for sure death isn't final, but intonations have been there.

Birth and death—in these transitions we find joy and sadness. Joy in joining us, sadness in leaving us. To and fro. Cherry blossoms in the spring. Young calves taking their first steps. Mothers and fathers leaving the world. There's a sadness in the passing of things, what the Japanese call *mono no aware*, the pathos of things. We see our two natures, idealized poles that mind presents to us from a deep intimacy of the wild working on our minds, knowing the giving of animal and plant life means we get to live; feeling the importance of the blip of life yet knowing, at rock bottom, we are just knots in the process of being tied and untied simultaneously. The wild teaches us how to die; beyond the bloom, after the funeral. We get attached to life and its manifestations, but before the we, before we developed, there was no attachment.

My father died in the fall of 2023, of prostate cancer, and my mother would pass the next fall, of Lewy Body dementia. Both were, and this is an understatement, rough ways to pass. For them, for us; gutting, exhausting, all the words. I was aware it was a moment for me. I needed to get myself sorted. I had had friends who lost a single parent in this manner and they hadn't recovered. They fell into depression, the bottle, or felt the sadness for years. I didn't want that. And so, I doubled down on looking at my mind for about three years straight with as much focus as I had given anything in my life. It felt like a worthwhile gamble.

As my mother was dying, I took a lot of walks, having learned with my dad how essential it was for my grieving. I walked in the morning, in the afternoon, at night. It became my main grieving process. There is no more beautiful place to be in the world than Maryland in the fall. There was a small path near the woods behind their house, and I'd walk the path back and forth. On my last visit, the leaves hit their peak, especially the maples. I'd stop and just stare at them. Unlike aspen leaves in their prime, a Colorado specialty, maple leaves turn every color. It's extraordinary. I wouldn't venture far from my mom's house, lest I'd get the call to rush home for her final breath, and so I walked in orbits. After thirty minutes or so, I'd go back inside and be with her, by the couch. One thing she loved, which relaxed her greatly, was having her hair brushed, and so for hours we'd brush her hair, her husband Jim and I. Then, one time, I noticed her gray hair was coming through, about a half inch of it. It was the first time in my life I'd seen her gray hair. She had always dyed it, and we had made arrangements to get her hair colored until the very end, but now the time had come. At this point, she wasn't able to talk to us, and so we brushed and brushed her hair. As I watched the brush go through, I realized the incoming gray transitioned into another color before it reached her dyed hair, an auburn brown. It was a spectrum. One new color, gray, of finality, and then an older "layer," of appearance, of cultivation. Then, on my walks, I started noticing the leaves differently. I noticed an analogous color transition, from vibrant green to yellow to bright red. The beauty and strangeness and intricacy stunned me. I just couldn't believe it. Going from the leaves to my mother made a deep impression on me, just as the time I went for a run and came across all those puddles. The wild was speaking to me, or, I was getting myself out of the way to such a point that I was now witness to all the comings and goings, as opposed to moving toward or away from the things in the goings. These leaves allowed me to see her death with clarity. A perfect case of sensatio—sensation indistinguishable from insight: the essence of skillful means. I knew that being with her during her final time was part of the oldest process life could offer, and it was all around me. Did the trees lament the falling of their leaves? No, they sure didn't. Was it possible to accept her death as the trees accepted the falling of their leaves? Likely not, but I knew the wild was suggesting I try.

Try I did. She deserved a good death. She didn't want me falling apart at the seams. I needed to be there not for her, but with her. It was one of the best decisions of my life, because from this non-fighting arrived the moments I'd remember the most, moments so clear and full I would have dismissed their possibility, and luminosity, years earlier.

What is insight if not the unfolding of the stories nature implants to us about our own lives? The wisdom of the wild. I say to Heraclitus, nature does not hide. It does everything but hide. Only we can hide. The moment we hide from ourselves is the moment nature is occluded from our perception.

Intertwined trees—lovers. A flower in a cleft—hope. Dry leaves in the sun—old age. A wet flower after a storm—infants.

That nature suggests and seduces is long a staple in the nature writer's quiver. In his essay "The Poet", Emerson writes, "Things admit of being used as symbols, because nature is a symbol, in the whole, and in every part. Every line we can draw in the sand has expression; and there is no body without its spirit or genius." He is right; nature is the original theater, the limitless giver, but this doesn't mean the giver is representing itself accurately. The wild gets layered in the murky world of the symbolic not by accident. It is in the nature of mind to find the *symbolic*—a thing standing for another thing; perhaps expressing a human thing—and perhaps it is in the nature of nature to sprout the symbolic, and thus we need to look closely at this *doing so*, between the perception and the sensation, as it is here, a here without a here, where modern neuroscience and ancient philosophy and theology find common ground.[84]

The finding of the symbol occurs in a sliver of time so miniscule as to be imperceptible ("almost simultaneously," said Yongey Mingyur Rinpoche), in which we start to see the basic function of mind. On the one hand, this is an act of cosmic import, likened symbolically to the creation of the world. On the other hand, it also tracks to the source of the human mind, the ever-generating moment of personal death and rebirth, where the ground zero does its dance, where small mind is born and dies. The bardo, from chaos to order, darkness to light, writ small.

We love and adhere to symbols on a daily basis; concepts and metaphors and language require them. Nature, however, doesn't traffic in symbols, per se; but this isn't to say what we see and feel, as we swim in a cold river, correlates to an objective world out there. It doesn't. Our worlds are being constructed at every level; what makes the wild unique in this process is that it has provided the original constraints for construction itself.

When the poet talks about dancing waves or when the nature lover sees a tree in the breeze and imputes the soul of a departed husband, they are partaking in an ancient practice of anthropomorphism—seeing the human in the non-human.[85] The impulse to do so accounts for the vast majority of ancient and modern religion: Christ the sun god; the Greek gods of thunder; Mother Earth, and so on. The imputation process is so powerful and so slippery it is nearly impossible to see, on account of being a foundational, unconscious practice of mind.

What, then, is the state of mind that tries to capture the *doing so*, the anthropomorphic impulse? Religious art is the best place to start looking.

The God of Harmonia

Relationship is a concept culled from the wild and applied elsewhere, far from its crib.

As a rule of thumb, when you approach religious art, you need to ask yourself a simple question: what state of mind is the deity symbolic of? Answer that question, and you've cracked the code.

The main Christian deity, Jesus, is typically represented as approachable, patient, sometimes suffering, often teaching, but always moving beyond the pain. Do a scan of his images in art history and you'd be hard pressed to find a wrinkle in his brow or squinty eyes; in contrast, his face is placid, a smile as rare as a smirk. It's no coincidence this is *the Christian ideal* too, a primary statement on our fundamental nature—we are essentially good, patient, forgiving beings, able to transcend human suffering when we align with divinity; we especially need to be so when the world presents injustice. We, with small minds sharing in the goodness of God (Christianity's version of big mind), partake in divine energy as enfleshed radio towers, standing sentinel in the world, the God-vibes always around, but it being a matter of choice—aka our will—if we want to tune in and distribute the "good news." Jesus' depiction is a state of mind. On the other hand, consider Kali, the Indian god of wrath—a decapitated demon head in her left hand, blood profusely dripping, her left arm catching the blood in a pan. In her right arm, a bloody sword. A necklace of skulls around her neck, a skirt of severed arms. Mouth open, sometimes with fangs, hissing, Kali is primal nature, beyond good and evil; like us, according to the Hindu system. The state of mind that Kali symbolizes is one of the torn human mind, perennially jockeying from good to evil, viciousness to love. Kali is the evil part, like Hades for the Greeks; Krishna is the part of love, like Eros.

Whereas some religions present the base constitution of the human soul as one of goodness, as Christianity does, an equal number of traditions acknowledge we *can* be good, *should* be good, but, in the end, at the basest levels of our animal selves, we *are* neither. If you strip off all the layers of family, social and cultural conditioning, there's no ethical commandments branded in our hearts. No essence. No moral code in the basement. Beyond our good and evil, both of which are expressions of judgments, concepts and rationale, there is an immutable original nature, wiped clean of karmic debt and cultural accumulation. We are patient, sure, and compassionate, yep, but we are equally treacherous, tribal, prone to violence, greedy, and envious. We are like the wild, no better or worse. We have to work for our goodness; homeostasis, which can be misconstrued for goodness, is not a morality. Morality is what our small minds layer over a homeostatic principle, the latter based in our psycho-somatic biology. It is a matter of *belief* if one thinks we are essentially good, because we are manifestly both in any given day, year, hour or lifetime, across the globe. What we *should be* is a different question from what we *are*.

In many ways, the "essentially good" hypothesis isn't just the prism through which the West has viewed itself, but also the pair of glasses through which we viewed nature. It's the reason we didn't wake up to the beauty of the natural world until the 18th century. Yes—going for a stroll in a forest to soak up the primitive vibes of *au natural* wasn't a sentiment lodged in people's consciousness for the large majority of history, as a lot of things needed to take place for the assumption to be engineered. This isn't to say people didn't stroll near rivers, or that farmers didn't find the mist on the fields to be pretty. I'm sure there was a power there, if unsaid and undocumented, and this perceived power and mystery spawned gods of nature. But overall, the Greeks, who gave us our terms, logic, political architecture, and so much more, didn't speak about nature much, at least not as we do today.[86] Frederich Schiller's 18th-century observation that nature for the Greeks had "no more special involvement of the heart than the depiction of a dress, a shield, a weapon, a household tool, or some sort of mechanical object," seems to hold correct. And only now are we learning the ecological lessons of Native American stewardship, the land and us as co-implicated in a primal relationship. But that's *our* Western ancestors. Across the Pacific, Shinto would worship nature like a god and Tibetan Bon folded the high Himalayas seamlessly into their mountain spirituality. In any survey of the world around, what you don't find is an idea of nature as irrelevant or a population that is indifferent ... with the exception of the modern West.

E.R. Hughes, an early scholar of Chinese culture, would write, "The main distinction between a western and a Chinese tradition is the western has tended to see reality as substance, the Chinese to see it as relationship."[87] Relationship is a concept culled from the wild and applied elsewhere, far from its crib. Citing and extending Hughes' work, Dolores LaChapelle, a mountaineer and an early leading voice of deep ecology, believes the "ultimate development" of the substance model was the Industrial Revolution—the collection of wild materials for the manufacturing, buying and making of discrete things, premised on the notion that these discrete things are perceived and valued as discrete entities. No one in the modern world, for instance, would buy a new car if once parked on the street anyone could drive off with it. Discretion enabled possession, and possession enabled property. It didn't take long until the natural world got lumped into the substance model as well, as a thing to be appreciated by an individual who appreciates it. This was made possible by nature's increasing irrelevance as urban life took hold, in addition to people's, and entire cultures', self-understanding. I inherited this technological and cultural baggage, which explains my desire to get *close* to nature, given as I felt, foundationally, that I was apart from it. However, my entire method was misguided. "It is not a matter of being 'close to nature' ... The Earth is, in a very real sense, the same as ourself (ourselves)," writes Paula Gunn Allen, a Laguna Pueblo writer and scholar. "That knowledge, though perfect, does not have associated with it the exalted romance of the sentimental 'nature lovers,' nor does it have, at base, any self-conscious 'appreciation' of the land ... It is a matter of fact, one known equably from infancy, remembered and honored at levels of awareness that go beyond consciousness."[88] We need to stop appreciating the land. We need to start sensing the land at multiple levels of awareness: from the everyday moment to the discoveries of neuroscience.

But when you don't appreciate the land, what are you left with?

Though there are worse things to do, appreciating nature is still consuming her flora and fauna as if it's a new movie or good steak. The problem—we don't stay in appreciation, we leave. We appreciate art, then leave the museum. We don't step back and appreciate our children, except in moments; rather, we live with our children, together, in the thick of it, as a unit, relying on each other, co-implicated in health and shared experience. I knew, however, whatever it was an Indigenous individual felt in the desert or jungle or savanna, born there, living there, was inaccessible to me. I, we, are in limbo. I was trapped between two worlds, neither of which were home.

According to the overarching Western mythos, humans are special, and created by God in his likeness, but nature is crude (substance) and subordinate (because not containing soul, thus not containing intelligence, and we have sadly based our qualitative judgments on just about everyone on the degree to which it has intelligence). This rough sketch was adopted by Islam, Christianity and Judaism. Human nature was essentially good, but later, after declaring his material was "good" too, God put humans in charge, granting them "dominion" over the animals of the earth, and, by default, the fish, vegetation and waters he just created, technically omitting the "other nature"—streams, hillsides, stands of aspen. An omission of note. Apparently, these items weren't even worth mentioning as a thing we needed power over. I'd argue, they hadn't even yet achieved "thing" status.

The dominion argument appealed to common sense, and

still does. If I want to bulldoze a piece of land to install a pool, I can do it. Why shouldn't I? I'm not hurting any *one*. The wild is powerless to stop me; as pure materiality, the wild appears to be unagented. I can cut down trees, trap and kill animals. It will not fight back. The wild is no match for the human mind, thus says mind. Because I have power over it, thus says mind, I must be superior, and, thus, the human mind appears to occupy a privileged position within the life of nature. It is a common-sense line of affirmations.

This historical back and forth is alive today, within us and within our neighborhoods. One neighbor will have no problem cutting down a hundred-year-old maple for a better view of the park, concluding, largely unconsciously, that their right to have the view is more important than the life of the tree. They will do this without even so much a thought as to what the tree deserves. Even to ask the question—does a tree have rights?—strikes a majority of us as novel, even though in some parts of the world rights are being granted to nature's limbs, such as the Whanganui River in New Zealand.[89] In 2007, in India, a high court ruled that a few sacred rivers, as well as some features, are a "legal person," and, as such, have an innate right to do what rivers do—flow.[90] In US water law, the water in a river has a "right," but on account of the animals that need it, not the river itself. Most rivers in the U.S. are dammed and choked up and very, very few flow today as they did thousands of years ago. We do respect trees, especially big and beautiful ones, but that just confirms the impurity of our perception. We grant more rights to things we see ourselves reflected in: the bigger the animal, the more rights it gets. Think of squirrels vs. elephants. The more human it is, the better, and the more common it is, the less important; we value scarcity, like gold. Think of silverback gorillas vs. a threatened type of tree frog in Bolivia, with population numbers no different than the gorilla. Without question, the world will move to protect gorillas. But the frog will be lucky if it gets a few local headlines. If we are ever to see life's manifestations as equal, we need to fight divisive, and discriminatory, tendencies in our small minds.

When the West woke up to the wild in the late 1700s, nature was crude because it was unfinished; a ragged hillside with mismatched trees had no symmetry nor consistency. Humans had to finish it, prune it, extract from it the fodder for civilization. The Garden of Versailles it was not. This was all at a time when the city, the great accomplishment of civilization, began the march to its modern form.[91] Nature's powerlessness and unsophistication was pegged as the city's foil. But the cities took their toll, and, in not too long, some started to seek a salve outside its walls. At a time when Charles Dickens was writing about the morose, clogged, smoke-infested boroughs of London, other writers vacated those very same cities in search of fresh air, cold streams and turquoise skies, a new place to start, a place where, it was felt, the human soul could find its clear reflection. Mankind, surely, wasn't designed by God to live in London smog. That's not what God meant in Genesis. Cue the wild.

At first, the wild didn't share the "essentially good" hypothesis—nature was as savage as it was unpolished, good and bad, without ethics or morality other than the law of survival. The sixteenth- and seventeenth-century debates about the "state of nature" exemplify this, and constantly blur into debates about the nature of the human soul. Is our nature peaceful, like the dove, or are we the lion?

As late as the 1700s, the valley where Chamonix—one of the most visited mountain towns in the world—is located, was a blank spot on the map. A fine illustration of Europe's convalescence was the birth of mountain climbing, whose summits and vistas have long been held up as *natural supreme*. Just outside Chamonix, Mont Blanc, the highest peak in western Europe, wasn't climbed until 1786, by Michel-Gabriel Paccard and Jacques Balmat. Before this, it hadn't been attempted. No one cared. People stuck close to home. Geneva, for instance, had been continuously inhabited for over 2000 years, and yet, roughly 40 miles away as the crow flies from the city center was Mont Blanc; as late as the 1700s, dragons were reported to live in the vicinity of the massif, and great adventurers waxed at length of this primeval wilderness, and the beasts roaming it, not far from Paris.

Untrammeled nature had no allure for most of our history, and this is largely because we didn't consider the wild, without makeup, beautiful or worthy. Japanese Zen, for its part, never got sucked into idealizing the purity of wilderness, or placing a higher value on it the more isolated it was from our influence. For the West, the value of the wild's "self-willed" qualities were defined against our knowledge that our will might not always be as good as we thought it was. Nature was without a trace of our will. In contrast, for Zen culture, the wild and the human were a symbiotic pair, benefitting each other. Humankind could improve the wild—think of a rock garden—and the wild could, in turn, improve us. Our nature existed between our minds and the breeze; the rock garden is this medium manifest, except it is not manifested for the purpose of appreciation, but to see mind itself. As it turns out, the value of untrammeled nature rises in direct proportion to our cognizance, as developers and consumers, of our harmful effect on nature; it becomes more pure, thus more appreciated, the more we find our acts to be impure. In America, for instance, from whom the world has since got its technical notion of wilderness, the preservation of the wild wasn't a problem at first, since there was so much of it; in fact, there wasn't an idea of wilderness at all. It wasn't wild, of course, as it was the home of Native Americans. Wilderness in the U.S. became an issue, and a technical term, when it started to run out—when we realized what we were doing to the land wasn't good for it.

At the same time as mountains and their wildness were approached, and writers like Emerson and Thoreau waxed lyrical about nature's transcendent allure, terms like "conquest" were introduced into the mountaineering lexicon. In the 1800s, and courtesy of prevailing sentiment flamed by the Romantics and fueled by urban discontent, the mountains garnered interest. As soon as nature become beautiful and inspiring, climbing mountains became a privileged site to experience big beauty—rugged, mystical, soul-filling stuff. In the first half of the 20th century, mountains, especially those in the Himalayas, were "conquered," effectively ignoring the Romantic impulse to climb mountains in the first place. Both perspectives, however, remain enchained to notions of consumption. In contrast, Tibetans had been living deep in the Himalayas for millennia and never once considered climbing a mountain to be of benefit for the soul. Tibetans saw right through the exercise—the top or the bottom of a mountain is irrelevant. What matters is how well you know your mind. Climbing a mountain and thinking the summit will provide wisdom or resolve or add a bit of street cred to your "self" is a classic case of a ground zero taken to disastrous extremes. I know from first-hand experience.

Today, we are beholden to a variety of watered-down Romanticism—a benevolent, impersonal arena, regenerative for the soul, valued by us for its non-humanness. A good thing to know, better yet to experience. A place we can experience deep, if abstract, connection, despite not knowing what, exactly, we are connecting with. A place we need to be in to tap into its beauty. A place to recreate in. A place which, given time, will do more healing than not. A place like a curious reflecting pool where civilization can go to look at itself, find its faults, admire its achievements, or, at its mystical core, go to find itself in a falling leaf. A place in which we can see aesthetic, and singular, beauty. In the twenty-first century, thousands upon thousands of articles have proven this aesthetic remedy, in phrases such as the "nature cure," "nature prescription," and so on.

With few exceptions, the lot of Western nature writing is beholden to the mythos of nature as a courteous, wise uncle who is always ready to talk, a bountiful mother caring for her young, or a mystical, beautiful, practical *other* who delights us with her idiosyncratic performances. Such assumptions have impaired the West for centuries. Caught in and embodying cycles of separation, isolation, development, exploitation and beautification, but also embodying centuries of debate, I too was beholden to this when I went for a swim that night. I thought the harmony in nature would bring harmony to my body. But the wild isn't, in essence, relaxing or stressful, neither all wise nor all murderous; if it appears so, it is due to our biology and the assumptions we scaffold it with. The wild is a killer. The wild is romantic. The soft gushing of a mountain stream is only pleasing when we are safely on the shore. Put us in that very same water in winter, in sub-zero temps, and nature, just like that, goes from friend to foe. Once, while trekking in Botswana, my wife and I slept out in the bush, in backpacking tents in the middle of a game park. It was fun and glorious seeing hippos and giraffes and lions panting in the sun during the day, but as soon as the sun dipped below the horizon, lions started roaring and pacing. This was no Abbey country where the fire flickers on dried juniper and you stare at the stars, prop up your feet on a log and wait for the universe to speak to you. With just a thin piece of canvas between me and a real pack of hungry lions, all I wanted was to survive the night. I wanted to get out of there. I had never wanted the sun to rise so badly in my life. If I was in a log cabin, the situation would have changed. But that's just it. Because the wild has been managed and declawed in so many ways, with our wildest places now developed with Wi-Fi and luxury lodges and fully accessible by car, our assumption is that nature is our friend. It is only when you experience all sides of the wild that this assumption falls to the wayside. Snow is lovely when it falls softly in the gaze of a lamppost, but when it buries your sons and daughters alive in the mountains, you get the stark lesson that it cares not. Nature is not your friend.

The listener and climber ground zero, I'd later realize, taught me these lessons early. They kept each other in check, dueling personas of the wild, fully dependent on each other. The climber, immersed in the harsh reality of mortal threat, kept at bay the nature as "pleasing mystical uncle" archetype. The climber had to navigate death constantly. Mountains *do* try to kill you. The listener, on the other hand, reminded the climber that the wild had something to say and was not just an apparatus for my shallow achievements and goals. The ego builder and the appreciator. Both were traps. The whole eluded me.

Art is a great place to explore, and understand, how we become actors in the wilds of our own lives, and it was in one German painting in particular, *Monk by the Sea*, where I first saw myself.

A Tale of Two Images

All beauty fades, and we shouldn't be so crass as to hitch a ride to a car that rarely starts.

I. *Rügen, North-east Coast of Germany, 1808*

In 1809, German artist Caspar David Friedrich started on a painting that would take a few years to complete. The painting was finished between 1808–1810 and given the title *Monk by the Sea*. The title isn't fancy, nor ironic, but describes the painting as one would typically describe the scene; there is, indeed, a monk by the sea, along with clouds, murky water and a few birds. One thing is peculiar, though: you can't tell it's a monk, as the robe-clad figure could be anything, and, should someone look at it and claim they don't see a monk, they could be forgiven. The figure is hardly prominent and could be mistaken for a tree stump with a tan bird on top.

Absorption of the figure by the vastness of the sea is, indeed, the point.

Receiving little acclaim in the artist's lifetime for the composition, the painting would later be loved by Hitler then ignored by art historians because of the Nazi's praise. When abstraction took hold during the turning of the 20th century, however, it was heralded as radical, genius, singular and would even be considered, according to some critics, to be one of the first pieces of Modern art, an honor placing the German up there in the ranks of Van Gogh.

I first encountered the painting when I was doing graduate work on the relationship between art, nature and religion. *Monk by the Sea* kept making appearances in the literature. I kept looking at it, circling it, but I can't say it impressed me at first. Its simplicity baffled me. I knew to respect it on account of artistic innovation, but in terms of a personal connection, the clouds failed to draw me in. The sea did not embrace me. The monk was drab and unexciting. The composition just didn't have the vibrancy and thrill of a Michelangelo. But I kept coming back to it and realized one day that I was indeed fascinated by the monk standing there, on the shore. So, I started to ask him questions. What do you see? What do you feel? Why are you there? I figured he felt like anyone standing on the shore on a windy day—he worried about getting his feet wet in the soggy soil. He enjoyed the salt-encrusted air for a few minutes, then got distracted. The whitecaps were lovely, momentarily, but surely became rote in time. The sounds of the seagulls overhead pierced the dull whoosh of the offshore breeze, and that provided a minute or so, ten at max, of delight. Did he experience more? Was he having a mystical experience?

It finally occurred to me, in writing *this* book, that my preoccupation with people staring into natural places was but a projection of the questions I, myself, was plagued with. I was fascinated with what other people saw and heard in the wild, or, to be more honest, I was insecure, and so, fueled by my vulnerability, I defaulted to accumulation—reading about the traditions, sayings, philosophy, myth and stories of how people approached the wild across the world, through history, prehistory, and into the future. I tracked down every lead. No book or idea or strategy was safe.

In the monk, and in time, I saw myself. I saw my own ground zero standing there on the windswept shores of the Rugen. As I was doing more reading on David Caspar Friedrich for this book, I discovered he lost his mother at age seven, watched his brother drown and die after falling through ice, and lost two sisters. All before he was eighteen. What else do you do when you have lost so much, other than go to the sea and stare out? I think Friedrich saw himself in the monk. I think, now, with my losses compounded, I see myself in Friedrich, who wanted the peace the monk had.

Monk by the Sea isn't just a work of Romanticism. In as much as religion is an attempt to wrangle the relation between the visible and the invisible, the finite and the eternal, body and soul—and to make such dualisms irrelevant—it is a *religious* painting. As such, we need to ask the question: what is the state of mind he represents?

For centuries, philosophers put a premium on contemplation. As Aristotle writes in the Nicomachean Ethics, "For contemplation is both the highest form of activity (since the intellect is the highest thing in us, and the objects that it apprehends are the highest things that can be known), and also it is the most continuous because we are more capable of continuous contemplation than we are of any practical activity."[92] We should not be surprised by his assertion, as this is like the mathematician claiming computation is the most sacred act of human life, or a writer insisting the act of filling up a white page with words is the supreme act of creation. We all have our biases. Aristotle was fully aware of contemplation's lack of use value, which, bluntly, he called useless;

without use value. Aristotle's contemplation wasn't directed toward flowering lilies, tiny rivulets or a herd of mountain sheep, Emerson's was—it was directed inward. It was, in a way, thought without an object. Pure thought. Whether it was thinking, or thinking of God, the idea was the same in what it wasn't—and it wasn't contemplating nature. The natural world had nothing to offer. No fodder in the trees for the soul. About two millennia later, and alongside the popularity of Romanticism, in 1880, Auguste Rodin's *The Thinker* would enflesh Aristotle's contemplation. Rodin's *Thinker* stares at the floor, caught in an internal feedback loop. The sublimity of pure contemplation wouldn't die easily, however, and it lingers in our nature writers in the sentimental obtuseness of nature's hidden wisdom. Oddly, the valorization of disembodied cognition allowed the concept of nature as an untouchable mystical source to survive, even through the Enlightenment, which, ironically, allowed us to foster the extractions of the Industrial Revolution at the same time, as we were only hurting the letter of the wild, not the spirit. In like manner, tourists atop Mt Sinai didn't need to care for the mountain, but what it represented. Mind can contemplate anything, and it can hurt the thing in the process with no degradation in said contemplation.

Friedrich's *Monk* is radical because it is the opposite of two thousand years of tradition. Christianity has had a strained, if not hostile relation, to the stuff of nature, as noted earlier. And it was barely fashionable, maybe even heretical, to place a man of God before the void of the sea and imply the green, chaotic frothiness was worthy of contemplation. Yet the monk stands there. We can't really say for sure that the monk is contemplating, but it is definitely suggested; the monk's hands are brought to his chin, and in his line of sight is the void of the horizon. He is a monk after all, and monks tend to contemplate. God and nature are blurred. Friedrich's *The Cross in the Mountain*, from 1808, makes an even more direct nod to nature and the divine by painting the crucifix like a tree—on a mountain top, the cross just another pine tree. The base of the crucifix even has little shoots from its base, turning the Roman symbol of torture into a mountaintop conifer.

Some peculiar color work needs to be brought to attention in *Monk by the Sea*. In terms of elements, we have land, sea and air, in order, respectively, from bottom to top. In no coincidence, the head of the monk is the same color as the earth and the robe of the monk is the same color as the sea. There is, should we borrow a phrase from French philosopher Gilles Deleuze, a "becoming-human" of the sea and a "becoming-sea" of the monk. The composition is progressive in the sense of how undifferentiated the landscape is, in contrast with most landscapes of the era, and it is Modern in the way a Mark Rothko is: the bold disfiguration, an emphasis on honest, earthy color and muted shape, mood over story. And yet, there is within it a very human story.

The earth on which the monk stands is wavelike, softly cresting, small grasses. Birds fly overhead, white seagulls we must presume. If you take away the monk, the painting changes dramatically. The monk is a crucial ingredient.

Repoussoir is a technique artists use for directing our vision. When a large black object on the side or top of a painting, such as a large vertical tree, for instance, keeps your eye from falling off the canvas, it is *repoussoir*. When a painter drops a person into a painting, and that person is gazing or acting on something, and we are drawn to what they are looking at, it is *repoussoir*. It is human nature to look where others are looking (extended mind); our minds play with what might be in another mind (agency detection). We want to know what the other mind is looking at, should it be knowledge we need as well. When a painter places an individual in the foreground of a seascape, and in front of them is the wide expanse of the sea, and we empathize with the figure by way of intimacy and intrigue, there is *repoussoir*. When, under the stars, on a Tuesday after midnight, the wild gives you an image of yourself floating face-up in a reservoir on the outskirts of Baltimore, then toggles to a bedroom door opening, it is *repoussoir*.

I had never identified with a figure in a work of art more than the *Monk by the Sea*—that is, until I came across Sutton's story.

II. *Columbia Island, Long Island Sound, New York, 2019*

For a *2019 New York Times* article on his private island, titled, "He's Spent Just One Night on His Private Island. He's Had Enough," the New Yorker stood for a photo. Outside, facing the camera, his arms in his pocket.[93] The photographer snapped the photo from inside the house, and the inside of the house is dark except for a subtle reflection on the floor. It is a true Shakespearean frame within the frame: the blackness of the interior space, and then the second frame of the bay window. A black tee hangs over the developer's thin shoulders. He stands beside a dry tree. It must be fall. Above and right of his head is a seagull, its wings outstretched. Behind him is Long Island Sound, the water fading from speckled white to dark blue until it abuts civilization. Sutton is not smiling.

As we saw, a common trope in Romantic art was that of the solitary individual staring into the wild. Except here is a modern Romantic, in every sense of the word, and he is staring at the camera.

Sutton was the pilgrim who had traveled thousands of miles in search of his master and then—*oh no!*—he found him. He stood face to face with his fantasy, with his guru at the end of the journey. There is nothing better to speak truth to the mind than to present to the mind, front and square and honest, the thing it has dreamed about. Getting what you want is a curse for the mind. Not long after Sutton finished his house, he sold it. When compared to Friedrich's,

I'm tempted to say Sutton's portrait is the more honest piece of art. He didn't have the great thoughts he'd thought he'd have. But then, I don't think the monk did either. Instead, Sutton looked at the camera, not trying to pretend.

The monk by the sea was Sutton's fantasy; it was mine too, but Sutton found out the emperor had no clothes. He thought, like I did, that simply being there in front of beauty would be enough. Sure, it's beautiful, and beauty gives good feelings. But all beauty fades, and we shouldn't be so crass as to hitch a ride to a car that rarely starts. We all thought it would just speak and we'd just listen and finally, eternally, we'd get that never-fading gem of light.

Dreams, just dreams.

In the West, one reason for the centuries of nature appreciation, or nature rejuvenation, where we chase the wild for beauty, relaxation and medicine, is that we are experience hunters at our core, enchained to a decidedly modern way of accumulating experience. It is no wonder, then, that we have turned toward the wild in our epoch of urban decay or civilizational discontent, as many did in the eighteenth century. You apply an antidote when you are sick, and the point is to not be sick.

Let it Realize Itself

Be careful what you wish for…
because you might get it.

Zen philosophy directs us nowhere other than *here*, a here without assumption, without contemplation, without appreciation, with clarity and sobriety, pure eyes; a here that it takes work, a lot of work, to arrive at. But we don't need to build a 13-million-dollar luxury home to get us there. Money is irrelevant to *this* place.

On the one hand, there's loads of irony when you try to square Sutton's observation that, "You get on the island, even if it's a wreck, and it's just gorgeous—the sky, the tide, the birds, everything," with him then building a multi-million-dollar home to better appreciate these things. Do birds and tide and sky get *more beautiful* when you can sip a latte on a three-hundred-dollar lounger? I venture to say no. Quite the opposite. This isn't to say, however, that nature can't become more beautiful with human intervention. It can. Nature is empty, we are empty, and thus we are not degrading it except in our concepts of purity. A lovely trait of the human mind is that it makes beautiful things. The trap is in thinking the accoutrements or designs we place onto nature, whether it is a garden or a bonsai tree, suffice, as if the experience is in the things.

Sutton's ground zero wanted to be a verb, and he imagined it in visual terms, him both the *repoussoir* and the wild. Except the ground zero fallacy never quits—we chase the dramatic scene (the developed island, for instance) in our zeros rather than the state of mind of the zero. We do this because we are ignorant and have never been taught how to develop different states of mind.

Sutton's failure writ large is our failure writ small. Sutton was beholden to classical utopian thinking, whereas in our daily lives we are enchained to *microtopias.*

Microtopias are what we expect to get out of each moment when we anticipate, desire and grasp. Assuming we are largely unaware, which the majority of us are, we never know we are involved in microtopias until we are disappointed they don't pan out. Disappointment, in fact, marks the presence of a microtopia like a wet sidewalk is a sign of rain. We often do it every night—"tomorrow will be better." Tomorrow won't be better. Sadness and yesterday's pain has a time-tested ability to find you anywhere. You might forget it for a few hours, but return it will. Before vacations we envision a time of deep relaxation where we are unharried, unbothered, where we are our best selves: patient, appreciative, calm, centered. And when we finally arrive at the doorstep of any microtopia—whether it is Hawaii or the donut shop—a feeling of unease arises. We don't see it at first, because we are thrilled just to be in a new place. And then, once you get it you are forced to confront, in a manner impossible before, that the thing isn't what you thought it was. Its identity didn't suddenly change. You changed; it deflated on account of what you put into it. Item or experience received, the mind instantaneously finds a new target. Bait and switch accomplished. If you stop expecting, you will stop being disappointed.

Opposite every microtopia is a shit plant. Microtopias propel our fiercest careerisms and creations, but the nearby shit plant—that is, the jing and jang of both existing simultaneously in all aspects of experience—is the fundamental reality. The shit plant is what adds the characteristic humanism to all art. It is the irony; the search for meaning; the blend of the infinite and finite; and the struggle to overcome dualistic, judgmental thinking. In understanding how the struggle to go beyond opposites relates to others, we can consider compassion and forgiveness, the main two stalwarts we have of human ethical activity. These can be defined as concepts describing the act of absorbing the toxicity of the world (of others) into our being, and, miraculously, not becoming toxic as a result. To be compassionate isn't to be unfeeling, but rather, to feel deeper than you did before, since it is only in this deeper and emptier place that we can develop a self to which nothing sticks. To forgive is to consume and disintegrate feelings inside of yourself; to not let the seeds of hate grow. As for being compassionate towards ourselves, we can learn through accepting toxic sensations to accept the unpleasant parts of ourselves, without judgment, as organic components of our karma and history. We let them be. We accept them. We recognize a beautiful tree has many broken limbs.

Of course, a shit plant is only a shit plant from the perspective of the microtopia, and a microtopia is only so from the perspective of the shit plant: each is hatched in the dreams of its opposite. Each is basic, small mind at work. Eventually, microtopias coalesce into greater, more seductive fantasies, such as ground zeros—a human-engineered gravitational field pulling everything toward itself—perception, others and money included—in the hope of accessing an experience defined vaguely as "better than now." Sutton's story is about the dangers of utopic thinking. Utopic thinking is not something only visionaries do, not the stuff of grandiose skyscrapers, Dubai's rotating buildings or the Gardens of Versailles. It is not relegated to creative exercises on how to reorganize the structure of society, but rather, it is something we all do every day. We need to see this clearly. Visionary utopias are just bigger microtopias.

Utopian thinking is defined by a specific vision, whether it be a method to organize society, a town, or an ideal sketch of humanity. The word comes from the Greek, and means *nowhere*. Though Plato riffs at length on the ideal Greek city state, and how its justice system would be organized and deployed, the British humanist Sir Thomas More defined utopia, as we understand it today, in 1516. Like Sutton, he imagined an island as a backdrop in his opus on utopian thinking. Note the utopic Garden of Eden—it was a garden. Nearly all utopias, some sci-fi tech versions excluded, put the wild at the center of their system, either a garden or an island; boundaries make this possessable and enable us to keep things out, such as the shit plants. Utopias have no shit plants. Of course, there's nothing wrong with making the world a better place, but on the level of ordinary experience "better" operates differently; much more often than not, there is no better.

What we do know, from his interviews, is that Sutton was bewitched by the beauty of the island and yet sought to "make it beautiful and let it realize itself," as if it lacked something. Sutton was right and wrong in developing the island. Right in that it *does* take a lot of work to find beauty in the world; it does require "engineering," in a sense. But he was wrong in needing to build a 13-million-dollar structure to find it. In yet another twist, which makes Sutton all the more relatable, he did say, after the build out, "A simpler solution for my desire for a Zen retreat would have been to rent a row[ing] boat from City Island for US$10, get out there whenever I wanted, stick a fishing pole in the water, look at the sky, look at the birds, and say 'Isn't this gorgeous.' I've often thought that.'"

He should have listened to that thought. The work he needed to do was on himself, prepping his mind and body to receive his island paradise with new eyes and a holistic attunement inclusive of the senses. Not so much an addition, but a subtraction. As Emily Dickinson aptly penned, "Not 'Revelation'—'tis—that waits/But our unfurnished eyes—."

What about these unfurnished eyes?

* * *

The most powerful motivator in life is one of a better experience, defined by the experience we are not having at the moment.

There is no greater motivator in life than the desire for a greater experience. This motivator is all the more powerful when we are not aware we are being driven by it. Whether we are talking about buying things (capitalism), moving to another country (migration), or camping in the Grand Canyon (wild lust), all of us are seeking a better experience, because, so we think, a better experience leads to a better life, and a better life means we will be happier. We think we will thrive, find our homeostasis, with a better experience.

Throughout history, we have gods to ask for things, gods of death, gods of life, gods of addition. But we are lacking one genre of gods. We are lacking a god of subtraction.[94]

Luxury Assumption

Change habit and you change the world.

Experience curation is our contemporary god of addition, the god with no name.

As self-conscious creatures, every action we take is, in one way or another, a proxy for experience hunting; to and fro, toward and away. Away from a shit plant, toward a zero. Our jobs, how we choose significant others, the outfits we wear, the neighborhoods we live in, are all the end results of choice. Each choice has a desired end, whether that end was hashed out consciously or unconsciously. We can be forgiven for our ruthless pragmatism. Our brains are hardwired to seek out, analyze and adapt. Contemporary neuroscience has a term to describe this: predictive brain. The brain is a "predictive machine," it is said frequently. "The term 'predictive brain' denotes one of the most relevant concepts in cognitive neuroscience, which emphasizes the importance of 'looking into the future', preparation, anticipation, prospection, and expectation in various cognitive domains."[95]

But we are not, of course, just our brains. Big mind haunts us at every turn.

I've been guilty of experience hunting for the majority of my life, not least because it never occurred to me that it was a problem. What's wrong with desiring to have an experience? Isn't that a good thing? Something isn't working out, and we make moves to fix it. We want to have a better experience than the current one. We are poor and try to get rich. We are rich and try to gain authenticity. We are selfish and try to make ourselves more grateful. What's wrong with this? The other day, I noticed my kids were bored. That bothered me. It bothered me because I felt that on a nice day, a ten-year-old boy shouldn't be complaining there's nothing to do when, in fact, there's plenty to do. We live in the heart of the Rocky Mountains, after all. I didn't like my experience of feeling his experience was subpar. So I cajoled him into the car to show him there was a better experience somewhere and all he had to do was go out and get it. We went for a swim in a local hot spring. We had a good time, and, presumably, a better experience than one of staying at home and annoying his sister. On the weekend, when you are trying to decide where to go on Friday night, or where to hike on Saturday morning, you are unconsciously dipping your mind into a future experience, and then, based on how that feels, you either commit or continue to shop around (microtopia). Often, the ground zero you chase gives the thumbs up or thumbs down to the potential experience, like the macro filter it is.

It doesn't have to be this way, but it largely is. This is not to say you shouldn't do anything, but, in the end, there's nowhere to go, and, because there's nowhere to go, you should go somewhere. But we need to arrive at places open, because the experience we want is rarely, if ever, the experience we need. When we are open, an experience unfolds, as opposed to us folding it.

We seek to relieve the tension, but we are still adding. Subverting this property of mind is unsettling at first, but in order to understand mind, you have to see it with absolute clarity. The cognitive dissonance of our experience hunting is profound. Worse, it is now a deeply entrenched habit, and there is no stronger actor in our world: not government, not Hollywood, not famine or disease. Habit is our most revolutionary and powerful agent of change. Change habit and you change the world; change your habit and you change your world. Coincidentally, one of the most powerful psychological and economic trends in the twenty-first century is the feverish pitch for luxury. Luxury goods. Luxury experiences. Better. More. This doesn't just mean more expensive either. Luxury is about value and time and appreciation, the very thing Sutton and I sought.

The luxury assumption is the unchecked concept lurking in our experience hunting.

If the world were a giant religious painting, luxury would be the main figure; its *repoussoir*. You and I are that figure staring out into the void. Just as all religious art is a state of mind, luxury is the sum-total aesthetic of our ground zeros, and the latter are aesthetic because we adorn them, caress them, place nice things in their proximity. And, since it is a work of religious art, we need to ask what the state of mind is of the painting?

The purchasing of a luxury, whether we do it with money or labor or time, is a form of experience hunting for a desired state of mind. Because it is a desired state of mind, it isn't our current one. A luxury is, in many ways, defined by the power of expectation attached to it. When you buy paper towels at the store, you don't expect much from them, aside from cleaning up a mess. In many ways, purchasing paper towels is an unthinking habit and thus considered, in terms of consumer economics, a necessity good: we need them. A luxury, in contrast, is not a necessity good, which means it's an elective purchase, and because it's elective, it comes with a price. A hallmark of luxury items is inflation.

But what is inflated, and where? Remember that story I was telling you about, when I was in Syracuse with the fire and the house was crackling, and the hungry ghost inside of me was inflating? The price tag is only the *obvious* inflation. The more relevant inflation is a tax on our current experience. The tax is levied against reality as it is presented to us, to be deducted from the lived moment by the hands of expectation and anticipation—qualitative words symbolizing a change in the way time is experienced. A debt against the present courtesy of an investment in the future.

Luxury hard goods adorn our physical places, but they also adorn our inner spaces. When we think we are in the midst of luxury, we act differently, in part because luxuries have a design, an intention baked into them, and our minds want to align with that intention. We slow down. We try to appreciate. We might take a picture. We also get possessive. We also project them as a proxy for our lack. Time enters our lives in a way it does when we are with our children or with a loved one before they depart. As a psychological and material phenomenon, luxury is the eternally unfulfilled promise of presence. Luxury is a moment curated and tailored for our taste, engineered to align perfectly with the idiosyncrasies and wish-fulfillments of small mind.

The luxury assumption spans our consumption of nature's jewels, too. In an age of decreasing wild places, we have placed the wild on a pedestal—green architecture, the nature cure, the National Park craze. So too, in an age of distraction, where our information economy consumes attention, we have put time on a pedestal. Our assumption of being in nature is one of time slowed down. Luxury is about attention, and it is not a coincidence that luxury items are, in essence, the items of post-capitalism, a driving force in our epoch. The queues lining up on the fabled vistas of Angel's Landing in Zion, or the thousands cramming a Mediterranean island vacation into a long weekend to "rest and recover," are under the spell of the luxury assumption. I see it play out in hometown of Carbondale, Colorado, an idyllic mountain town in the heart of the Rockies. Surrounded on all sides by mountains, trails galore, two rivers intersecting, a historic Main Street—from all places people are *coming* to Carbondale, renting AirBnbs, soaking in the small-town mountain vibe. Locals, whenever they get the chance, are *leaving* in equal numbers, either for a desert trip or another part of the mountains. We are all chasing the same thing, in different places. It reminds me of an old Zen parable of the impatient person rushing and trying to cram as much they can into a trip to … you guessed it … relax.

We need to escape the act of escaping.

Our inner lives can be altered in a variety of ways, due to a variety of factors. The existence of a thing can create the need for it. No shocker there. In the 1600s, no one desired a car for the simple reason that cars didn't exist. When cars were invented, even for cultures who didn't share in their invention, the desire for one spread like wildfire. Now, cars are a status symbol and it's hard to imagine someone who doesn't give thought to their car; not caring about a nice car is, still, making a point, since it's hard to imagine someone unaware that a car is a status symbol, and, thus, the rejection of it is still a form of desire. But that is an example of a thing creating a desire. Luxuries are more powerful because they don't create a desire for a thing, but exploit an inbuilt structure of desire, to which our habits assume shape. Luxuries have "changed the way we interact," according to Dana Thomas. They have "become part of our social fabric."[96] Not just that, but they are changing the way we interact with ourselves, each other, and nature.

As it was with the supernormal stimulus, to which we have outsized responses based on our biological evolution, the structure of desire that luxury exploits is part of mind itself. In fact, it is as old as time—as old as golden goblets in a mud hut or jeweled statues in stone-block temples. It was just dormant; the supernormal stimulus never dies, just awaits. Innovations in manufacturing, shipping and design made the first wave of luxury commodities possible (early capitalism), but the second wave of luxury unmasked the true impulse behind the first—it was a grasping for experience. In much the same way that NASA didn't invent the impulse to travel in space but merely realized it, luxury has resuscitated what Buddhists have, for millennia, called the hungry ghost. The next time you feel unfulfilled by a particular thing, or experience, and thus chase down another thing to fill the emptiness the formerly unfulfilling thing left, you are a hungry ghost. That's all of us, really. What undergirds our hungry ghosts is the ability to sense our suffering, plot the pleasure and be aware of how we think an experience might or might not fulfill our desires.

Remember the first and second noble truth in Buddhist philosophy: life contains suffering; the cause of suffering is desire.

The Experience Economy

More is not more when it comes to toys and nature.

While extravagance and opulence are nothing new, ostentation has historically been confined to the upper classes. Think Chinese and Roman emperors with marble bathrooms and gilded toilets. In the early eighteenth century, things started changing; enter the "democratizing" of luxury … which, at least in my mind, culminated in a New York bathtub carved from the same block of Carrara marble that Michelangelo used to create the Pieta. Is a hot bath just that much dreamier when the steaming waters are held in embrace by Cararra marble? I'd ask Sutton.

Just as the ability to buy goods created new forms of identity based on material accumulation—an identity based on possession, ownership and status—the ability to purchase experience is likewise creating an ever-newer form of identity based largely on material accumulation, but with profound variations. This new form of identity has arisen with what was termed, at least in 1998, the experience economy. Historically, it is an outgrowth of previous forms of attaching value to things. For some, it is the fourth iteration of buying and selling. In many ways, luxury created the practice of stores selling goods with a side of experience. Now, experience itself, a fundamental unit of mind, is being monetized.

The experience economy is reactive. It is as if, in the face of failing to define ourselves against others because there is no exclusivity in luxury anymore, we have retreated to a *pseudo* inner sanctum: where we still accumulate, except we accumulate experience and differentiate by experience; where we still seek exclusivity, except it's no longer the unique object, but the *unique experience.* The experience economy animates our ground zeros and it could be the final act in the play before we enter neurologically-designed experience: erasing bad memories, rewiring our brains for happiness, creating synthetic experiences, and so on. Neuroscience will undoubtedly be the frontier of our future experience economies.

Because of the premium, and pressure, we are putting on designer experiences, it makes sense that so much social tech is around prediction, or managing expectation. Tourism has become experience-designed on the brand side. Eco-tourism. Drug tourism. Cultural tourism. Voluntourism. Travel has always sold experience wrapped in place, but now they are aware of the behavioral economics and are explicitly selling experience to buttress a common ground-zero archetype: the resource hoarder.

But what's wrong with having a good experience? You had a great day with your children. You feel good about that fact. The good feeling lingers and you hold onto it. You want to repeat it next weekend. The problem is that, at least for deep seekers, the good experience fades and needs to be replaced, and it fades because it is attached to a ground zero, and thus any indulgence of this zero merely entrenches it more, producing its equal and opposite reaction. Or, we discover that we seek as much as we avoid. And that's exhausting. The harder you fall, the more you grasp to get back on. It is a cycle of seeking resolution but never finding it, of our monkey minds being our default mind the majority of our lives. The problem is we are not free. In fits and starts, I found this freedom in the wild. The luxurious rivers brought me home, the deep mountains closer to the source. I tried drugs too. That didn't work. I came down. But I could never hang onto the experience, couldn't make it last.

For me, I learned I had indulged the very thing occluding me from seeing the wild.

Consuming the stuff of the world, and the experiences it offers, has, in many ways, altered the way we all approach and/or consume the wild, which is really what the majority of people are doing today. Appreciation is a form of consumption for the modern experience hunter. It's no wonder the visitation rates of Natural Parks in the U.S., or the global growth of the outdoor industry have an analogous shape to the luxury market—they keep going up. They keep going up because the two trends are inseparable. We keep demanding more idiosyncratic and luxurious natural experiences in the belief we know what a premium wild experience is. The outlandish marketing material is without parallel. One of my favorites is of the man driving his truck through a backcountry river; off road and rugged, the car bounces, swerving here and there. The river splashes, the cobbles torn asunder. His arm is out his window, the wind in his hair. *This is what it's like to be in nature*, the commercial conveys. It's hyperbolic, but it's illustrative. The images and ads are pure "nature" porn. These people are in front of amazing places, having loads of fun, smiles all round, framed by the proscenium of the wild, whose theater provides the most enigmatic actors we can imagine: sherbet sunsets, towering cliffs, billowing clouds. Freedom. Individualism. In the ski industry, for instance, powder is starting to become a real commodity, with some resorts charging upwards of $800 for fresh tracks before the lifts open to the public.[97] The assumption? Skiing powder is the premium experience. You have more fun in powder. That's both true and definitely not true.

The irony is profound: the more we try to glean from the wild, the less we get to know it. The more we try to consume it, the more we deceive ourselves. There is no better way to *avoid* having an intimate experience with the wild than driving your truck through a pristine stream. That's tourism on Mount Sinai writ small. It is the shell of an experience. Coffee without caffeine. Small mind experience in the place where big mind wants to be realized.

Porcupines and Wine

But how can consciousness catch consciousness?
The same way porcupines make love—carefully.

I sought freedom, but the problem was the I. I sought big wild, a wild that no longer hid in the Heraclitean sense. But I sought it while I was small, and thus only saw small things, small pleasures, small band aids for my discontent, and so on, despite trying to compensate by living and training in big nature: running and climbing in the mountains, trekking in the Jordanian desert, etc. As Suzuki said, "you cannot practice true zazen, because *you* practice it."[98] Suzuki meant this: the moment you are aware of your practice, either in seated meditation or any other practice, you become self-aware, and when you are self-aware you are on the outside of the intensity of time and place. Outside of the moment the practice becomes untrue and impure. It is impure because the gravitation field that is the "I," the "you," experiences only a portion of the possible. Or as Annie Dillard writes, "Experiencing the present purely is being empty and hollow; you catch grace as a man fills his cup under a waterfall." It is not *your* experience anymore, and this realization quiets the judging mind and allows you to choose your reaction, should you decide to have one. But when you are in the wild seldom is a reaction required, and thus the mind can be even more quiet, the senses even more alive.

At a young age, I would be exposed to one of the great Chinese poets, Li Po, who, as legend would have it, died drunkenly while trying to embrace the moon's reflection.

Li Po would write of drinking as much as of the wild. In *Reverence-Pavilion Mountain, Sitting Alone*:

Birds have vanished into deep skies.
A last cloud drifts away, all idleness.
Inexhaustible, this Mountain and I
gaze at each other, it alone remaining.

In *Drinking Alone Beneath the Moon*:

Among the blossoms, a single jar of wine.
No one else here, I ladle it out myself.
Raising my cup, I toast the bright moon,
and facing my shadow makes friends three,
though moon has never understood wine,
and shadow only trails along behind me."

Moon has never understood wine; nature and civilization do not speak the same language. Emerson, on the other hand, can write ten pages on a falling leaf, and he does this because it is about using your eyes and heart and soul to align to the mysterious expressions of the wild. Emerson's nature is a baroque cathedral, delightful and symbolic, and Zen's is a rock garden. In the Buddhist, Shinto and Confucian traditions, all of which influenced Zen, nature was depicted as unforgiving, uncaring and unsentimental, and all the more mysterious and abstract for it. The qualities of the *impersonal* tuned the eyes, ears and minds of the Zen poets to the savage *detail*, the thing without relation or symbolism; relationality is judgment manifest. The wild has no soul and has no ears to listen, should St. Francis begin preaching. In an empty mind, the smallest drop makes the biggest echo.

Japanese poet Hokushi writes, "I write, erase, rewrite, / Erase again, and then / A poppy blooms." We busy about, thinking, calculating, judging the quality of our actions. Small mind clamors. Then a poppy blooms. The detail doesn't set a scene. It is that which is immanent, *there*, a thing resisting a relation to something else. It is vertical relationality between depths that cultivates transcendence, and transcendence breeds the formless obsession. In our production of writing and erasing and rewriting, a poppy blooms. It mocks our efforts. It mocks art. It mocks the symbolic. It mocks mind's nature to incorporate, to extend.

When we look at someone's angry face, what do we see? "I see anger," would be a common response. But that's not true. What you see are eyebrows drawn in close; a focused gaze, perhaps a squint; tightened lips. Your pattern-matching mind has taught you these traits, taken together, indicate a state of mind called angry, and so you apply the concept of angry to them, which also occludes all the other non-angry aspects. Thus, your awareness narrows, and when awareness narrows, some call it knowledge, which is true to a point, but others call that blockage.

The best method to dispel the illusion of knowing something is to fully experience it; without trying to set up a prop (luxury home); without expectation the experience will amend or correct or create a future self. If you experience something without supposition, nor assumption, but with full body, with tantric senses, then you will have a hard time knowing anything about it. This is a good thing, because you have unmoored the knower. The world will, quite literally, become alive in new ways. Rather than you trying to leverage the wild, it will leverage you.

* * *

"Things are truth itself to be used for removing delusion," said Dongshan Liangjie.[99] The truth of the thing, to see the thing or a person or a mountain-top vista, is a subtraction of our default small mind. The delusions are many: the ground zero, the belief that the shit plant isn't there, the formless obsession. The Zen tactic is to see mind, to catch it in the act, prior to mind's pattern-matching reflex, before value, concept, judgment, or ground zeros generate negative self-talk in us on account of not measuring up to what people want us to be or what we want to be. The sky is there behind the clouds, and the sky is perfect. Suzuki writes that Zen concerns when "time has not yet come to its own consciousness. Zen is where this consciousness is about to rise. Or it may be better to say that consciousness is caught at the very moment of rising from the unconscious."[100] It's a luxurious moment, infinite potential.

But how can consciousness catch consciousness? The same way porcupines make love—carefully.

Coda: The Sweet Spot

Nature is a method, and all methods are traps.

He tried hard but failure and alienation nagged. He thought he knew who he was. He thought he knew what he needed. He needed the wild. He needed nature. It had worked since he was a child. Why wouldn't it work again?

At a breaking point, he went for a run, desperate to feel deeply. It was midnight, outside Baltimore. On the run a curious thing happened—the shit plant. He'd ignore it, but it was a transmission, the wild doling out skillful means. He was ready. "Pain is the breaking of the shell that encloses your understanding," said Khalil Gibran. It cracked the shell of his precious expectation, and expectation is a form of understanding. He ran to a forested peninsula, stripped down and went for a dip. The night was quiet, and the water was warm. He had the company of ducks, their beaks nestled into their feathers, and the stars and the maple and birch trees arching over the slanting shoreline. In his heart and mind were Emerson and Muir and the Zen poets. The mud squeezed through his toes.

Languid, floating under the stars, a vision of himself appeared. With clarity, he saw the person he was running from and the person he was running to. He was running from the boy who lost a love and his friends and the feeling of home. He was running to the wild, to a place that wouldn't ask questions, a place without bad feelings and ill intentions, a new home, to a place he thought could never be outdone, a place of his childhood and adulthood. He was running from the highly personal to the impersonal.

The wild rebuffed him, personally.

He still didn't listen. Undeterred, he moved again to Colorado. He climbed more, ran more, skied more, tried to court nature's mystical embrace. He'd get as deep as he could as often as he could, onto the summits, in the valleys, on ribbons of ice and stone. The strategy couldn't fail, he told himself. He buttressed his mind with fantasies of what everyone else must have seen. *The Monk by the Sea*. Muir. Siddhartha. Abbey. Their words haunted him. Nature was a luxury he couldn't afford to lose.

It was beautiful and the experiences stacked up, one on top of another, but ultimately his strategies failed. He finally got the message. "Move on from me," said the wild. He was heartbroken.

His heart would be broken until it was broken twice more. The death of his father and the death of his mother, in quick succession. The loss of a job, the confrontation of someone he had been trying to avoid. He was cornered, hanging off the root of a tree—lions waiting for him on one side, and the void on the other. He just wanted to make it through each day. He found an alcove in the shape of a strawberry.

The strawberry was an insight. He realized who he had set up inside of his mind, the ground zeros he was striving for, why they were there, how they got there and what they wanted. He also realized what these zeros surrounded themselves with. On one hand was the zero at one with nature: a well-read romantic, a student of history, of thought, philosophy and ideas, who prided himself on the search for the bleeding heart of the forest and who, on most accounts, had tasted its elite, sublime offerings. On the other hand was the climber—the listener of stone and ice, fully in tune with the mountains, how its verticality felt, and how to move in and out of its terrain; person who sought big and beautiful nature, thinking bigger and more beautiful experiences were to be found there. Each zero had its merits, two parts of the same journey. But he'd learnt a hard lesson: the very things he'd been chasing, constructed from the chaser, were the very things keeping him ignorant. A third zero presented itself—the good son. Turns out this good son had to do the very thing he didn't want to do. He had to let go of his parents. So he did.

His story was universal. He was caught in the patterns of desire, inbuilt from philosophical, evolutionary and historical forces alike. "Three things cannot be long hidden: the sun, the moon, and the truth," said Guatama Buddha. It was time for truth to reveal itself.

As his parents died, his zeros died alongside them. "The value of a thing sometimes lies not in what one attains with it, but in what one pays for it—what it costs us," said Nietzsche. If there was indeed a truth earned, it cost him *him*.

Heraclitus said, "nature loves to hide." But for nature to reveal itself, *we* need to hide.

He mourned himself … but only for so long. The wild rejected him, yes, but, sprouts and green grasses gradually began to punch through freshly burned soil. In thinking he had lost the relationship he once had with nature, what was once only to be found in the wild expanded into everything he saw and touched. His senses rediscovered their origin and purpose. The big beauty of the wild, now shrunken, became the big beauty of the world, there in each moment, with no remainder.

Nature was a method, but all methods are traps. The greatest methods self-destruct, and we need to be brave enough to let them do so. "If you see the Buddha, kill him," it is said. Your weaknesses are best expressed in your attachments. I was attached at the hip to the wild.

* * *

All of the innovations in this book are meant to highlight areas where we need to let go. To let go out of vitality, not out of resignation, is a brave, and seldom practiced esoteric art. We need to let go of expectation, of our zeros, of the formless obsession, of judgment, of our controlling minds, of experience hunting, of what we think nature is. All of these assumptions block true understanding. Ground zeros are concepts like any other, but they are tools of self-destruction; they are an exercise in not just seeing through our scheming mind, but the things it surrounds itself by, and in seeing both you can be doubly liberated—from the gravitational field of self-centered living *and* from the objects it feeds on. It is in the soil of our zeros where the modern diseases of self-criticism, negative self-talk and feelings of unworthiness are germinated. Remove judgment from the calm waters of the alcove and these feelings, the hallmarks of our time, are robbed of fuel.

In this journey of mine, I needed not just to see the mind, but to understand why it was so, what biology had given us and what neuroscience could offer. Or, put differently, I was asking, can nature help us awaken with more expediency than other methods? Yes, I think so, but with caveats. The contours sketched here provide enough clarity that the artifice can be discerned: the wild was the sculptor of the mind. It built what we sense, how we sense and the small mind interpreting all the sensations. Feeling this in a deep way is enough to break the dualism between self and the wild. Lucky us, the wild left a turnkey for us, an expedited way out of small mind: our body. Small mind is reliant on body and body is reliant on environment. There are many avenues to see small mind, meditation being one of them, but because the wild laid the avenues for our sensations prior to mind, it offers a privileged method for non-dual experience, for releasing us from judgment. These privileged pathways manifest in delight, lightness, exhortations to beauty, inexhaustibility, hard-to-describe feelings of kinship, but the practice doesn't stop there. "To study the self is to forget the self," said the thirteenth-century founder of the Soto school of Zen, Dogen Zenji, also known for his deep engagement with the wild. But Dogen kept going: "To forget the self is to be actualized by myriad things." In the wild, we see the full myriad of things on display, each unable to be otherwise, each actualized by all that came prior; each is not itself, but transparent interdependency. Our modern methods and means of enlightenment, whether in Eastern or Western varieties, have merely adopted this natural principle and dressed it up into concepts for our minds. Spiritual truth and biological truth converge.

The wild, always already awake, goads us on.

Pablo Picasso was once in a restaurant sketching on a napkin. A woman recognized him and asked how much she could pay for the napkin. Picasso said $20,000. The lady was aghast. "But it only took you two minutes to draw," she said. "No, it took me my whole life," the painter replied. He was right. Practice creates potency and capacity in experience.

In our perennial strivings to mimic in mind the creative death–rebirth of the wild as unphased or unattached to things, we are often equally impressed with the boldness of its impermanence. Fluorescent blossoms one day, pedals on the grass the next. It strives so, so hard, animals fighting for their very lives, for … just a few more breaths. A few more minutes *here*. I felt this urge when my mother and father passed. I could see the clawing desire for more time in my mind. Just a few more hours, it said, as she was slipping away. But this wasn't about my loss; this was about her transition. Rather than fight her journey, I embraced it. I held on the only way I knew how—by letting her go with a smile. For her last week of life, I volunteered to stay up with her through night, turning her, giving her the doses of morphine every two hours, adjusting the pillow under her hip. I barely slept. On the couch, in those long hours of darkness, I witnessed her return under the dim light of the chandelier. On one night, after the lights were out and we were alone, I laid my head beside her. She was unable to talk or move her body, or make any meaningful gestures at this point. I pulled her frail hand onto my head and let it rest there. *It was wild*. She was hanging on by a thread, as was I, but, through her hand, her energy, my mother, the myriad of all her things—she arrived in full. An image kept coming to my mind too—of her falling to the earth like the leaves from the maples outside her window. I didn't like the image, but it stuck. I fought it ... then it occurred to me, she was bestowing her final lesson. Skillful means.

During these nights, to center my mind, I would focus on her breath, rather than mine. It wasn't so much breath, as air through a windpipe, soft at times, heavy at times, with erratic pauses. It was her only sign of life. In the quiet, I listened, hour after hour. One night I was awoken not by her breathing, but the lack thereof. The silence jolted me to consciousness. I sat up and looked over. No more breath. Her chest was not rising. I ran upstairs and got Jim. She took one more breath, each of us by her side, and then returned.

Living deeply and living well for a night—or for sixty seconds—takes all the time before it, all the practice, whether you are in the forest or in a room with your dying mother. The next day, it occurred to me to return to Loch Raven, to the peninsula, to close the loop. I got my stuff ready, then I stopped. It wasn't necessary. I didn't need anything else. I took a walk instead and marveled at the leaves.

Endnotes

1 Yongey Mingyur Rinpoche. *In Love with the World: A Monk's Journey Through the Bardos of Living and Dying*. New York: Spiegel & Grau, 2019.

2 *Food Wastage Footprint: Impacts on Natural Resources.* Food and Agriculture Organization of the United Nations. Rome: FAO, 2013.

3 Møller A. P., Thornhill R. 1998. Bilateral symmetry and sexual selection: a meta-analysis. *Am. Nat.* 151, 174–192 10.1086/286110

4 Twohig-Bennett C, Jones A. "The health benefits of the great outdoors: A systematic review and meta-analysis of greenspace exposure and health outcomes." *Environ Res.* 2018 Oct;166:628-637. doi: 10.1016/j.envres.2018.06.030. Epub 2018 Jul 5. PMID: 29982151; PMCID: PMC6562165.

5 Hansotia P. A neurologist looks at mind and brain: "the enchanted loom". *Clin Med Res.* 2003 Oct;1(4):327-32. doi: 10.3121/cmr.1.4.327. PMID: 15931326; PMCID: PMC1069062; David Eagleman, *Incognito: The Secret Lives of the Brain* (New York: Pantheon Books, 2011)..

6 Eagleman, David. 2021. "The Real Difference Between the Mind & the Brain, Says a Neuroscientist." *MindBodyGreen.* July 13, 2021. https://www.mindbodygreen.com/articles/difference-between-mind-and-brain-neuroscientist. Accessed May 2025.

7 John Tooby, Leda Cosmides, "The past explains the present: Emotional adaptations and the structure of ancestral environments," *Ethology and Sociobiology, Volume 11*, Issues 4–5, 1990,Pages 375-424, ISSN 0162-3095.

8 Suzuki, Shunryu. *Zen Mind, Beginner's Mind: Informal Talks on Zen Meditation and Practice.* Edited by Trudy Dixon. New York: Weatherhill, 1970.

9 In particular, the concept of "nature deficit disorder" was popularized by Richard Louv in *Last Child in the Woods: Saving Our Children from Nature-Deficit Disorder*. Chapel Hill, NC: Algonquin Books, 2005.

10 Voon, Claire. "Marina Abramovic's Infamous Naked Doorway Will Be Restaged for Her Royal Academy Show in London." *Artnet News,* September 4, 2019. https://news.artnet.com/art-world/marina-abramovics-naked-doorway-coming-royal-academy-london-1642153. Accessed May, 2025.

11 Nadler, Steven, ed. *The Cambridge Companion to Malebranche.* Cambridge: Cambridge University Press, 2000, p. 42.

12 Marc Bekoff, "Animal Emotions: Exploring Passionate Natures: Current interdisciplinary research provides compelling evidence

that many animals experience such emotions as joy, fear, love, despair, and grief—we are not alone," *BioScience, Volume 50,* Issue 10, October 2000, Pages 861–870.

13 There are more than a few natural philosophy and taxonomy texts. One of the most class is: Linnaeus, Carl. *Systema Naturae per Regna Tria Naturae: Secundum Classes, Ordines, Genera, Species, cum Characteribus, Differentiis, Synonymis, Locis.* 10th ed. Vol. 1. Holmiae (Stockholm): Laurentii Salvii, 1758.

14 Mynott, Jeremy. *The Story of Nature: A Human History.* Yale University Press, 2024. Hadot, Pierre. *The Veil of Isis: An Essay on the History of the Idea of Nature.* Belknap Press, 2008.

15 Thomas, Sue. Technobiophilia: Nature and Cyberspace. A&C Black, 2013.

16 *Daily Mail.* "Incredible Pictures of One of Earth's Last Uncontacted Tribes Firing Bows and Arrows." Accessed May 27, 2025. https://www.dailymail.co.uk/sciencetech/article-1022822/Incredible-pictures-Earths-uncontacted-tribes-firing-bows-arrows.html.

17 White, Lynn, Jr. "The Historical Roots of Our Ecologic Crisis." Science 155, no. 3767 (March 10, 1967): 1203–7. https://doi.org/10.1126/science.155.3767.1203.

18 Hadot, Pierre. *Philosophy as a Way of Life: Spiritual Exercises from Socrates to Foucault.* Wiley-Blackwell, 1995.

19 The Greek word for truth, *aletheia*, incorporates the word for "forgetting"; *a-letheia* might be translated as "unforgetting" or "remembering."

20 Riitta Hari, from "Brain–Environment Connections to Temporal Dynamics and Social Interaction: Principles of Human Brain Function," *Neuron*, Volume 94, Issue 5, 2017, Pages 1033-1039, ISSN 0896-6273, https://doi.org/10.1016/j.neuron.2017.04.007.

21 Pyne, S.J., Goldammer, J.G. (1997). "The Culture of Fire: An Introduction to Anthropogenic Fire History." In: Clark, J.S., Cachier, H., Goldammer, J.G., Stocks, B. (eds) *Sediment Records of Biomass Burning and Global Change.* NATO ASI Series, vol 51. Springer, Berlin, Heidelberg. https://doi.org/10.1007/978-3-642-59171-6_5

22 Ibid.

23 Ahmad, Hafiz Ishfaq, Muhammad Jamil Ahmad, Farwa Jabbir, Sunny Ahmar, Nisar Ahmad, Abdelmotaleb A. Elokil, and Jinping Chen. "The Domestication Makeup: Evolution, Survival, and Challenges." *Frontiers in Ecology and Evolution 8* (May 8, 2020). https://doi.org/10.3389/fevo.2020.00103.

24 Winston R, Chicot R. The importance of early bonding on the long-term mental health and resilience of children. *London Journal of Primary Care* (Abingdon). 2016 Feb 24;8(1):12-14. doi: 10.1080/17571472.2015.1133012. PMID: 28250823;

PMCID: PMC5330336.

25 Tomasello M, Rakoczy H. What makes human cognition unique? From individual to shared to collective intentionality. *Mind Lang.* 2003;18(2):121–147.

26 As cited in, Nussbaum, Martha C. The Therapy of Desire: Theory and Practice in Hellenistic Ethics. Princeton University Press, 2009: p. 13.

27 Berger Lee R, Makhubela Tebogo, Molopyane Keneiloe, Krüger Ashley, Randolph-Quinney Patrick, Elliott Marina, Peixotto Becca, Fuentes Agustín, Tafforeau Paul, Beyrand Vincent, Dollman Kathleen, Jinnah Zubair, Gillham Angharad Brewer, Broad Kenneth, Brophy Juliet, Chinamatira Gideon, Dirks Paul HM, Feuerriegel Elen, Gurtov Alia, Hlophe Nompumelelo, Hunter Lindsay, Hunter Rick, Jakata Kudakwashe, Jaskolski Corey, Morris Hannah, Pryor Ellie, Mpete Maropeng, Roberts Eric, Smilg Jacqueline S, Tsikoane Mathabela, Tucker Steven, van Rooyen Dirk, Warren Kerryn, Wren Colin D, Kissel Marc, Spikins Penny, Hawks John (2023) Evidence for deliberate burial of the dead by Homo naledi eLife 12:RP89106, https://doi.org/10.7554/eLife.89106.2

28 This is not to say that all traits are beneficial. They are not. Some traits are valuable in some contexts, or environments, and not in others.

29 Sahn, Zen Master Seung. *Only Don't Know: Selected Teaching Letters of Zen Master Seung Sahn.* Shambhala Publications, 1999.

30 Sumner, William Graham. Folkways: A Study of Mores, Manners, Customs and Morals. Dover Publications: 2002. In the original text of 1906, the quote appears on page 2

31 Witoszek, Nina, and Andrew Brennan. *Philosophical Dialogues: Arne Næss and the Progress of Ecophilosophy.* Rowman & Littlefield, 1999: p. 3.

32 Lutz, Jaime. "Prospect Park It! Neighbors of Brooklyn's Backyard Sue, Say Tower Would Cast a Shadow." Brooklyn Paper, December 20, 2013. https://www.brooklynpaper.com/prospect-park-it-neighbors-of-brooklyns-backyard-sue-say-tower-would-cast-a-shadow/. Accessed May, 2025.

33 Sudimac, S., Sale, V. & Kühn, S. How nature nurtures: Amygdala activity decreases as the result of a one-hour walk in nature. Mol *Psychiatry* 27, 4446–4452 (2022). https://doi.org/10.1038/s41380-022-01720-6

34 Franco LS, Shanahan DF, Fuller RA. "A Review of the Benefits of Nature Experiences: More Than Meets the Eye." *Int J Environ Res Public Health.* 2017 Aug 1;14(8):864. doi: 10.3390/ijerph14080864. PMID: 28763021; PMCID: PMC5580568.

35 Ibid.

36 Simpson, Jon. "Finding Brand Success In The Digital World." *Forbes,* August 25, 2017. https://www.forbes.com/sites/

forbesagencycouncil/2017/08/25/finding-brand-success-in-the-digital-world/. Accessed May 2025.

37 For the statistics, see United Nations. "68% of the World Population Projected to Live in Urban Areas by 2050, Says UN." United Nations. Accessed May 27, 2025. https://www.un.org/uk/desa/68-world-population-projected-live-urban-areas-2050-says-un. See also Peen J, Schoevers RA, Beekman AT, Dekker J. The current status of urban-rural differences in psychiatric disorders. *Acta Psychiatr Scand.* 2010 Feb;121(2):84-93. doi: 10.1111/j.1600-0447.2009.01438.x. Epub 2009 Jul 13. PMID: 19624573.

38 Manus, M.B. "Evolutionary mismatch." *Evol Med Public Health.* 2018 Aug 8;2018(1):190-191. doi: 10.1093/emph/eoy023. PMID: 30159142; PMCID: PMC6109377.

39 Barrett, Deirdre. *Supernormal Stimuli: How Primal Urges Overran Their Evolutionary Purpose.* W. W. Norton & Company, 2010.

40 Biswas, Aviroop, Paul I. Oh, Guy E. Faulkner, Ravi R. Bajaj, Michael A. Silver, Marc S. Mitchell, and David A. Alter. "Sedentary Time and Its Association With Risk for Disease Incidence, Mortality, and Hospitalization in Adults." *Annals of Internal Medicine 162*, no. 2 (January 20, 2015): 123–32. https://doi.org/10.7326/m14-1651.

41 Marselle, M.R., Bowler, D.E., Watzema, J. et al. "Urban street tree biodiversity and antidepressant prescriptions." *Sci Rep 10*, 22445 (2020). https://doi.org/10.1038/s41598-020-79924-5

42 Roger S. Ulrich, "View Through a Window May Influence Recovery from Surgery." *Science 224*,420–421(1984). DOI:10.1126/science.6143402.

43 Gruebner O, Rapp MA, Adli M, Kluge U, Galea S, Heinz A. "Cities and Mental Health." *Dtsch Arztebl Int.* 2017 Feb 24;114(8):121-127. doi: 10.3238/arztebl.2017.0121. PMID: 28302261; PMCID: PMC5374256.

44 Sanzaro, Francis. *Society Elsewhere: Why the Gravest Threat to Humanity Will Come from Within.* Zero Books, 2018.

45 Scarry, Elaine. *The Body in Pain: The Making and Unmaking of the World.* Oxford University Press, USA, 1985.

46 Jelle Bruineberg, "Adversarial inference: predictive minds in the attention economy," *Neuroscience of Consciousness,* Volume 2023, Issue 1, 2023, niad019, https://doi.org/10.1093/nc/niad019

47 Mormann, Florian, Julien Dubois, Simon Kornblith, Milica Milosavljevic, Moran Cerf, Matias Ison, Naotsugu Tsuchiya, et al. "A Category-Specific Response to Animals in the Right Human Amygdala." *Nature Neuroscience* 14, no. 10 (August 28, 2011): 1247–49. https://doi.org/10.1038/nn.2899.

48 This quote appeared in an interview with Dr. Anna Lembke, of Stanford University, titled, "The Science Behind Social Media's Hold on Our Mental Health." *Teen Vogue*, November 10, 2021. https://www.teenvogue.com/story/the-science-behind-social-medias-

49 Buss, M. David. (1989) "Sex Differences in human mate preferences: Evolutionary hypotheses tested in 37 cultures." *Behavioral and Brain Sciences.* 12: 1 – 49.

50 See *Lion's Roar*. "Let Your Mind Move," by Francis Sanzaro. March 24, 2024. https://www.lionsroar.com/let-your-mind-move/. Accessed May, 2025.

51 From the author's website. Mettler, Barbara. "The Language of Movement." Accessed May 27, 2025. https://www.barbarametttler.org/The-Language-of-Movement.

52 Aknin, L. B., Dunn, E. W., & Whillans, A. V. (2022). The Emotional Rewards of Prosocial Spending Are Robust and Replicable in Large Samples. *Current Directions in Psychological Science,* 31(6), 536-545. https://doi.org/10.1177/09637214221121100 (Original work published 2022)

53 Blake, William. "Eternity."in *Notebook*, c. 1793.

54 Capra, Fritjof. *The Tao of Physics: An Exploration of the Parallels between Modern Physics and Eastern Mysticism.* Shambhala Publications, 2010, p. 24

55 Of course, in our century, even in the deepest of wild places there is always the trace of the human, but for the average observer, the fact of managed wildlife doesn't enter their consciousness, and so does not affect their experience.

56 Kühnen, Ulrich & Kitayama, Shinobu. (2021). "Agency-Detection," in *Encyclopedia of Evolutionary Psychological Science* (pp.1–8) Publisher: Springer International Publishing10.1007/978-3-319-16999-6_3011-1.

57 "The Symbolic Self in Evolutionary Context"; Antonio Damasio, Hanna Damasio; Feelings Are the Source of Consciousness. *Neural Comput* 2023; 35 (3): 277–286.

58 For starters, see this Sohn, Hansem, Devika Narain, Nicolas Meirhaeghe, and Mehrdad Jazayeri. "Bayesian Computation through Cortical Latent Dynamics." *Neuron* 103, no. 5 (September 2019): 934-947.e5. https://doi.org/10.1016/j.neuron.2019.06.012. Also of importance is: Antono, Jessica Emily, Roman Vakhrushev, and Arezoo Pooresmaeili. "Value-Driven Modulation of Visual Perception by Visual and Auditory Reward Cues: The Role of Performance-Contingent Delivery of Reward." *Frontiers in Human Neuroscience* 16 (December 23, 2022). https://doi.org/10.3389/fnhum.2022.1062168.

59 Ptito M, Bleau M, Bouskila J. The Retina: A Window into

the Brain. Cells. 2021 Nov 23;10(12):3269. doi: 10.3390/cells10123269. PMID: 34943777; PMCID: PMC8699497.

60 Potter, M.C., Wyble, B., Hagmann, C.E. *et al.* Detecting meaning in RSVP at 13 ms per picture. *Atten Percept Psychophys* 76, 270–279 (2014). https://doi.org/10.3758/s13414-013-0605-z

61 Milders M., Sahraie A., Logan S. (2008). Minimum presentation time for masked facial expression discrimination. Cognition and Emotion, 22, 63–82. See also Neath K. N., Itier R. J. (2014). Facial expression discrimination varies with presentation time but not with fixation on features: A backward masking study using eye-tracking. *Cognition & Emotion*, 28, 115–131.

62 Gustafson C. Bruce Lipton, PhD: The Jump From Cell Culture to Consciousness. Integr Med (Encinitas). 2017 Dec;16(6):44-50. PMID: 30936816; PMCID: PMC6438088.

63 See Appleton, Jay. *The Experience of Landscape.* Chichester [Eng.] ; New York : Wiley, 1975.

64 Being in a body is the result either of a reincarnation (Tibetan Buddhism, for example), revelation (the Earth, and us on it, *is the revelation*), or some other process we will never know about. For some Christian theologians, the earth itself is a revelation. For Australian Aboriginals, life is viewed as an acting out of the Dreaming. Or, for some indigenous peoples, our lives are a way to serve the creator. For some ancient Greeks, our lives are a performance of the god of Fate, which has preordained All. It is of course possible that life is entirely random, but, for their part, spiritual traditions tend to view the fact of our existence as a good thing, a tool in our advancement, one we need to learn and leverage. In short, you being alive isn't a total accident for the lot of religious belief. You are here to learn something only life on earth can teach you. Whether or not this is actually the case, it doesn't hurt to pretend it is, to add a variation to Pascal's wager. Body is, therefore, essential to any spiritual enterprise.

65 Mattson MP. "Superior pattern processing is the essence of the evolved human brain." *Front Neurosci.* 2014 Aug 22;8:265. doi: 10.3389/fnins.2014.00265. PMID: 25202234; PMCID: PMC4141622. https://www.ncbi.nlm.nih.gov/pmc/articles/PMC4141622/

66 Quote found in "The Symbolic Self in Evolutionary Context" in *Personality and Social Psychology Review* 1997, Vol. 1, No. 1, 80_102.

67 Antonio Damasio, Hanna Damasio; Feelings Are the Source of Consciousness. *Neural Comput* 2023; 35 (3): 277–286.

68 "The self serves as the repository of mental structures that store and organize self-relevant information." "The second capacity of the self is executive and involves the regulation

of its relation with the social and physical environment." and "Finally, the third capacity of the self is its reflexivity, defined as the organism's ability to depict itself in its ongoing relation with other objects." These quotes were pulled from: Sedikides, C., Skowronski, J. J., & Dunbar, R. I. M. (2006). When and Why Did the Human Self Evolve? In M. Schaller, J. A. Simpson, & D. T. Kenrick (Eds.), *Evolution and social psychology* (pp. 55–80). Psychosocial Press.

69 For the original studies, see the work of Nikolaas Tinbergen. More recently, his work was brought to attention in *Supernormal Stimuli: How Primal Urges Overran Their Evolutionary Purpose.* W. W. Norton & Company, 2010.

70 MD, DFAPA Grant Hilary Brenner. "Why Poor Sense of Self Underlies Dark Triad Traits." *Psychology Today*, May 17, 2021. https://www.psychologytoday.com/us/blog/experimentations/202105-why-poor-sense-self-underlies-dark-triad-traits.

71 "Land as a Social Relationship." *Briar Patch Magazine.* By Mike Gouldhawke. Sep 10, 2020. Accessed May 28, 2025. https://briarpatchmagazine.com/articles/view/land-as-a-social-relationship.

72 *National Parks Traveler.* "Family of Man Killed By Mountain Goat in Olympic National Park Sues National Park Service." Accessed May 28, 2025. https://www.nationalparkstraveler.org/2011/11/family-man-killed-mountain-goat-olympic-national-park-sues-national-park-service8977.

73 News, ABC. "More People Visit National Parks but Spend Less Time in Them." ABC News, July 11, 2012. https://abcnews.go.com/Travel/people-visit-national-parks-spend-time/story?id=16755260. Accessed May, 2025.

74 This is not the same as approving access for those who need it. We need to encourage and support that trend.

75 A popular term now, see its origin in *Supernormal Stimuli: How Primal Urges Overran Their Evolutionary Purpose*, by Deirdre Barrett published by W. W. Norton & Company in 2010. Also see "Supernormal Stimuli: How Primal Urges Overran Their Evolutionary Purpose." Southeastern Naturalist 10, no. 1 (March 1, 2011): 196. https://doi.org/10.1656/058.010.0121.

76 Billman, George E. "Homeostasis: The Underappreciated and Far Too Often Ignored Central Organizing Principle of Physiology." Frontiers in Physiology 11 (March 10, 2020). https://doi.org/10.3389/fphys.2020.00200.

77 See the 27:30 timestamp on "The Origins Podcast," with Joseph LeDoux. See also LeDoux J. Rethinking the emotional brain. Neuron. 2012 Feb 23;73(4):653-76. doi: 10.1016/j.neuron.2012.02.004. Erratum in: *Neuron.* 2012 Mar

8;73(5):1052. PMID: 22365542; PMCID: PMC3625946.

78 Schuman-Olivier, Zev MD; Trombka, Marcelo MD; Lovas, David A. MD; Brewer, Judson A. MD, PhD; Vago, David R. PhD; Gawande, Richa PhD; Dunne, Julie P. PhD, RN, PMHNP-BC; Lazar, Sara W. PhD; Loucks, Eric B. PhD; Fulwiler, Carl MD, PhD. Mindfulness and Behavior Change. Harvard Review of Psychiatry 28(6):p 371-394, 11/12 2020. | DOI: 10.1097/HRP.0000000000000277

79 See Damasio, Antonio R. *The Feeling of What Happens: Body and Emotion in the Making of Consciousness.* Houghton Mifflin Harcourt, 1999. Also Peper A. "A general theory of consciousness I: Consciousness and adaptation." *Commun Integr Biol.* 2020 Jan 30;13(1):6-21. doi: 10.1080/19420889.2020.1713967. PMID: 33149800; PMCID: PMC7591160. and Consciousness as a Trigger to Adaptation, Massimo Cossentino (1National Research Council of Italy (CNR), Via Ugo La Malfa, 253, Palermo 90146, Italy), Luca Sabatucci (1National Research Council of Italy (CNR), Via Ugo La Malfa, 253, Palermo 90146, Italy), and John Mylopoulos (2University of Toronto, 40 St George St, Toronto, ON M5S 2E4, Canada, *Journal of Artificial Intelligence and Consciousness* 2023 10:01, 27-47

80 Heartney, Eleanor. *Postmodern Heretics: The Catholic Imagination in Contemporary Art.* Midmarch Arts Press, 2004.

81 Brown, Peter R. *Treasure in Heaven: The Holy Poor in Early Christianity.* University of Virginia Press, 2016.

82 See this for starters: Moser MB, Rowland DC, Moser EI. Place cells, grid cells, and memory. *Cold Spring Harb Perspect Biol.* 2015 Feb 2;7(2):a021808. doi: 10.1101/cshperspect.a021808. PMID: 25646382; PMCID: PMC4315928. See this also: Madar, A.D., Jiang, A., Dong, C. et al. Synaptic plasticity rules driving representational shifting in the hippocampus. *Nat Neurosci* 28, 848–860 (2025). https://doi.org/10.1038/s41593-025-01894-6

83 From the back cover of Thích, Nhát Hanh. *The Heart of Understanding: Commentaries on the Prajñaparamita Heart Sutra.* Parallax Press: 1988.

84 From Yongey Mingyur Rinpoche's *In Love with the World:* "Misunderstandings about the source of sensation occur because the perception and the interpretation arise almost simultaneously, so close together that the strong but incorrect impression is created that the interpretive reality—good-bad, attractive-aversive—is lodged within the object itself and not in the mind. It can be very difficult to accept that the source of what we like or do not like arises in our mind....When we relate to the world with a mind full of preconceptions, we erect a barrier between us and reality as-it-is."

85 Damiano, Luisa, and Paul Dumouchel. "Anthropomorphism in Human–Robot Co-Evolution." *Frontiers in Psychology* 9 (March 26, 2018). https://doi.org/10.3389/fpsyg.2018.00468.

86 Payne, Mark, 'The Natural World in Greek Literature and Philosophy', Oxford Handbook Topics in Classical Studies (online edn, Oxford Academic, 1 Apr. 2014), https://doi.org/10.1093/oxfordhb/9780199935390.013.001, accessed 28 May 2025.

87 LaChapelle, Dolores. "Educating for Deep Ecology." Journal of Experiential Education 14, no. 3 (November 1991): 18–22. https://doi.org/10.1177/105382599101400305.

88 Booth, A.L. (2003). We are the Land: Native American Views of Nature. In: Selin, H. (eds) Nature Across Cultures. Science Across Cultures: The History of Non-Western Science, vol 4. Springer, Dordrecht. https://doi.org/10.1007/978-94-017-0149-5_17

89 Heinrich Böll Stiftung. "The River as a Legal Person: The Case of the Whanganui River in New Zealand." Accessed May 28, 2025. https://www.boell.de/en/2025/01/29/river-legal-person-case-whanganui-river-new-zealand.

90 Chandran, Rina. "India's Sacred Ganges and Yamuna Rivers Granted Same Legal Rights as Humans." Reuters, March 21, 2017. https://www.reuters.com/article/world/indias-sacred-ganges-and-yamuna-rivers-granted-same-legal-rights-as-humans-idUSKBN16S108/. Accessed May 2025.

91 "The Romans did not share the same vision of cities as the Greeks: cities (and especially Rome) were seen as places of filth and sin, and the "good life" was in the countryside villas (an ideal of bucolics), in a manner surprisingly close to the modern American view of insane cities contrasting with safe residential suburbs": from Ducarme, F., Couvet, D. What does 'nature' mean?. Palgrave Commun 6, 14 (2020). https://doi.org/10.1057/s41599-020-0390-y

92 See page 322 of Snow, Nancy E. *Cultivating Virtue: Perspectives from Philosophy, Theology, and Psychology*. Oxford University Press, 2014.

93 Barron, James. "He's Spent Just One Night on His Private Island. He's Had Enough." *New York Times*, July 2, 2019 https://www.nytimes.com/2019/07/02/nyregion/island-sale-nyc.html. Accessed May 2025.

94 And, come to think of it, we are lacking a god of addition too, though this god is ever-present. Some spirits take away, such as gods of death, loss and destruction, and there are deities of birth. But there is no god that adds. There are gods of happiness, which bring happiness, and various spirits can be appealed to such that we accumulate things, but these gods are always specific, such spirits of fertility, wealth, etc.